Corporate Governance in China:
Research and Evaluation

Corporate Governance in China:
Research and Evaluation

Li Wei-An

WILEY

John Wiley & Sons (Asia) Pte. Ltd.

Other Wiley Editorial Offices

John Wiley & Sons, Inc., 111 River Street, Hoboken, NJ 07030, USA
John Wiley & Sons Ltd., The Atrium, Southern Gate,
    Chichester PO19 BSQ, England
John Wiley & Sons (Canada) Ltd., 5353 Dundas Street West, Suite 400, Toronto,
    Ontario M9B 6H8, Canada
John Wiley & Sons Australia Ltd., 42 McDougall Street, Milton, Queensland 4064,
    Australia
Wiley-VCH, Boschstrasse 12, D-69469 Weinheim, Germany

Library of Congress Cataloging-in-Publication Data:

ISBN-13: 978-0-470-82340-8

Typeset in 11-13.5 point, Palatino by Superskill Graphics Pte. Ltd.
Printed in China by WKT Co. Ltd.
10 9 8 7 6 5 4 3 2 1

Contents

Abstract

Corporate governance evaluation is designed to make a rating and judgment of governance structures and mechanisms, and the corporate governance index is a quantitative description of the governance status quo. In this book, we first propose a governance evaluation system and establish a corporate governance index system, and then we appraise the *status quo* of the listed companies' corporate governance from the six dimensions of behavior—of controlling shareholders, board of directors, supervisors' committee, management, information disclosure and other stakeholders. Finally we conduct empirical research on the relationships between the corporate governance index and corporate performance.

The research can provide theoretical guidance in order to perfect corporate governance mechanisms. The application of a governance index in analyzing the corporate governance *status quo* of listed companies can help the management to pinpoint existing problems and make related improvements on the one hand, and on the other hand it can provide investors with a sound evaluation tool and standards, which can help to evaluate the governance efficiency of investment objects and reduce the information asymmetry. It can also put some kind of effective reputation restraints on the companies and help supervisory authorities to exert valid supervision.

The book is oriented to scholars and students majoring in economics and management as well as readers from listed companies, supervisory authorities, stock exchanges and so on, and anyone who is interested in corporate governance.

Preface

Chinese listed companies have established modern corporate governance structures and governance mechanisms gradually. For both academic and operational circles, it is an urgent matter to understand which governance model is more suitable for the governance environment where Chinese listed companies survive.

Issues of importance include:

- the quality of corporate governance of listed companies in China
- whether the interests of shareholders and other stakeholders are effectively protected
- how to improve corporate performance through the management of the shareholder structure of listed companies
- how to regulate shareholders' conferences and ensure the independence of listed companies
- how boards function to form the perfect decision-making and supervisory mechanisms
- what incentive and restraint mechanisms should be implemented to effectively reduce agency costs and promote agent endeavor for the long-term development of the company
- how to establish and improve information disclosure systems
- what kind of mechanisms of stakeholders' participation in corporate governance should be established to enhance corporate performances
- what the factors determining the quality of corporate governance are
- what the relationship is between the quality of corporate governance and corporate performance.

The core action to address these issues is to establish a corporate governance appraisal system adapted to the outside environment. Through the operation of the system, we can view the functioning of corporate governance, and observe and analyze the status of and problems related to the behaviors of the controlling shareholders, the board functioning, manager-incentive constraints, supervisors' committee supervision and information disclosure. Based on this, we can carry out a series of empirical studies. Through the empirical and normative research, we can explore Chinese corporate governance model, regulate the governance structure and the behaviors of the boards of listed companies, and thereby establish good incentives and restraint mechanisms for top managers, perfect the information disclosure system, protect the interests of shareholders and other stakeholders, and ultimately accomplish good performance.

Based on the objective requirements of the theoretical development of corporate governance and the practices accumulated by listed companies in China, funded by the national natural science fund projects, national social sciences fund projects, and higher outstanding young teachers teaching and research projects incentive fund, we launched the stage results about corporate governance applications and evaluation for the first time in April 2000, namely, "Chinese corporate governance principles." This production was adopted by the "China listed company governance norms," established by the China Securities Regulatory Commission, and the "East Asia corporate governance principles" established by Pacific Economic Corporation Council (PECC). The Organisation for Economic Cooperation and Development (OECD) also paid attention to it. After three years of systematic study, we launched the second stage results of Chinese corporate governance applications and evaluation in April 2003—"Chinese corporate governance evaluation indicators system"—achieving international practice in corporate governance evaluation. The indicators system based on the theory of corporate governance, aimed at protecting the interests of stakeholders, emphasized the core role the board plays in corporate governance, attended to the impact of information disclosure for corporate supervision, and evaluated the situation of corporate governance from six dimensions of the behaviors of controlling stockholders, the board of directors, the board of supervisors, the managers layer, information disclosure and other stakeholders. Based on the successful launch of the evaluation indicators system, using scientific methods and evaluation criteria we introduced CCGI^{NK}, shortened from Chinese corporate governance index, and designed the questionnaire survey aiming at Chinese listed companies. In support of the relevant departments of the China Securities Regulatory Commission, as well as through the cooperation with the Shenzhen Stock Exchange, we successfully retrieved the questionnaires. With the survey-based data, we conducted a comprehensive evaluation of the situation of corporate governance for Chinese listed companies.

This book takes the combination of corporate governance theory and practices as a starting point and aims to establish a scientific decision-making mechanism. Based on the analysis of the basic theory in the evaluation of corporate governance, we put forward the corporate governance evaluation indicators systems and created an evaluation index model for Chinese listed companies. According to the survey-based data from Chinese listed companies, we conducted a comprehensive systematic evaluation for the governance status of Chinese listed companies.

Chapter 1 addresses corporate governance evaluation system design. From two aspects of power separation in modern companies and the goal of corporate governance research, we state the reasons for corporate governance evaluation and the theoretical foundation of it in the theory of economics. On the basis of setting principles for creating a corporate governance evaluation index system, the book shows the content of the corporate governance evaluation index system, evaluation criteria and evaluation measures, and establishes a corporate governance model also. Finally, we make a non-parameter test for system design, with the support of data on corporate governance in Chinese companies.

Chapter 2 introduces the application of the corporate governance evaluation system. According to the investigating data about corporate governance of Chinese listed companies, this chapter makes a descriptive analysis on the general governance status and industry governance status of Chinese listed companies, and includes relativity analysis on the influence of ownership structure and the nature of majority shareholders on the quality of corporate governance by using CCGI. And we conducted empirical study of the relationship between the quality of corporate governance and firms' performance on the basis of discussing the corporate governance performance.

Chapter 3 introduces the study of the evaluation and index of controlling shareholders' behaviors. This chapter considers four aspects, which are shareholders' equal treatment, the systematic inducement of negative externalities of controlling shareholders' behaviors, the restriction mechanisms of the negative externalities effect of controlling shareholders, and the negative externalities of controlling shareholders' behaviors. And we also appraise the general status of controlling shareholders' behaviors from aspects such as related transactions, independence of listed companies, shareholders' meetings, and the protection of minority shareholders. Then we analyze the relationship with the index of controlling shareholders' behaviors and firms' performance.

Chapter 4 introduces the research on evaluation and index of directorates' governance. This chapter considers five dimensions: directors' rights and obligations; directorates' operational efficiency; directorates' organization; directors' compensation; and independent director system with an angle of efficient operation of directorates and scientific decision-making. We take the effective operation system as our key point for systematic evaluation of the overall condition of directorates' governance of Chinese listed companies, comparison among industries, and the relationship between directorates' governance and firm performance.

Chapter 5 introduces the research on evaluation and index of supervisors' committee governance. This chapter takes efficient regulation as our target and designs an index evaluation system based on positivism, effectiveness, independence, integrity and objectivity, which is supplemented by the independent director system. This evaluation system has two dimensions as a guarantee of supervisory capacity and operational efficiency of supervisors' committees for the evaluation of the supervisors' committee index, firm performance and impacts on supervisors' committee governance from controlling shareholders.

In chapter 6 we introduce the research on indexing and evaluating top management governance. We make the evaluation on three aspects: removal and appointment; guarantee of operation; and incentive and restriction mechanism. On the basis of establishment of an evaluation system of top management governance, we make the descriptive evaluation on the status of top management governance of Chinese listed companies and make empirical analysis of the relationship among corporate performance and the engagement of top managers, incentive and restriction, and other factors.

Chapter 7 contains research on information disclosure evaluation and the associated index. On the basis of establishing an information disclosure evaluation index system, we examine authenticity, timeliness and integrity of information disclosure, the overall condition of information disclosure in Chinese public companies, key factors for information disclosure, and its industrial features. In addition, we look at empirical research on the relationship between information disclosure quality and corporate performance and corporate governance mechanisms.

Chapter 8 contains research on stakeholder governance evaluation and the associated index. Depending on the position and function of stakeholders in corporate governance, and considering the scientific evaluation of the index and features of Chinese public companies, the book sets a stakeholder governance index system to measure their participation in corporate governance and protection of their benefits. We also conduct empirical research on the influence on corporate performance that stakeholder participation in corporate governance has.

In chapter 9 we introduce the research on the index and evaluation of private-oriented listed enterprise governance. On the basis of the evaluation of Chinese listed companies governance, we focus particularly on the status of private listed enterprise governance, making the comparison of governance characteristics of private listed enterprises, with the comparative analysis based on industry characteristics. We also look at the relationship between the status of private listed enterprise governance and corporate performance.

Notice of Correction

The first paragraph of the Acknowledgements is corrected as follows:

"This book is the working result of three years of effort by the corporate governance evaluation project, headed by Prof. Li Wei-An of Nankai University of China. I am grateful to major team members of the project, including Prof. Cheng Xin-Sheng (General Coordinator, Nankai University), Associate Prof. Liu Xiao-Lun (English Version Coordinator, Beijing National Accounting Institute),Prof.XieYong-Zhen (Shandong University), Associate Prof. Wu Li-Dong (Nankai University), Prof. Ma Lian-Fu (Nankai University), Doctor Zhang Guo-Ping (Nankai University), Doctor Zhang Yao-Wei (Nankai University), Doctor Xu Wei (Nankai University), Doctor Niu Jian-Bo (Nankai University), Doctor Tang Yue-Jun (Fudan University), Doctor Wang Shi-Quan (Northeast University), and Doctor Li Ya (Nankai University)."

Acknowledgments

This book is the working result of three years of effort by the corporate governance evaluation project, headed by Prof. Li Wei-An of Nankai University of China. I am grateful to major team members of the project, including Prof. Cheng Xin-Sheng (General Coordinator, Nankai University), Associate Prof. Liu Xiao-Lun (English Version Coordinator, Beijing National Accounting Institute), Prof. Xie Yong-Zhen (Shandong University), Associate Prof. Wu Li-Dong (Nankai University), Prof. Ma Lian-Fu (Nankai University), Doctor Zhang Yao-Wei (Nankai University), Doctor Xu Wei (Nankai University), Doctor Niu Jian-Bo (Nankai University), Doctor Tang Yue-Jun (Fudan University), Doctor Wang Shi-Quan (Northeast University), and Doctor Li Han-Jun (Central University of Finance and Banking).

The project was supported by the national natural science fund projects (Project No.: 70272026, 70141011, 70372028); state key program of national natural science fund projects (Project No.: 70532001); national social sciences fund projects (Project No.: 02BJY127); MOE Project of Key Research Institute of Humanities and Social Sciences in Universities (Project No.: A03301); higher outstanding young teachers teaching and research projects incentive fund, "211" project and "985" project, of Nankai University.[1]

I wish to express my appreciation to my students, including Sun Juan, Chang Juan, Wang Qiao, Xie Reng-Ming, Wang Lei, Xu Hao who draft translated the context into English.

---

[1] The "211" project is a national education-supporting project which is aimed at developing 100 top universities for the 21st century in China, and the "985" project is a higher level national education-supporting project aimed at building world-class universities in China, as announced by then president of China, Jiang Ze-Min in May 1998.

I am also especially thankful to Prof. Lin Run-Hui and Prof. Zhou Jian, whose efforts make the publication of the book possible.

Finally, I wish to thank Michael Hanrahan, the copyeditor of the book, and everyone at John Wiley & Sons, Inc., including Nick Wallwork, Adeline Lim, Janis Soo, Joel Balbin, and Wayne Wang, for helping to make this book possible.

The Framework of Corporate Governance Research

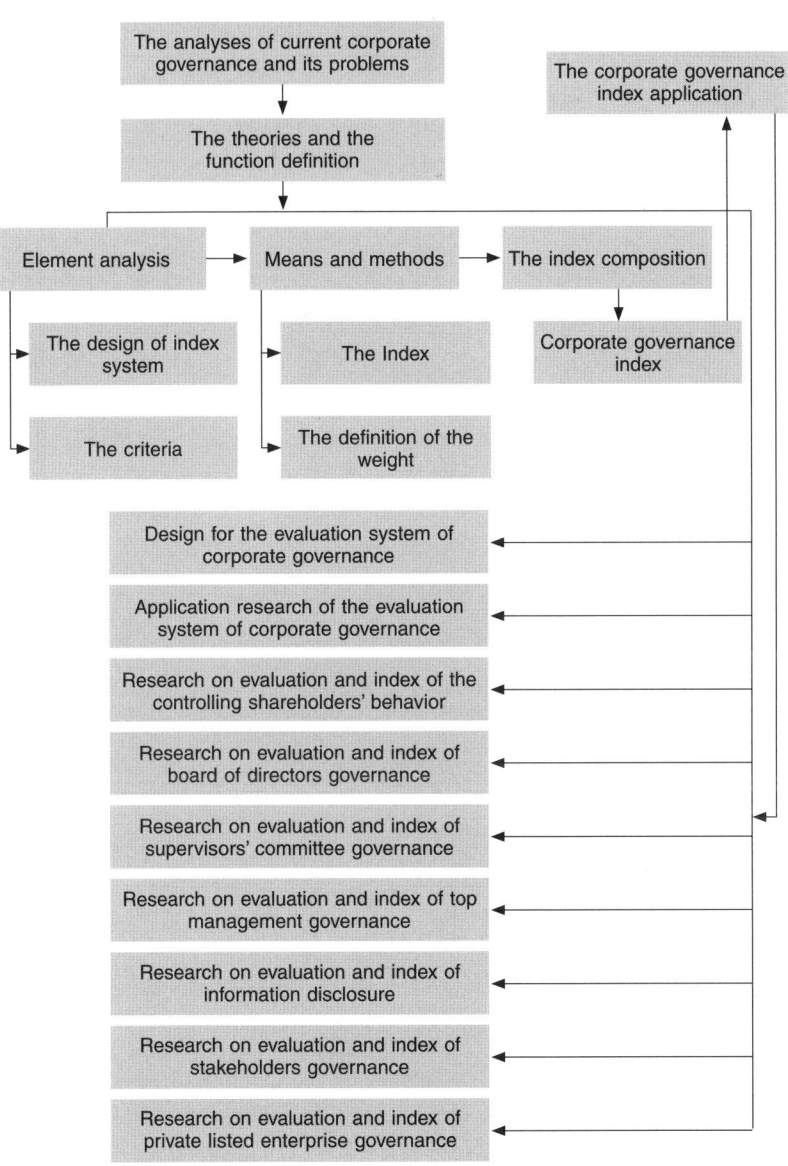

The Design of a Corporate Governance Evaluation System

Taking the description of corporate governance evaluation theory as the foundation and the environment of corporate governance in China as the background, we design the system of corporate governance evaluating criteria, establish corresponding evaluating rules, and establish the evaluation model of the Chinese corporate governance index with a combination of subjective and objective weights. We also test the stability and the reliability of the model, using the method of non-parameter examination.

The rationale of corporate governance evaluation

The rationale of corporate governance evaluation plays a key role in its practice, which should be established on the foundation of the latter.

Agency theory and corporate governance evaluation

The rising up of agency problems is attributed to the separation of controlling rights from ownership. There are layers of principal–agent (request–act) relationships, of which the most critical two are the agent relationship between shareholders and the board of directors, and the board of directors and the top managers. The deviation of the principal's goal from the agent's and information asymmetry lead to the problem of "moral hazard" and "adverse selection," which will reduce the benefit to principals. To solve these two problems, a power check-and-balance system is necessary—such as an incentive and restraint system—to guide the agent's behavior as well as to force him to make the effort required for the realization of the principal's maximum benefit. Principal–agent relationships in corporations comprise the logical boundary of corporate governance evaluation and the incentive and the condition of incentive and restraint system comprise the main content of corporate governance evluation.

System theory and corporate governance evaluation

System theory focuses on accurate description and profound learning of the features of complicated systems, using thoughts of system theory. That requires regarding factors—such as every element and every link inside the system, as well as the inside and outside environment—as dynamic relationships in which they relate to and restrict each other. That also requires deciding and acting with a developing and dynamic view, and finding the proposal that leads the system to the most satisfactory condition. An enterprise is essentially a series of contracts made by stakeholders, the life force of which comes from the cooperation of stakeholders. Entities of property rights might invest their special property in different forms, but enjoy the "retained earnings" as a whole. That is to say, the material basis of corporate "surplus production" is composed of physical assets from shareholders, liabilities from creditors, human resources from employees, special human resources from managers, and customer value from customers. Therefore, they all have the right to share the retained earnings in accordance with the matching principle between the yield and the contribution.

Meanwhile, the limited liability of shareholders—which means shareholders' loss will never be more than their investments in the company—makes them not the only sharers of the retained earnings. Information asymmetry, decentralization of shareholders, and "free rider" behavior which comes from the previous meaning that corporate owners have neither the capability nor incentive—according to the theory of new classical property rights—to monitor the managers effectively. However, employees who hold more information about the company than shareholders, and whose personal interests correlate highly to the interests of the company, have the capability and incentive to monitor the company, and even get more efficiency than shareholders.

The factors above determine that corporate governance should conciliate the relationship among the stakeholders and realize the scientific nature of decision-making through formal as well as informal rule design, and as a result maximize the value of the company. The corporate governance evaluation system should be designed in accordance with the structure and mechanism of corporate governance, and in the condition of fully considering the dynamic and interacting relationship among all stakeholders. In the course of establishing a corporate governance evaluation index system, the condition of each constituent attaching themselves to corporate governance activities should be affected totally, and their interrelationships considered fully. The system should be comprehensive, systematic, scientific and feasible.

Multi-goal planning and corporate governance evaluation

A public company is a complicated system, and its ultimate goal is the realization of maximum stakeholder benefit, the concrete representation of which is the benefit of shareholders, creditors, suppliers, customers, community, government, and so on. Companies realize these benefits by way of participating in corporate governance activities and establishing a specific corporate governance structure and corporate governance mechanism; that is, shareholders' meetings, board of directors, supervisors' committee, managers, and information disclosure principles. Corporate governance evaluation is the quantified representation of the integrated result of such elements. The course of integrating should comply to a multi-goal planning principle, consider comprehensively the integrated function direction and degree of every element, and as a result reflect comprehensively and systematically the condition of every element which determines the quality of corporate governance.

Contingency theory and corporate governance evaluation

The contingency theory of management, which formed in the U.S. in the 1970s, fully considers the relationship between environmental variables and corresponding management concept and technology. The theory requires playing to the core with the change in the inner and outer managing environment; that is, seeking different management patterns, projects, or means in different specific conditions. The choice of a corporate governance pattern is the result of the interaction between inner and outer environmental variables and managing variables. In general, corporate governance's outer environment includes society, technology, the economy, politics, and laws, while the inner environment includes suppliers, customers, competitors, employees and shareholders. As a formal organization system, variables of the inner environment are correlated to the outer environment. Managing variables in corporate governance—such as decisions, information communication, incentive and restraint—has a fundamental connection with corporate governance environmental variables. Hence the interaction of corporate environmental variables with their management lead to different corporate governance patterns.

Recently there has been a trend that corporate governance patterns in different countries appear to be converging, but there is always a difference in specific patterns because variations exist in different countries' political and economic rules, their fundamental approach to corporate law, and the structure and design of corporate departments. When designing the corporate governance index, the setting of an index system and choice of evaluating method are determined by the corporate governance structure and corporate governance mechanism under a certain pattern of corporate governance. Different corporate governance patterns lead to different evaluation index systems and evaluation methods; therefore, there is neither a uniform governance pattern nor a perfect corporate governance evaluation system. In the transition period in China, domination by a single shareholder, insider controlling, and other special phenomena came into existence in Chinese public companies which do not exist in the U.K., U.S. or other countries that have a developed economy, nor in Russia or East European countries which are also in a period of transition. All of these features should be considered in the course of establishing Chinese corporate governance index, and proper adjustment should be made to index systems when the corporate governance environment changes. Meanwhile, it is also necessary for the weights that indicate the significance of each evaluation criteria to be adjusted with the change of the criteria pool in the evaluation system and variation in extent of each criteria's numerical value. In addition, the evaluating factors of each criterion should also be adjusted dynamically.

Research into corporate governance evaluation

Theoretical research of corporate governance is extended to empirical research by professors at home and abroad, and then to the research of corporate governance quality evaluation.

Theoretical research of corporate governance

Professors in foreign countries have done trailblazing research in corporate governance theory. For example, R.H. Coase (1937) and Jensen and Meckling (1972) studied the nature of the firm; Berle and Maynes (1968), John Cubbin and Dennis Leech (1983), Harold Demsetz and Kenneth (1985), Oliver Hart (1995), Fama and Jensen (1983), and others have done systematic research in the theory of ownership and control; Jensen (1976), Fama (1980), Meckling (1976) and Williamson (1996) and others have studied the problems of agency cost; Davis and Kay (1990), Williamson (1988) and others did research from the aspect of transaction costs, raising the thought that projects in which capital has low specialty should be financed by debt. Professors in China referred to this research field in the 1990s; Li Wei-An, Qian Ying-Yi, Wu Jing-Lian, Zhang Wei-Ying and others have done deep research into the meaning of corporate governance. This research focused on the property right institution, corporate governance patterns, manager incentive and restraint, and impelled the revolution of state-owned companies into a deeper stage. Recently, there has been a trend that research into actual practice of corporate governance has been developed, including management, economics and sociology.

Research of corporate governance

On the basis of theoretical research on corporate governance, scholars extended the research on corporate governance to the field of actual practice. For example, Armen A. Alchina and Harold Demsetz (1972), Robert E. Hoskisson, Charles W.L. Hill and Hicheon Kim (1993) and others have done detailed research on corporate structure and internal corporate governance. Fama (1980), Jeremy (1993), Hart (1995), Edward J. Zajac and James D. Westphal (1996), Barry Baysinger and Hoskisson (1990), Kwnneth J. Rediker and Anju Seth (1995), George P. Baker, Michael C. Jensen and Kevin J. Murphy (1998) and others have done research on the aspects of inner structure and working procedure of boards of directors; Peter J. Buckly and Mark Casson (1991), John H. Dumming (1998), David J. Teece (1986) and others have done systematic research on multinational corporate governance. James B. Quinn and Hilmer Frederick G. (1994) have done research on the relationship between corporate governance and corporate management from the angle of strategic management. T. Carter (1992), Robert C. Pozen (1994), John Pound (1988), John C. Coffee (1991), Stephen D. Prowse (1990), Helen Short and Kevin Keasey (1997) and others have studied the role of institutional investors in corporate governance. Schliefer and Summers (1988) and Jensen (1988) referred to the influence of capital markets on corporation monitoring. Henry G. Manne (1965), Sanford J. Grossman and Oliver D. Hart (1980) and Amar Bhide (1993) and others have done systematic research on the impact of markets on corporate governance. In China, Li Wei-An (1998) systematically studied multinational corporate governance, network governance and corporate group governance, and made the first corporate governance principle in China. His works provide a guide for research on actual practice about corporate governance. There are also other scholars in the researching field of corporate group governance, such as Xi You-Min.

Empirical research on corporate governance

The third research aspect of corporate governance is empirical research on the relationship between corporate governance structure, corporate governance mechanisms and company performance. This includes the relationships between the structure of stock ownership and performance, governance structure and information disclosure, and governance structure and performance. For example, Jensen and Meckling (1976) studied the relationship between inner shareholders' ownership proportion and company value. Demsetz (1983), Holderness and Sheehan (1988), McConnell and Servaes (1990), Myeong Hyeon Cho (1998) and others have done research on how corporate governance structure relates to corporate performance. Catherine M. Daily and Dan R. Dalton (1993), Michael C. Jensen (1990), Rosenstein and Wyatt (1990), Kline (1999), Bhagat and Black (1999) and others have focused on the relationship between executive directors' and CEOs' payment and corporate performance. Shivdasani (1993) and Perry (1996) studied the influence of directors' reputation and compensation plan on their behavior. Liptonand Lorsh (1992), Jensen (1993), Eisenberg (1998) and Yermack (1996) and others have done research on the relationship between the size of the board of directors and company value. Nikos (1999) focused on the frequency of the board of directors' meetings and company value. Morck, Shleifer and Vishny (1988), Jensen (1993), Pound (1995), William and Brown (1996), Weisbach (1998) and Perry (2000) and others have done research on the relationship between incentive to independent directors and corporate value. Aram and Cowan (1983), Baysinger and Bulter (1985), Hambrick and Finkelstein (1987), Judge and Miller (1991), Dalton (1991), Pound (1992) and Solomon (1993), Rechner and Boyd (1995), Goyal and Park (2001) and others found out how the combination of two positions relates to company value. George J. Benson (1982), Geoffrey Whittington (1993), John J. Forker (1992), David B. Citron (1992) and others focused on the empirical research on corporate governance and information disclosure.

In China, Hu Qin-Qin and Shen Yi-Feng (2002), Gao Ming-Hua (2002), Zhan Hong (2003), Wu Jian-Xiong (2002) and Tan

Jin-Song (2003) and others have studied the relationship between independent directors' incentive and company performance in Chinese public companies. Tian Zhi-Long and Yang Lu (1998) researched company performance from the aspect of shares held by managers. Gu Qi and Yu Dong-Zhi (2001) and others studied corporate governance, the behavior of the board of directors, and operating performance. Li Wei-An and Li Jian-Biao (2003) and others have done research on the governance of the board of directors and corporation credit. Xu Xiao-Nian (1999), Sun Yong-Xiang, Huang Zu-Hui (1999) and others focused on structure of share ownership and company value; He Jun (1998), Zhong Ye-An (1999), Wu Shu-Kun, Xi You-Min (1999), Hua Jin-Yang (2003) and others studied the relationship between the size of the board of directors and a company's value. Wu Shu-Kun (2001), Yu Dong-Zhi (2003) and others have done empirical research on corporate leadership structures.

This empirical research provides guidance for the development of a public company governance structure and the improvement of corporate value.

The rise of corporate governance evaluation

According to agency theory, modern companies are composed of two groups of people: one is shareholders as the principal, the other is directors and managers as the agent. In the pattern of a dual system, supervisors' committee—which is also entrusted by shareholders—takes the duty of monitoring the board of directors and the managers. However, the board of directors sits in a special position, as both the agent of shareholders and having the right to choose as well as incentivise and control managers. On one hand, shareholders are not able to monitor managers because of the lack of correlated knowledge and experience, or their time and vigor are not available to do this work because of their jobs. On the other hand, they have no motive to monitor managers with the intendance of a "free rider." Therefore, the task of monitoring managers (directors) and maximizing shareholders' benefits is set on the shoulders of directors who act as the agent. As early as 1776, Adam Smith posed that what the directors control is others' money, so they will not be as diligent as when they manage their own money. Thus, negligence and waste by directors are foreseeable in the form of the "company," and it is rational that shareholders pay much attention to the value of the capital they have invested and the performance of the company. Due to the decisive effect of corporate governance on corporate performance, more and more investors pay more attention to the quality of corporate governance structures and corporate governance mechanisms—which are the source of company value—in addition to the performance evaluation of public companies. Then, evaluation of the quality of corporate governance becomes the objective of shareholders, and it is on the basis of the objective requirements of principal investors that corporate governance evaluation occurs.

Evaluation is a judgment of a certain objective and activity which can help people to learn and master objective things and their rules, improve organizations, and enhance efficiency with effective measures. Corporate governance evaluation is the judgment of corporate governance structures and corporate governance mechanisms. Specifically, it is designing a corporate governance evaluation system according to the corporate governance environment, and evaluating the condition of corporate governance objectively and accurately with scientific measures. Using theories of statistics and operational research according to a certain index system, comparing with certain standards, following scientific procedures, and through quantitative and qualitative analysis in the form of an index, a corporate governance evaluation index evaluates public companies governance systematically, objectively and accurately. Since the beginning of production activities, human beings have been aware of the concept of evaluation. Taking a view from the history of modern economics, the true meaning of evaluation was put forward by company's owners with the intention to strengthen their control over capital rights hereafter the appearance of the corporate institution in middle and later period of 19th century. The separation of ownership and managerial authority and principal–agent relationship are the basic reasons of corporate governance evaluation. Taking a view from the history of economics and management science, corporate governance evaluation and corporate governance indexes emerged with the appearance of the corporate institution and the separation of ownership and managerial authority which came with this, with the intention of capital owners to strengthen their control over a company and the demand from investors for good investments.

At first, the position of corporate manager was often taken by one of the partners or the senior shareholder, so there was no principal–agent relationship. With the development of industry and commerce this system doesn't work; with the increasing size and complexity of companies, the position of manager is usually taken by managing experts paid by salaries. They are usually employed by a board of directors who represent the owners and they are not usually major shareholders of the company themselves. The privileged commercial company in the 1700s had the features of a modern corporation; for example, the East India Company (based in Holland) had shareholders' meetings as the top power organ; the board of directors was composed of 60 directors selected by a shareholders' meeting and took charge of decision-making; the daily managerial activities were charged by a board of managers which consisted of 17 members. Specializing companies, joint-stock companies and other forms of company came up subsequently. However, the real modern company appeared in the form of railway companies in the 1840s, and then extended to companies in finance and communication, and into modern industry and all comers. Accompanying the birth of the modern company came corporate ownership separate from managerial power. Berle and Means (1932) pointed out—in their book called *The Modern Corporation and Private Property*—that in a large public company there are many shareholders who have small numbers of shares, little managerial knowledge and no control rights or power, and it is this situation that causes the departure of ownership and control. Ownership is held by shareholders and control by the directors, and the direct result of this is the agency problem.

The practices in corporate governance after the 1980s forced the development of corporate governance research. In the 1980s, companies under the Japanese–German pattern attained better performance, which attracted attention to this pattern whereby banks and several companies form a corporate group and members in the group take shares in each other. However, in the 1990s economics in America revealed a better path, which brought attention to U.K.–U.S. corporate governance patterns. Large amounts of literature comparing the efficiency of corporate governance patterns arose, with the purpose of finding high-efficiency corporate governance systems and guiding governance practice more effectively. At the same time, corporate mergers and acquisitions happened frequently, and managers' compensation increased by a large extent. The increase in compensation didn't bring better company performance, and stakeholders' benefits were still damaged. Therefore, with the purpose of protecting minority investors, public companies in the U.S. established the independent director to strengthen the check-and-balance mechanism on boards of directors. Independent directors monitor the legality and reasonableness of board decisions, provide constructive opinions for the company's development, and provide better decision-making through the use of the independent director's expertise and objective judgment. Recently, financial scandals in large American companies such as Enron and WorldCom attracted the attention of scholars to corporate governance working conditions and quality evaluation; for example, diagnosis and evaluation of the governance of boards of directors, evaluation of the effect of directorate governance, and evaluation of the governance of public companies.

Development in the field of corporate governance practice in many countries produced the demand for evaluation of corporate governance from investors, government, and public companies. For investors, they care much about their investment's underlying value, to which corporate governance is critical. To corporate performance, corporate governance is as water to human life. Companies will have ongoing competitiveness and create more value only if they have a healthy governance structure and mechanisms. The reason why investors are willing to pay more for companies which have higher quality corporate governance is that corporate governance plays a decisive role in a company's value. To satisfy the focus on corporate governance by institutional investors, the Council of Institutional Investors (followed by some international institutions) designed a form evaluating the procedures of boards of directors, aimed at helping investors find out more about the condition of public companies' corporate governance, analyzing investing risk and underlying value, thus improving the scientific focus of decision-making. Meanwhile, corporate governance evaluation also gave timely awareness of problems existing within companies, helping them to control critical factors in order to carry on corporate governance activities more effectively.

Corporate governance evaluation in Thailand is conducted with the encouragement of the government. For public corporations, corporate governance is an essential factor for competitiveness, and in order to improve governance quality, generate better corporate performance and attract more investors, it's necessary for businesses to pay attention to corporate governance in their company, their position in the industry, and existing problems. Corporate governance evaluation is borne from the spontaneous demands of investors, governmental monitoring departments and public corporations, and the demand generates the evaluation of corporate governance by research institutions and scholars.

The attention on corporate governance evaluation from scholars at home and abroad is based on the demand for development of corporate governance practice, especially from institutional investors. Corporate governance evaluation germinated from analysis of directorates' performance by Jackson Martindell. In 1950, it rose through commercial organizations. The earliest and canonical corporate governance evaluation research is the procedures used to formally evaluate a board of directors, designed by the Council of Institutional Investors. Subsequently, research resulted in corporate governance diagnosis and evaluation; for example, Walter J. Salmon (1993) created the 22 diagnostic problems for a board of directors, while Standard & Poor's, Deminor and Credit Lyonnais Securities Asia each created a corporate governance evaluation system in 1998, 1999 and 2000 respectively. Institutional Shareholder Services also built a worldwide corporate governance database for public companies, providing services to member investors of monitoring public companies' governance situations. In addition, there were the different corporate governance evaluation systems from Brunswick Warburg, the Institute of Corporate Law and Corporate Governance (ICLCG), the Information and Credit Rating Agency (ICRA), the World Bank, Thailand, Korea, China Taiwan, and others.

Table 1.1:   Primary corporate governance evaluation systems existing at home and aboard

Evaluation organization or individual	Evaluation content	Scope of application	Evaluation methods
Jackson Martindell	Social contribution, service to stockholders, analysis of directorate performance, corporate financial policies	Corporate evaluation	The larger the core, the better the corporate governance condition
Standard & Poor's (S&P)	*State evaluation:* Foundation of law, regulations, rules of information disclosure, market base *Corporate evaluation:* Ownership structure, rights and interrelationship of financial stakeholders, transparency and information disclosure, the structure and running of directorate	State evaluation and corporate evaluation	The larger the core, the better the corporate governance condition
Deminor	*State evaluation:* Analysis of law relating to corporate governance *Corporate evaluation:* Stockholders' rights and obligations, the scope of takeover defences, information transparency, structure of directorate	State evaluation and corporate evaluation	The larger the core, the better the corporate governance condition

Evaluation organization or individual	Evaluation content	Scope of application	Evaluation methods
CLSA	*State evaluation:* Transparency, comprehensive regulation and supervising discipline, exercise of relative rules, politics and regulation environment affecting corporate governance and ability to maximize company value, adoption of the U.S. Generally Accepted Accounting Principles, institutional mechanism of corporate governance culture *Corporate evaluation:* Managerial constrain, transparency, minority stockholders' protection, the independence and accountability of directorate, core business, debt controlling, cash return to stockholders and corporate social liability	State evaluation and corporate evaluation	The larger the core, the better the corporate governance condition
ISS	Structure and composition of directorate and its subordinate committees, corporate law and institution, law of state where the corporation is located, compensation of managers and directors, relative financial performance, "lead" corporate governance practice, proportion of shares held by senior managers, education background of directors	Corporate evaluation	The larger the core, the better the corporate governance condition

Evaluation organization or individual	Evaluation content	Scope of application	Evaluation methods
Davis and Heidrick	Stockholders' rights, corporate governance committee, transparency, corporation administration and audit	Corporate evaluation	The larger the core, the better the corporate governance condition
Brunswick Warburg	Transparency, the degree of share dispersal, capital transferring and transfer price, merger/ reorganization, bankruptcy, limit of ownership and controlling, managerial attitude to the external staff, nature of enrollment	Corporate evaluation	The smaller the core, the smaller the corporate governance risk, and the better the corporate governance condition
ICLCG	Information disclosure, ownership structure, directorate and management structure, shareholders' rights, expropriation risk, corporate governance history	Corporate evaluation	The larger the core, the better the corporate governance condition
ICRA	Ownership structure, management structure (including the structure of each directorate committee), quality of financial report and other disclosures, satisfaction of financial stakeholders' benefits	Corporate evaluation	The smaller the core, the better the corporate governance condition

Evaluation organization or individual	Evaluation content	Scope of application	Evaluation methods
Corporate governance evaluation system in Thailand	Stockholder rights, director quality, effectiveness of corporate internal control	Corporate evaluation	The larger the core, the better the corporate governance condition
Corporate governance evaluation system in Korea	Stockholder rights, structure of directorate and committee, directorate and committee procedures, disclosure to investors and equality of ownership	Corporate evaluation	The larger the core, the better the corporate governance condition
Corporate governance evaluation system in China Taiwan	*Macro-evaluation:* Clearly integrated laws and regulations, effective performance of laws and regulations, political environment, accounting standards, institutional factors of promoting the recognition of corporate governance culture *Corporate evaluation:* Composition of directorate (supervisors' committee), ownership structure, managerial participation in trading with second largest shareholder and people with special relationships, the degree of big shareholders' referring to stock market	Macro-evaluation and corporate evaluation	The larger the core, the better the corporate governance condition

There are four common features in the governance evaluation systems above:

1. All the evaluation systems are composed of a series of detailed indexes, and include factors such as shareholders' rights, structure of the board of directors, and information disclosure.

2. Grading methods are the same in these systems, except for two. In general, a low grade means poor quality of governance, and vice versa. The ICRA evaluation system works contrarily; that is, grade CGR1 means the highest level of governance condition and grade CGR6 the lowest. Another exception is Brunswick Warburg's governance risk analysis, which makes grades in the form of castigatory scores. The higher the grade, the higher the governance risk.

3. Most grading systems adopt a weighting method; that is, set different weights to factors that have different importance.

4. The methods to get grading information are the same, which is from publicly available information and some from interviews with key employees of companies.

There are two differences among different evaluation system. Some evaluation systems, like Davis and Heidrick and Brunswick Warburg, aim to evaluate the corporate governance of a certain foreign country, and others, like Standard & Poor's, Deminor and CLSA which include national level analysis, refer to several countries. Evaluating standards used in these systems are similar. Standard & Poor's offer a four-factor evaluation on the effectiveness of laws, regulating, information disclosure and market base; Deminor services by way of providing a nation analyzing report which includes a juristic analysis and a reporting of corporate governance practice in several countries. Their service is available in 17 European countries. CLSA's grading, which includes 20 to 25 new markets, mainly uses six decisive factors referring to monitoring and institutional environment. Recent research of the World Bank compares national level analysis on the basis of six comprehensive indexes about corporate governance; the same work is also done by Davis and Heidrick (2002) in a different way, in which they consider mainly the average level of corporate governance of different countries on the basis of corporate governance practice and corporate governance conditions of separate companies.

There are great distinctions among these evaluation systems in the aspects of emphasis, standards adopted and structures of the index systems. Specifically, under the guidance of OECD corporate governance guidelines and CalPERS's corporate governance principles, Standard & Poor's classify corporate governance evaluation in two parts: evaluation of government and evaluation of corporation. The former evaluates from what the law is based on, monitoring information disclosure and market base. While the latter includes ownership structure and its influence, financial stakeholders' relationship, transparency and information disclosure as well as the structure and working process of boards of directors. It focuses on the influence from outer forces on the macroscopic picture and corporate inner structure and workings of corporate governance. Deminor designed its index system on the OECD corporate governance guidelines and the World Bank's corporate governance directions. Its evaluation is from three dimensions—shareholders' rights and obligations, scope of takeover defense, and transparency and directorate's structure and function. It focuses on the influence on corporate governance quality from the corporate governance environment, especially from the defensive measures against corporate takeover. CLSA's evaluation system pays more attention to transparency, independence of the directorate and protection of minority shareholders, emphasizing corporate social obligation. Evaluation is from eight aspects: transparency, managerial control, independence and accountability of the board of directors, minority shareholders' protection, core business, debt control, cash return to shareholders and corporate social responsibilities.

All of this research enriches corporate governance theory, and at the same time provides guidance for corporate governance practice.

The rise of corporate governance evaluation systems in China

Corporate governance structures and corporate governance mechanisms are determined by the corporate governance environment, and the evaluating extent and evaluating standards change sharply with a different corporate governance environment; therefore, there is great distinction between corporate governance evaluation systems in different governance patterns. So far, a number of different evaluation systems have been established, such as evaluation systems of Standard & Poor's, Deminor, CLSA, ISS, DWS, Brunswick Warburg, Thailand, Korea, City University of Hong Kong, Fu Jen University of Taiwan. Different systems need different environments; evaluation systems brought in from other countries can't work as satisfactorily as in the original country because of the distinctions in corporate governance environments and the developing condition of China compared to others (for example, the typical phenomenon of "dominant shareholder" and a board of supervisors, which are different from that of U.K.–U.S. patterns). We should refer to international experience when designing an evaluation index system unique to China, integrating the legal environment, institutional environment, market conditions and public companies' own development, and make objective and accurate evaluation of public companies by scientific measure. Only in this way can our evaluation reflect Chinese public companies' governance conditions faithfully. Therefore, China should establish a set of corporate governance evaluating systems that fit to its governance environment satisfactorily.

The Corporate Governance Research Center of Nankai University is always working in the combination of corporate governance theory and its application. Taking the improvement of corporate governance quality as the ultimate goal, the research team turned gradually to research of corporate governance application from fundamental theoretical research and began to study corporate governance evaluation in 1999. They first extended the theoretical research to the field of the corporate governance principal and its application, and then to research of evaluation and indexing. The researching field is extended from corporate governance structure to corporate governance mechanism, from theoretical research to practical research, from national research to international research, from traditional corporate governance to network corporate governance, from modern corporations to private companies, from one who is the governance objective to one who executes corporate governance, and so on. In the field of theoretical research, the center established a theoretical framework and extended the researching scope from single corporation to corporate group, multinational corporation and network, and from governance objective to executors.

The positioning of the Chinese corporate governance index

Using theories of statistics and operational research, comparing with certain standards, following scientific procedures, and through quantitative and qualitative analysis, a corporate governance evaluation index is the systematic, objective and accurate evaluation of public companies which is in the form of an index. Taking a view from the history of economics and management science, corporate governance evaluation and corporate governance indexes are put forward with the appearance of the corporate institution and the separation of ownership and managerial authority and of ownership and control power, with the intention of the capital owner or owners to strengthen their control over the company and the demand of investors for good investments. A corporate governance index is the deepening of corporate governance evaluation, and its functions are as outlined below.

Enhancing monitoring and promoting the development and quality of the capital market

Through the setting and periodical publication of a corporate governance index, monitoring departments can get timely information about public companies' corporate governance structures and corporate governance mechanisms. Monitoring is therefore assured to have a definite objective in view of the feedback of information, and stock monitoring departments can analyze timely corporate governance conditions and executive conditions in relation to guidelines and principles in Chinese public companies. Using the system, stock monitoring departments can be aware of the establishing and ongoing conditions of the objectives in the aspects of:

- controlling shareholders' behavior
- the selecting procedure of directors
- directors' obligations
- the constitution of the board of directors
- duties of the board of directors
- special committees of the directorate
- duties of the board of supervisors
- information disclosure
- performance evaluations
- incentive and restraint.

This is propitious for monitoring departments to implement their duty; for example, to test the executive condition of the directing opinion about establishing independent directors institutions in public companies proclaimed in August 2001 in China, and China listed company governance norms in January 2002.

Providing to investors a tool to evaluate an investment, and directing investment decisions

A corporate governance index which is quantified and timely makes it convenient for investors to compare corporate governance levels and recognize the underlying corporate governance risk of an investment, and the dynamic number sequence can be used to test the developing trend and investing value of corporate governance in public companies and improve decision-making. The rise of corporate governance in foreign countries is the result of investors' attention to it, and the goal is to decrease information asymmetry and advance decision-making. Traditionally, financial ratios are the main consideration of investors, but serious problems have consequently arisen, such as the frequent occurrence of financial scandals at the end of the 1990s and beginning of the 2000s. These lower the rate of return greatly, and sometimes even cause total loss of an investment.

Investors now take more care on the underlying value of an investment, which is determined by the quality of corporate governance. Research on the relationship between corporate governance and share price shows that there is close relation between them. Establishing and publishing periodically a corporate governance index will enhance the dissemination of information and reduce information asymmetry. With the signals provided by corporate governance, investors will be more rational and no longer invest speculatively. For investors, the key value of corporate governance evaluation is the offer of comprehensive information; evaluating this information can help with assessing investment value and support decision-making. McKinsey & Company's investigation on investors' intentions in June 2000 found that three-quarters of investors regard directorate behavior as important as financial performance; investors in Latin America even think the former is more important than the latter, and 80% of them are willing to pay more for shares with good corporate governance. The LENS Investing management company is finding from aspects of financial evaluation and corporate governance evaluation the undervalued company whose value can be increased by corporate governance. A worldwide database about corporate governance in public companies is built by the Institutional Shareholder Services (ISS) to provide monitoring of public companies' governance for their members. For investors, periodical publication of governance information offers them timely realizing of governance conditions and existing problems of invested objects, and they can reduce the investing risk by timely and effective measures.

Improvement in scientific decision-making

Corporate governance evaluation systems offer both investors and the companies timely information on the general condition of corporate governance and detailed information on the aspects of controlling shareholders' behavior, board of directors, board of supervisors, managers, information disclosure, and so on. It can also help companies to diagnose possible problems and take proper measures for remedy, and as a result assure public companies' corporate governance structure and corporate governance mechanisms are in good condition and strengthen their competitiveness.

Helpful in forming reputation control of public companies and improving the quality of the stock market

Considering corporate financing and continuing development, public companies must take care of their performance in the stock market and with investors. The establishment of corporate governance evaluation systems can track conditions of corporate governance comprehensively, systematically and in a timely fashion, and periodically make public the evaluation result and make up for the shortcoming of weak outer environmental control in Chinese companies. The reputation constraint comes from timely publication of corporate governance details, which encourages public companies to improve corporate governance and reduce governance risk, and ultimately improves the stock market's quality. Public companies' credibility is founded on the basis of a good corporate governance structure and corporate governance mechanisms, and a public company with good corporate governance is certain to have good corporate credit.[1] The periodic publication of relevant information can track the condition of corporate governance, forming a strong reputation constraint and ultimately improve the stock market's quality. Dynamic comparing of the corporate governance index of different periods

---

[1] Li Wei-An, *Research of corporate credibility internal controlling mechanism from the view of corporate governance.* pp 107–121. China National Natural Science Fund Emergency Project. Project number: 70141011.

reflects the fluctuation of corporate governance quality in public companies and forms the dynamic reputation constraint.

Building the platform of empirical research of corporate governance and improving corporate governance researching standards

The establishment of corporate governance evaluation systems builds the platform for the change from normative research to empirical research, which turns the theoretical research to quantitative and practical research, and measures corporate governance quality exactly. Meanwhile, the series of research results in the course of evaluation is an important data resource for Chinese public companies to favorably accept empirical research on corporate performance. The building of this platform provides the chance for corporate governance theoretical research to integrate to governance practice, and then take a further step to improve the guidance of theoretical research to governance practice.

Design principles of evaluation systems in Chinese companies

The design principles of corporate governance evaluation systems must be based on the specific corporate governance environment in order to reflect Chinese companies' corporate governance comprehensively, objectively, and accurately.

Purpose

Evaluating the purpose determines all the factors of an evaluating system, such as the design of the system, selection of evaluating method, and method of attaining information on evaluating objects and forming value judgments. Therefore, the designing of a corporate governance evaluating index system should consider firstly the goal of the evaluation. There are three goals of corporate governance evaluation in public companies, the first of which is providing reference for government and monitoring departments to set corporate governance policies; the second is providing reference for public companies to improve corporate governance quality; and the third is offering information to investors for their selecting investment objects.

Scientific basis

The setting of corporate governance evaluation indexes should adapt to the characters of public companies themselves and the requirements of corporate governance guidelines, principles and criteria, and be scientific, rational and reflect governance conditions accurately and comprehensively. This is also the basic starting point of designing corporate governance evaluation indexes.

Comparable

The setting of corporate governance indexes should not only fully reflect public companies' corporate governance, but also make them comparable. Comparability refers to every aspect of an index system, the most important of which is the extent, calculation caliber and calculation methods. The influence of the governance environment in different periods of corporate governance should also be considered for longitudinal comparing.

Combining qualitative research with quantitative data

The condition of corporate governance includes every aspect from corporate governance structure to corporate governance mechanisms. Some details which are hard to represent with exact numbers—such as accomplishment of directors' obligations, directorate structure and performance evaluation of directors—can only be described in qualitative ways. Therefore, when setting evaluation indexes, qualitative criteria should be combined with quantitative data. When evaluating comprehensively, governance index, which are quantitative data, reflect public companies' corporate governance after quantitating the qualitative criteria.

Integrality

The setting of an index should consider the relationship between each index completely and with no duplicate. Meanwhile, as an integrated index system, indexes should be related to each other in timing, space and decision methods, supplement each other, and ultimately assure the integration of the system.

Feasibility

The setting of an index system should be feasible, exercisable, and meet the needs of practical work. In this book, we try our best to be systematic when doing this work. However, we excluded content which is not essential and for which it is difficult to obtain accurate information.

The content of a corporate governance evaluation system

An evaluating index is the core of an evaluating system. The design of a corporate governance evaluating index must consider the institutional environment of Chinese public companies, which has the feature of "path dependence"; that is, the founding and development of a corporate institution is strongly influenced by the country's culture, political institutions, law and corporate practice. Chinese public companies have developed under the influence of "Confucian culture" and the planned economy, and this leads to strong "path dependence" of our public companies no matter what the arrangement of ownership structure or human affairs and related transactions.

Planned power arrangements carried over from the traditional planned economy mean the ownership structures of public companies represent the peculiarities of "parallel ownership"[2] and "national shares' majority position." Meanwhile, in the long-term influence of Confucian thoughts and relations, joint directors and related transactions appeared in public companies, which make corporate governance patterns in China unique from both the unitary pattern in the U.K. and U.S. and the dual one in Japan and Germany. The setting of Chinese corporate governance evaluating index system should be based on the characteristics of the governance environment faced by Chinese public companies.

The quality of corporate governance is revealed in the form of decision-making and monitoring and constraining

---

[2]   Hamada Michiyo, et al. *Corporate Governance and capital market supervision—compare and learn.* Beijing University Press, 1997. p 129.

mechanisms. Thus, corporate governance is through a set of formal and informal, inner and outer rules or mechanisms to harmonize the beneficial relationship between corporations and their stakeholders and assure scientific decision-making, and protect the benefit of every stakeholder. A company not only belongs to its shareholders, but is also of interest to the community. Corporate governance mechanisms are not limited to internal governance, which is based on corporate structure, but a joint-governance by stakeholders through a series of inner and outer mechanisms. The purpose of corporate governance is not only to realize shareholders' maximum profits, but also to assure the scientific decision-making, realize stakeholders' maximum profits consequently. So a corporate governance evaluation should consider the participation degree of stakeholders. Meanwhile, the essence of corporate governance—which comes from the agency problem—lies in the monitoring and check-and-balance of managers by governance entities such as shareholders, the result of which is solving the problems of moral hazard and adverse selection, which are caused by information asymmetry.

There are two objects of corporate governance. One is managers, the governance of which is from the board of directors—the goal is the properness of corporate management and judging is by a company's operating performance; the other is the board of directors, the governance of which is from shareholders and other stakeholders, aiming for the properness of important strategy decision-making judged by the return on investment of shareholders and other stakeholders. Therefore, evaluations of the board of directors and managers are the core of corporate governance evaluation, and it is the board of supervisors which is the special organization charged with supervising that plays the role. That's why evaluation of the board of supervisors is necessary to the whole evaluation system. Information disclosure, as a controlling mechanism, plays a key role in constraining the behavior of managers of public companies and protecting the benefits of stakeholders.

Complying with the designing principles of a corporate governance evaluation index system, integrating with the governance environment of Chinese public companies, based on Chinese corporate governance principles and China listed company governance norms, we make allowance for the company law, securities law, Guidelines on Articles of Association of Listed Companies, Establishment of Independent Director Systems by Listed Companies Guiding Opinion, Rules on Implementing Disclosure of Information Relating to "Share Transfer Companies", and other laws and codes concerning public companies and relevant files. Meanwhile, using existing corporate governance evaluation indexes of foreign countries, we set six aspects of evaluation: shareholders' rights and behavior of controlling shareholders, the board of directors and its members, the board of supervisors and its members, management group, information disclosure, and stakeholders. Each of these is composed of a series of evaluating indexes.

Shareholders' rights and controlling shareholders' behaviour

Shareholders' rights

Broadly, shareholders' rights refers to all kinds of rights to a company that can be exercised by shareholders, including the right to obtain economic benefit and take part in corporate governance activities. Classified by exercising purpose, shareholders' rights are divided into self-benefiting rights on one hand and common-benefiting rights on the other, which is accepted by scholars in China and Japan. Some scholars definite self-benefiting rights as the rights aiming to get economic benefits, and common-benefiting rights are aiming to manage the company. However, others think self-benefiting rights are only for individual benefit but common-benefiting rights are for both individual and corporate benefit. There is no intrinsic difference between the two descriptions, in that economic benefit is the main representation of individual benefits of shareholders, and there is a connection between shareholders' individual benefits and the corporate benefit of the shareholders participating in corporate management. The classification is the most important one, but there are no absolute boundaries between the two kinds of rights. This is because some common-benefiting rights are exercised as a way to exercise self-benefiting rights, which leads to double classification of these rights; for example, rights to check accounting files and accounting ledgers, or rights to acquire or stop issuing new shares.

Controlling shareholders' behavior

From the view of controlling shareholders' agency, the present ownership structure in Chinese public companies gives birth to two corporate governance problems. The first is the agency cost of controlling shareholders, which is in relation to ownership concentration; the second is the weakness of government in realizing the maximum value for shareholders, which is related to the identity of shareholders. Measures adopted recently target the first problem, while measures directly related to the second are rare. However, government is the direct or indirect controlling shareholder in most public companies, so the two problems coincide. Therefore, measures aimed at solving the problem of controlling shareholders will affect the power of the government when they exercise the extenuatory disposition right.

The corporate governance problems in China are closely related to the features of share ownership. The most important effect of the dominant position of state shares in Chinese public companies is the control of manager appointing and incentive, and the consequent influence on corporate behavior. Although it is not unique to China that corporate entities control publicly listed companies as the controlling shareholder, majority shareholders usually override shareholder meetings and the board of directors and exercise direct control on the companies. A feature of ownership of Chinese public companies is that influential families, individual shareholders, financial institutions and institutional investors play a minor role, while state shares dominate. In fact, 95% of public companies are controlled directly or indirectly (through state industrial corporations) by the government. In addition, 50% of public companies' ownerships are highly centralized; that is, the first three biggest shareholders take 60% to 80% of all shares. The highly centralized share ownership and relatively low proportion of outstanding shares means the competition for control rights in public companies is very limited, if it exists at all.

Shareholders' meeting

The shareholders' meeting is the top power organization in a corporation. However, there is no definite regulation on shareholders' rights in China. Although the right to select and fire directors is one of the ways that shareholders can influence corporate behavior, there is limited scope for minority shareholders to ensure there is one director who represents their own benefits on the board. According to the rules, independent directors should pay much attention to the benefits of minority shareholders, however the provision of holding at least 10% of shares to nominate independent directors excludes minority shareholders from nominating. It's impossible for independent directors to be loyal to minority shareholders without giving the nominating rights to the minority holders. In the present ownership structure, without ways to increase the chance for minority shareholders to select directors (for example, a cumulative voting system), nominating independent directors has almost no value. To protect minority shareholder benefits, provisions related to director appointment should be drafted to prevent majority shareholders from distorting voting results and breaching other rules.

On the basis of the analysis above, according to the regulations for shareholders' rights, regulations for shareholders' meetings and regulations for controlling shareholders' behavior in Chinese corporate governance guidelines and public company governance principles, we think it reasonable to evaluate controlling shareholders' behavior from shareholders' meetings, independence of public companies, benefit protection for middle and minority shareholders, and related transactions.

Corporate directorate governance evaluating index

Features of the board of directors

The directorate is the core of corporate governance. It's been proven that a good directorate is the center and precondition of improvement in corporate governance. Therefore, it's essential to attract more investors that improve the quality of corporate governance, and as for the efficiency of directorate corporate governance, the key is frequent evaluation of the legality of directors' behavior and quality of the directorate's performance, and additionally to supervise and urge public companies to better directorate governance. The National Association of Corporate Directors Blue Ribbon Committee (1999) even think it certain that as long as there is a proper directorate evaluation procedure, corporate performance can be improved. Therefore, a systematic evaluation of directorate governance becomes a critical part of corporate governance, and establishing a directorate evaluation index which aims at these problems is of great necessity.

The directorate has a specific legal status in corporate power structures, and then should take on specific legal duties and obligations as well. Directors' obligations can be divided into the hard work obligation—which requires them to carry out duties satisfactorily, including attending meetings and taking care of corporate running—and the credibility obligation, which demands that they act in the interests of the corporation and never engage in activities damaging corporate benefits. However, we must give them certain incentive as well, including material and spiritual incentive. In order to make this effective, scientific director performance evaluation standards and performance evaluations are indispensable.

With increasing power in public companies, institutional investors become more demanding of the capability and professional background of directors. CalPERS suggests directorates establish mechanisms to check directors' performance and set corresponding checking standards for directors' loyalty and attending, preparing for and participating in meetings. Generally speaking, a director should at least be capable in accounting or finance and international markets, have commercial or managerial experience, industrial knowledge, customer-based experience or point of view, threat-responding ability, and leadership or strategic planning experience.

Directors' qualifications have two categories: positive criteria on one hand and negative criteria on the other. The former is the indispensable features to be a director, and the latter is that which cannot be taken by directors. Usually, except for compulsory provisions for negative qualifications, there are few rules about directors' positive qualifications—this is left to shareholders. However, lacking enough information on director candidates, shareholders' selecting ability is constrained. In order to protect confidence in the market, for public companies some stock exchanges stipulate required abilities and professional knowledge of directors through setting rules for public companies coming into the market. For example, directors of listed companies of the stock exchange of Hong Kong should satisfy extra active provisions. They should give proof of their qualifications, experience, loyalty and adherence to certain professional standards. Non-executive directors in public company directorates should also prove independence besides the common qualifications of directors.

Directorate governance evaluation index system

In evaluating directors and the directorate's working conditions, differences exist among different countries. Combined closely with Chinese public companies' governance environment, when we design a directorate governance evaluation index system the focus is on the legality of directors' behavior and efficiency of the directorate's working, considering fully the duties charged to the directorate by law and the directors' characters from the five dimensions of directors' rights and obligations, the directorate's working efficiency, the directorate's composition, directors' compensation, and independent directors.

Evaluation index system of the board of supervisors

Features of the board of supervisors in Chinese public companies

Compared with foreign countries, there are certain special features of supervisors' committees in Chinese public companies. For the two acknowledged corporate governance patterns around the world there are no supervisors' committees, but there are flawless independent director institutions in U.K.–U.S. corporate governance, while a supervisory board is most typical in the Japanese–German pattern. However, supervisor committees in the Japanese–German pattern are defined differently from those in the Chinese system. In Germany, a supervisors' committee is composed of non-executive directors charged with monitoring, while a directors' committee is composed of executive directors and takes the duty of executing. A supervisors' committee is at the core of corporate governance. Thus in Japan, both the supervisors' committee and directors' committee are selected by shareholders' meeting, and as an independent department a supervisors' committee evaluates the directorate's performance.

The accountability provided by a supervisors' committee will improve the monitoring quality inside corporations. It's also agreed by foreign scholars that under the special background of China, the relative powerlessness of the court's sentencing makes supervisors' committees more important. However, the bringing in of independent directors leaves an awkward position and an uncertain perspective. A scientific and effective monitoring mechanism is important in the achievement of the goal of good corporate governance. A component of the supervisory mechanism is the orientation of supervisory departments, and attention should be paid to effective execution of supervisors' committee functions. An examination of modern corporate institutions in 2002 found that one of the most important components for good results is a supervisors' committee. The combination of the independent director institution with the present corporate governance structure in China influences the monitoring functions of supervisory departments.

Supervisors' committee governance evaluation index system

There are no supervisors' committees in corporate governance systems in Britain and America, so supervisors' committee evaluations are not included in these locations. Even in corporate governance evaluation systems in Chinese public companies— which is established by researchers of internal organizations of security combined with related law, provisions and policies in China—there is little content about supervisors' committees. In China, under the precondition that we still have supervisors' committees in the corporate governance system, evaluation should include the assurance of directors' capabilities as well as effectiveness of supervisor committee work.

Manager governance evaluation index system

Features of managers

As predicted by research conducted by foreign scholars on corporate governance and the associated problems, "agency problems" and "contract incompleteness" are two fundamental reasons for the existence of corporate governance. Borne with the emergence of the agency relationship are the inner conflicts between principal and agent, such as misalignment of goals, information asymmetry, and mismatch of duty and risk. Therefore, it's very likely to happen that the agent can't behave in the principals' interests, and can even pursue their own individual interests at the expense of those of capital owners. This is called the "agency problem". For the agent, corporate managers' deliberate or unintended damaging of the benefit of capital owners is the essence of the "agency problem", and is a major focus of corporate governance.

Increasingly, extension of the scope and aims of corporate governance requires managers to serve not only for shareholders' interests but also other stakeholders, with larger scope and assurance of stakeholders' maximum benefits. However, there are a lot of issues in the managers' governance of listed companies in China, such as incentive and supervisory mechanisms are lacking or are problematic, and simple and low-level compensation packages of senior managers run short of dynamic and long-term motivation to work hard. On the other hand, critical executives own almost ultimate control rights; that is, the "insider control" phenomenon appears obviously and seriously in Chinese listed companies, breaks the balance in the governance mechanism, destroys or corrupts managers' ability for decision-making and executing maintenance, makes the board of directors suffer, and hurts minor shareholders and employees' benefits. In addition, as the components outside the company—such as capital markets, product markets, professional managers markets and stock markets—haven't been established or are not mature, it causes further problems. Therefore, a manager evaluation index which evaluates comprehensively the appointment, incentive and constraints of managers in Chinese public companies is significant for learning the quality of managers' governance in public companies, finding out existing problems, improving corporate governance quality and perfecting the governance mechanisms in our public companies.

Managers' governance evaluation index system

There are differences in manager governance between our country and developed countries. First, compared with material markets of western countries the incompleteness of our capital market, product market and particularly the managers' market leads to poor incentive and constraints of managers and low dependence on external governance; next, contrary to developed countries' market governance, our government still plays a certain role in corporate governance; additionally, corporate governance in foreign countries has features of strong incentive and external constraining mechanisms, with both weak in our country; and last, the new economies place focus on scientific decision-making mechanisms, while our companies are still not paying enough attention to it. Therefore, there are two problems that our public companies need to resolve. Make managers willing and provide incentive to realize stakeholders' maximum profits through the realization of their own benefits, and prevent them from damaging any stakeholders' benefits deliberately; as a result, solve the problem of weak management and corruption, which can be done through good incentive and constraint mechanisms. And try to make capable managers make decisions which benefit the corporation's long-term development; this can be realized by proper appointing mechanisms and executive protection mechanisms.

On the basis of the analysis above, we designed certain evaluating criteria from three dimensions to evaluate managers: personnel appointment, executive protection, and incentive and constraints.

Information disclosure evaluation index system

Features of information disclosure in public companies

Information disclosure is extended from solely financial information to both financial and non-financial information which is used to evaluate corporate operations, public policy, risk prediction, effectiveness of corporate governance, and so on. There are four areas in an information disclosure evaluation system: financial information, auditing information, the conformity of the disclosed corporate governance information to related regulations, and the timeliness of information disclosure.

Companies should build websites for investors to search for related information as soon as it is available. The monitoring institutions and intermediary organs collect, analyze and test the authenticity of the information, the results of which can be used to evaluate the reliability of information disclosure. Taking a view from public investors, true, timely, comprehensive information disclosure will lead to rational investing decisions, while for the capital market timely information will help to adjust share prices on time, assure continuity and effectiveness of transactions, and reduce blind shifts in the market. The integrality of information disclosure requires public companies provide comprehensive information and not neglect or hinder critical information, so that users know about the corporate governance structure, financial conditions, operating results, cash flow, operating risk, and so on.

Information disclosure evaluation index system in public companies

For different purposes, public companies can adopt various disclosing methods to hinder critical information. It is a most serious problem to not disclose information accurately and reliably, which is required by regulations. Therefore, the evaluation should aim at these problems. Improving the incentive for public companies to disclose information, disclosing all events which are likely to influence economic decisions fully and in a timely fashion, and reducing information asymmetry can help information users make good judgments and assures equal treatment of all shareholders. Therefore, an information disclosure evaluation index system should be designed from accuracy, timeliness and integrity of information disclosure.

Corporate stakeholders governance evaluation index

Features of corporate stakeholders governance

It's quite common in Germany, Holland, Switzerland and other European countries that a typical stakeholder—such as an employee—participates in corporate governance. There is also research in China which argues that the "third capital"—that is, environmental capital, which is provided by environmental factors such as suppliers, customers, creditors, employees, government and community—is increasingly important to corporations. In 2002, the China Securities Regulatory Commission (CSRC) and State Economic and Trade Commission (SETC) established Chinese public company corporate governance guidelines, which regulate the scope of stakeholders, and their position, function and rights in corporate governance, and points out that stakeholders have rights to share benefits, obtain information and participate. The way they function in corporate governance is that corporations directly communicate with creditors, employees with the directorate, and supervisors' committee with managers. It's obvious that stakeholder problems are indispensable in modern corporate governance structures, and they must be included in corporate governance evaluation index systems in order to assure objectiveness and completeness.

Stakeholder governance evaluation index system

The evaluation index about stakeholders is not included in foreign corporate governance evaluation systems. That is because it's still at the theoretical level and it's hard to define the way stakeholders function in corporate governance as well as performance evaluation. Nevertheless, it's the developing trend of corporate governance practice that attention must be paid to stakeholders in a comprehensive corporate governance evaluation system; meanwhile, there are also regulations about it in the corporate governance guidelines, so it's necessary to consider a stakeholders' evaluation index in the whole evaluation system. Based on the position and function of stakeholders in corporate governance, and considering the science and feasibility of evaluation indexes, we set the evaluation index to reflect stakeholders mainly from the perspective of stakeholders participating in corporate governance and the harmoniousness of their relationships. The former mainly evaluates the extent of their participation, and the higher the extent the better the protection of the corporation and the better the decision-making; the latter evaluates the harmoniousness of the relationships between the corporation and stakeholders. For example, the participating extent of employees, exercise of corporate social duties, relationship of management, relationship between the corporation and monitoring department, corporate litigation and arbitrage.

Table 1.2:   Corporate governance evaluation index for Chinese public companies

Level 1 index	Level 2 index	Level 3 index	Index directions	Evaluation criterion
Index for shareholder rights and controlling shareholders' behavior	Condition of related transaction	1. Same-industry competition	Evaluates the same-industry competition between public companies and the controlling shareholders of other related organizations	Sitting in different industries, there is no same-industry competition
		2. Pricing foundation	Pricing foundation of related transactions between controlling shareholders and public companies tell the regulation of related transactions	Public companies should issue clear reports on related transactions
		3. Occupy of capital	Whether corporate capital is occupied by controlling shareholders reflects the external condition of controlling shareholders' behavior	No occupied capital

Level 1 index	Level 2 index	Level 3 index	Index directions	Evaluation criterion
Index for shareholder rights and controlling shareholders' behavior	Condition of related transaction	4. Loan guarantee	Whether public companies offer loan guarantees to controlling shareholders and other related entities reflects external condition of controlling shareholders	Not supply of guarantee
	Independence of public companies	5. Personal independence	Whether there is a personal relationship between public companies and controlling shareholders	Independent
		6. Business independence	Whether there is a business relationship between public companies and controlling shareholders	Independent
		7. Financial independence	Whether there is a financial relationship between public companies and controlling shareholders	Independent
		8. Capital independence	Whether there is a capital relationship between public companies and controlling shareholders	Independent
	Condition of shareholders' meeting	9. Participation of shareholders' meeting	Measure the participation of shareholders in shareholders' meeting	As much as possible

Level 1 index	Level 2 index	Level 3 index	Index directions	Evaluation criterion
Index for shareholder rights and controlling shareholders' behavior	Condition of shareholders' meeting	10. Regulation of shareholders' meeting	Measure the procedures of shareholders' meeting, evaluate participation of shareholders in shareholders' meeting	Comprehensive-ness of share-holder meeting's record
	Rights and interests of middle and minority stockholders	11. Provisional proposal in provisional stockholders' meeting	Adequate attention to the willingness of middle and minority shareholders	Exist
Evaluation index of directors and directorate	Directors' rights and obligations	1. Director selection	Measure the reasonableness of selecting procedures of directors	Comply with provisions and corporate law
		2. Examine the capability of directors	Check the situation that director fulfills responsibilities and participates in directorate's activities	Comply to related requirements from China Securities Regulatory Commission and participate in directorate activities
		3. Annual training of directors	Evaluate the improvement of directors' capabilities	The more, the better
	Effectiveness of the board of directors	4. Scale of board of directors	Check the reasonableness of directorate scale	Able to discuss effectively and make sure equal shareholders' benefit, contains 5 to 19 members

Level 1 index	Level 2 index	Level 3 index	Index directions	Evaluation criterion
Evaluation index of directors and directorate	Effectiveness of the board of directors	5. Personal constitution of directorate	Measure the reasonableness of directorate personal constitution	External director and independent director count for the majority, and be expert in different fields
		6. Quality of directorate meeting	Measure quality of directorate meeting	Comprehensive, specific, detailed, and signatures
	Organizational structure of directorate	7. Leadership composition of the board of directors	Examination power balancing condition of board of directors	Comply to relative laws
		8. Design of specialized committee	Measure designing condition of specialized committee	There is corresponding specialized committee
		9. Running state of specialized commission	Measure operational quality	Independent director is in majority at times of issuing independent suggestion
	Directors' compensation	10. Directors' compensation level	Measure the rationality of directors' compensation level	According with relative stipulation
		11. Form of directors' compensation	Measure the rationality of director incentive structure	Director ought to adopt long-term incentive mechanism
		12. Director performance evaluation	Measure the rationality of director compensation	Valid evaluation procedures

Level 1 index	Level 2 index	Level 3 index	Index directions	Evaluation criterion
Evaluation index of directors and directorate	Independent director mechanism	13. The proportion of independent directors	Measure rationality of the scale of independent directors	Independent directors ought to comprise one-third of board of directors
		14. Independent director incentive	Measure the working efficiency of independent directors	Incentive measures of independent directors
		15. The independence of independent directors	Measure the state of independent directors' fulfilling responsibilities	Relevant stipulation
Evaluation index for supervisors and supervisors' board	Guarantee to supervisor's capability	1. Nominate supervisor candidate who stands for non-workers	Measure the effect that parties who have rights to nominate non-worker supervisor candidate impact supervisor independence and capability	Person who has the rights should represent the benefits of all the shareholders
		2. Proportion of full-time supervisors	Whether the chairman of supervisor board takes two posts in company, and type of the other post is a key factor to influence independence of supervisor board	The chairman can take two posts properly, but should take post which is not close relative to directorate and manager group, to ensure the independence of his monitoring
		3. Working time guarantee of external supervisor in the company	Certain proportion of working time is the basic guarantee for external supervisor to effectively fulfill monitoring responsibility	The actual working time that external supervisor spends in company must not be lower than the certain limitation

Level 1 index	Level 2 index	Level 3 index	Index directions	Evaluation criterion
Evaluation index for supervisors and supervisors' board	Guarantee to supervisor's capability	4. External supervisor's compensation level	Measure means and amount of external supervisor's compensation which is important to quality of supervisor's work and independence	External supervisor should be paid based on the degree that supervisor discharges his responsibility
	Supervisor be able to run validly	5. Condition of calling provisional shareholder meeting in most recent three years	Whether supervisor board exercise corresponding rights to certain events	Corporations law stipulates that supervisor board suggests to hold provisional shareholder meeting, and corporate law charge it the rights to hold the meeting independently
		6. Efficiency of supervisors' board structure and scale	Check the base that supervisor fulfill the monitoring function	Ought to guarantee that supervisors have enough experience, capability and professional background, fulfilling the duties independently and effectively to monitor directors and managers as well as check and monitor corporate finance
		7. Validity of supervisor conference	Check that supervisor board fulfill their functions	Supervisor board should hold periodical meetings and supervisors assure frequency of attending meetings

Level 1 index	Level 2 index	Level 3 index	Index directions	Evaluation criterion
Evaluation index for supervisors and supervisors' board	Supervisor be able to run validly	8. Validity of supervisor board's monitoring	Measure condition of supervisor board monitoring function fulfillment of directorate, directors and managers	Supervisor has the right to demand directors, managers and financial officers attend supervisor meeting and question them about certain problems
		9. Integrity of monitoring record of supervisor board	Supervisor or supervisor board's records or specific review results are critical evidence to evaluate directors' and managers' performance	Each activity taken by supervisor board should be recorded carefully and records retained
Evaluation index for management corporation	Appointment and removal system	1. Means to choose and appoint president	Measure the openness of the source of president and competition degree	The board of directors takes open and transparent measures to choose president
		2. Means to choose other senior managers	Measure the openness of the source of other senior managers and competition degree	Chosen by president or nominating committee, through open and transparent measures
		3. Administration degree of senior manager group	Measure the degree that corporate administration is independent from government	Senior managers of modern corporations do not hold an official administration post concurrently provides the guarantee

Level 1 index	Level 2 index	Level 3 index	Index directions	Evaluation criterion
Evaluation index for management corporation	Appointment and removal system	4. Authority of president together with chairman of the board	Measure the relative independence of president's controlling position of operation	Separate authority of president from that of chairman of the board is good for directorate's monitoring and incentive to managers
	Carry out guarantee	5. Decision supporting	Measure the means and nature of senior managers providing decision information to directorate	It's good for directorate's decision effectiveness that senior managers provide real-time, periodic and meaningful decision information
		6. Operation controlling	Evaluate the governance results by means of valid degree of corporation operation controlling	Corporation manager group ought to implement effective operation controlling
		7. Double posts holding	Measuring possibility that senior manager is referring to related transaction	Double post holding is more likely to raise price transmission and other non-marketing trade, avoidance of which is an effective means to control related transactions

Level 1 index	Level 2 index	Level 3 index	Index directions	Evaluation criterion
Evaluation index for management corporation	Carry out guarantee	8. Insider control	Evaluate mutual constraint between managers and directorate by the proportion that directors with management positions account for in the whole number of directorate members	A certain proportion should be kept; a higher one will make managers override the board and result in no function of shareholder meetings and directorate
Evaluation index for management corporation	Carry out guarantee	9. CEO setup	Evaluate degree of centralization of the corporation operating rights through setup of CEO who is the agent of the board of directors	Set CEO who is in charge of monitoring and carrying out every operating decision which is managed centrally by directorate
	Incentive mechanism	10. Compensation standard	Evaluate the relative level which senior managers' compensation is set at in the same industry and country, as well as degree of relative variation as compared with other employees' compensation in the company	Higher compensation standard in the same industry and bigger variation in the same company will both lead to strong incentive of senior managers

Level 1 index	Level 2 index	Level 3 index	Index directions	Evaluation criterion
Evaluation index for management corporation	Incentive mechanism	11. Compensation structure	Compensation form and composition	Reasonable compensation with diversification and combination of long-term and short-term forms encourages managers to put effort into their careers
		12. Dynamic incentive of compensation	Measure dynamical degree of compensation incentive by measuring the relationship between compensation and performance	Linking compensation to corporate performance leads to dynamic incentive function of compensation
		13. Proportion of shareholding	Reflect the incentive intensity to manager group	The higher the proportion, the better
		14. Circulation of shares	Reflect effectiveness of incentive function to managers	The better the circulation, the better
		15. Ways of shareholding	Whether the way is active or not will lead to different incentive effects	The bigger the proportion of active shareholding, the better the effect of incentive

Level 1 index	Level 2 index	Level 3 index	Index directions	Evaluation criterion
Evaluation index for management corporation	Incentive mechanism	16. Decision reporting mechanism	Evaluate the decision controlling and authority degree of directorate to managers, reflect constraint degree of decision controlling rights	Proper proportion of managers' rights of investment decision can increase incentive, and before the maximum authority, amount within decision should not go over 10% of net capital
		17. Functionary consumption	Degree of incentive constraint from operating rights	It is the most powerful method to put an end to the functionary consumption paid by the company
Evaluation index for information disclosure	Complete disclosure	1. Whether the resolution of shareholders meeting is fully disclosed	Measure transparency of decisions, management and monitoring in public company	Complete disclosure
		2. Whether the resolution of directorate meeting is fully disclosed		
		3. Whether the resolution of supervisor board meeting is fully disclosed		

Level 1 index	Level 2 index	Level 3 index	Index directions	Evaluation criterion
Evaluation index for information disclosure	Complete disclosure	4. Financial information disclosure: whether the periodical reports in the previous three years are fully disclosed	Measure transparency of information disclosure in public company	Disclose completely
		5. Special topics and significant matters are disclosed (disclosure of entrust financing and so on)	Measure disclosure of significant matters in public company; reflect whether complies with related procedures that entrust financing in public company	Public company should disclose comprehensively the following content: 1. accounting policy, estimation, and combination scope in the notes of financial statement 2. use of collected capital 3. information about related transactions 4. information about contingent events 5. information about financial guarantees 6. information about segments 7. reason for frequent change of shares in short time

Level 1 index	Level 2 index	Level 3 index	Index directions	Evaluation criterion
Evaluation index for information disclosure	Faithful disclosure	6. Whether the annual financial report is given unqualified opinion of non-standard form or criticized openly	Measure reputation of public company, independence of auditor, regulation conformity of information disclosure, and transparency	Public company is seen to have regulation violating history if one of the following is met: 1. openly tried by the judicial organization 2. checked by China Securities Regulatory Commission 3. have been openly criticized, condemned, forced to rectify and so on by China Securities Regulatory Commission or security exchange 4. cumulatively three times given qualified opinion, denied opinion or refused to issue opinion by auditing office 5. regulation violation disclosed by mass media, professional researchers or open research results
		7. Whether there is a change in accounting policy or accounting estimation in previous three years		
		8. Whether replaced the certified accountant office in previous three years		
		9. Whether the replaced accounting office has given conflicting opinions or made appeals		
		10. Other service provided by certified auditing office in previous three years		
		11. Whether supervisor board has discovered and verified falsifications in the financial statement		

Level 1 index	Level 2 index	Level 3 index	Index directions	Evaluation criterion
Evaluation index for information disclosure	Timely disclosure	12. Timely disclosure of annual, half-yearly bulletin, quarterly report	Measure timeliness of information disclosure in public company	Ought to disclose in accordance with requirements the annual and half-yearly bulletin, and quarterly report, disclose other information in time
		13. Whether disclosed in time the resolutions of shareholder meetings		
		14. Whether disclosed in time the resolutions of directorate meetings		
		15. Entrust financing ought to be disclosed in time		
Evaluation index for stakeholder governance	Participation degree of corporate employee	1. Proportion of employees supervising	Measure participation in corporate governance of employees	The bigger the proportion of employee supervisors and employees holding shares, the greater the extent of employee participation in governance
		2. Proportion of shareholdings by employees		
	Condition of fulfilling corporate social obligations	3. Parliamentary donation of company	Measure contribution of public company to society and community it locates in through parliamentary donation	The more parliamentary donation, the more complete the environment protection measures, the better the fulfillment of social obligations
		4. Environment protecting measures	Measure attention and protection to the environment it locates in	

Level 1 index	Level 2 index	Level 3 index	Index directions	Evaluation criterion
Evaluation index for stakeholder governance	Corporate investment relationship management	5. Website establishment and update	Measure establishment and usability of information disclosure and communication to investors	The corporation ought to establish a website and update it regularly, to make it convenient for investors to gather information
		6. Whether the corporation sets up investor relationship management institution	Measure the establishment of investor relationship management institution	The corporation ought to establish complete investor relationship management institution, in order to harmonize investor relationships
	Relationship between corporate and monitoring and administrating department	7. The penalty disbursement and revenue	Measure the relationship between corporate and monitoring and administrating department	The less the penalty disbursement and revenue, the better
	Corporate lawsuit and arbitration	8. The existence of lawsuits and arbitration	Value the relationship between corporation and shareholders, suppliers, customers, consumers, creditors, employees, community and government, and so on	The fewer lawsuits and arbitration, the better

Corporate governance evaluation criteria and the significance rating of evaluation index

Corporate governance evaluation criteria

Evaluation criteria is one of the three key elements of the evaluation system and the foundation of establishing a corporate governance index. Clear evaluation criteria plays a decisive role in obtaining rational evaluation results. The selection of evaluation criteria depends on what the establishment of the index aims at. The goal of corporate governance rests on providing guidelines for investors' scientific decision-making, government's effective monitoring, and public companies' self-diagnosis and self-controlling. There is neither national standards about corporate governance nor industrial ones in our country at present, and even internationally there is no criteria that clearly defines affairs about corporate governance, such as stock ownership structure and proportion of independent directors. In fact, according to contingency theory, it's impossible that there will be unified criteria, with the large distance between governance environments in each country. A good corporate governance criterion should be a contingency-based criterion which considers the law, system, and culture along with the marketplace. We consider the empirical research at home and abroad, take as a base the generally acknowledged corporate governance rules and norms, and integrate them with the history of Chinese public companies. We consider as a standard requirement the Chinese public company corporate governance principles, along with corporate law, public company guidelines, public company independent director guidelines, securities law and other laws and regulations for Chinese public companies, along with results of other research. This is all taken into account to make the criteria for each evaluation index.

With the combination of "spot criterion" and "string criterion," corporate governance evaluation criterion is not only a "spot" but a "string" which is formed via combination of several points. A "spot criterion" is set according to related regulations; for example, proportion of independent directors is set directly with quantified criterion from public company independent directors institution guidelines. A "string criterion" is based on features of an evaluation index and curve which represents the relationship between an evaluation index and corporate performance, and composed of the inflection point of the curve. Compared with "spot criterion", the adoption of "string criterion" makes criteria of an evaluation index reflect features accurately, and more importantly provides accurate evaluation results. Compared with a quantity index, a quality index is more objective and likely to be influenced by knowledge, experience, and the judgment of evaluation staff. It's decided on the basis of cooperation of experts and with reference to research results and related regulations. To ensure scientific evaluation of a quality index, selection of high-quality experts in corporate governance is critical. We established a corporate governance expert quality evaluation index system and expert quality model, in the hope of selecting a high-quality expert.

Ascertaining the significance factor of evaluation index

The significance factor of a corporate governance evaluation index considers that every element has to be integrated into the evaluation, and plays a critical role. In the course of setting a corporate governance index, ascertaining the evaluation index significance factor is based on a multilayer evaluation index system, adopting the method of analyzing layer by layer and integrating subjective and objective valuations. That is, adopting subjective valuation at the target layer and main-principle layer, and objective valuation at the index layer. Subjective valuation is made on the basis of the experience of the evaluator or expert in this field and has no relation to actual numbers of the evaluation index. The Delphi Method and AHP are the two main examples of this, both of which are expert-based methods, but the latter is more suitable to evaluation of multi-goal planning problems. The key of AHP is to establish a group adjusting system to provide a foundation to set significance degrees of an index. The two-two grading criteria adopted widely at present is carried out by professor Satty, with grades from 1 to 9. The grading has poor coincidence with the qualitative recognition of the evaluator. Many scholars at home and abroad conduct research in grading using an AHP matrix, and it turns out that grading with a score is more objective and rational to reflect one's judgment than other grading.

The course is:

1. Make two-two comparison to each layer and element to establish judging matrix. Information basis of AHP is mainly the judgment of relative importance of each element. It is these judgments which bring in proper grading presented with numbers that form the judging matrix, elements of which reflect one's recognition of the importance of each element. Our system adopts scoring grades to construct a judging matrix, wishing to simulate one's feeling of judging relationships better.

2. *Fix on relative significance number for evaluation index and coherence test. Judge the corresponding eigenvector $A = (A_1, A_2, \ldots, A_k)^T$ of maximum characteristic root.*

    λ_{max}; that is, the relative significance number of each evaluation factor. Using random coherence index of the judging matrix, it's possible to do a coherence test. Usually, when it's smaller than 0.1, the matrix is regarded to have satisfied coherence; that is, weights allocation is reasonable; or else, the matrix needs to be rebuilt and the weights allocation reset.

Objective valuation method fixes on significance of coefficient according to actual number observed of evaluation index, hence is not influenced by subjective consciousness. At present, examples of it mainly include signs coefficient of variation, entropy weight coefficient method, and weighted sum of square method. Suitable to the governance environment of public companies in China is the Signs coefficient of variation. This method integrates the evaluation index's significance coefficient into its value variation, and sets bigger weight to the index with bigger variation. That is because these indexes mean bigger variation and poorer stability at present, reflected by evaluation—it's harder to attain the average level of the index.

Therefore, bigger weight is given to them to show performance variation of the evaluation object on this index. Indexes with smaller variation have better stability and it is easier to attain the average level of the index. Smaller weight is given when the evaluation reflects the smaller variation. Signs coefficient of variation valuate according to content of index system and index number, which shows dynamic features of index weight. Especially with the short and developing history of our public companies, great instability exists in many aspects, and significance coefficient of evaluation index which is fixed by this method is better for reflection of index variation.

Corporate governance index model and Nankai governance index grading

When establishing an evaluation index system, on the basis of fixing evaluation criteria and significance coefficient of evaluation index, we can obtain a corporate governance index by the following mode:

$$CCGI^{NK} = \alpha_1 CCGI_1^{NK} + \alpha_2 CCGI_2^{NK} + \alpha_3 CCGI_3^{NK} + \alpha_4 CCGI_4^{NK} + \alpha_5 CCGI_5^{NK} + \alpha_6 CCGI_6^{NK}$$

In this model: $CCGI^{NK}$ means corporate governance index; α_i ($i = 1, 2, 3, ..., 6$) means significance coefficient of each evaluation factor; $CCGI_1^{NK}$ means evaluation index for shareholder rights and controlling shareholders' behavior; $CCGI_2^{NK}$ means evaluation index for directorate governance; $CCGI_3^{NK}$ means evaluation index for supervisor board governance; $CCGI_4^{NK}$ means evaluation index for manager governance; $CCGI_5^{NK}$ means evaluation index for information disclosure; $CCGI_6^{NK}$ means evaluation index for stakeholder governance.

The public company governance index set by the course above adopts hundred form, with the biggest value 100 and the smallest 0. Specific evaluation grades are:

$CCGI^{NK}$ I: governance index 90%–100% (includes 90%; the same in following stages)

$CCGI^{NK}$ II: governance index 80%–90%
$CCGI^{NK}$ III: governance index 70%–80%
$CCGI^{NK}$ IV: governance index 60%–70%
$CCGI^{NK}$ V: governance index 50%–60%
$CCGI^{NK}$ VI: governance index <50%

Non-parameter of governance index setting in Chinese public companies

Rank-relating coefficiency test of governance index setting in public company

Testing rank-relating coefficiency of governance index setting in public companies shows that there is high positive relativity among the three results of sequence ordering, which means high coherence among the total grading direction of the three. See Table 1.3.

Table 1.3: Spearman rank correlation coefficient

Sequence		Sequence 3	Sequence 2	Sequence 1
Sequence 3	Coefficient	1.000	0.864(*)	0.820(*)
	Sig. (2-tailed)	–	0.000	0.000
Sequence 2	Coefficient	0.864(*)	1.000	0.946(*)
	Sig. (2-tailed)	0.000	–	0.000
Sequence 1	Coefficient	0.820(*)	0.946(*)	1.000
	Sig. (2-tailed)	0.000	0.000	0.000

* Correlation is significant at the 0.01 level, 2-tailed.

Summary

Corporate governance evaluation is quantitative analysis of corporate governance quality; this research is designed to develop a corporate governance evaluation index system under the guidance of corporate governance theory. Meanwhile, governance evaluation is established on the basis of governance practice. Corporate governance practice in each country and different corporate governance evaluation systems provide good references for our country's developing evaluation.

A corporate institution has the character of "path dependence". History, political institutions, laws, and so on play critical roles in the establishment and development of corporate institutions. The design of a corporate governance evaluation system in Chinese public companies must consider the institutional environment in which our companies sit. Establishing a corporate governance evaluation index system setting principles on the basis of a company's governance environment will make it objective and accurate and reflect the conditions in a Chinese company.

One of the key factors in an evaluation system is corporate governance evaluation criteria, which is also the basis for setting up a governance evaluation index. Scientific and reasonable evaluation criteria—the selection of which depends on the goal of setting up the index—is critical to the accuracy of evaluation results.

CHAPTER

Research and Application of the Evaluation System of Corporate Governance

In this chapter we use an evaluation system of corporate governance to appraise the governance status of Chinese listed companies. The results of the research indicate that during the transition period, the corporate governance level of most listed companies is low and the method for improving the governance quality is hard and wide ranging. The level of corporate governance also shows a great difference between industries. If companies are good in corporate governance, they will have higher security in financing, and can strengthen their profitability. Investors will pay a premium for companies that have good corporate governance.

Corporate governance of Chinese listed companies

The sampling of the research and evaluation of corporate governance of Chinese listed companies is sourced from two channels: one is the investigation about corporate governance on Chinese listed companies which was made in 2002 by the corporation of China Securities Regulatory Commission (CSRC), the other is annual reports of listed companies until April 2003. The principle of the sample filter is the information of the index is complete and does not contain abnormal data. Finally, we have 931 available samples.

Governance status of Chinese listed companies

The index of corporate governance has a normal distribution trend, and a big difference exists among individual companies. Observed data suggests that the mean value of the $CCGI^{NK}$ is 49.62 which belongs to the rank of $CCGI^{NK}VI$. The maximum value of $CCGI^{NK}$ is 78.81, the minimum value is 30.79 and the standard deviation of observed data is 5.33. Only 2.15% of sample companies reached rank $CCGI^{NK}III$, 8.59% reached rank $CCGI^{NK}IV$, 42.75% reached rank $CCGI^{NK}V$, and 46.51% reached rank $CCGI^{NK}VI$. The mean of the shareholder index is 53.70, the maximum value is 83.33, and the minimum value is 10.40, a difference of 72.93%. The mean of the board governance index is 43.40, which is the poorest of the six dimensions. The maximum of the sample companies' board indexes is 74.51, the minimum is 1.56, a significant difference of 72.95%. The supervisor committee has a weak governance status, with a mean value of only 48.64 and a great level of difference. It shows that supervisor committees of Chinese listed companies don't play the overseeing role well at present. The management index—which contains appointment, incentive and execution—has a mean value of 47.44. The maximum is 77.74, the minimum is 11.98, a difference of 65.76%. The information disclosure is better, with a mean value of 58.44, maximum of 97.69 and minimum of 4.72. There is 92.97% difference between the samples. Compared to others, stakeholder status is the worst, with an index of only 20.52. Few stakeholders take part in the corporate governance in listed companies.

Governance status of Chinese listed companies across industries

There are different characteristics of Chinese listed companies' governance status between different industries. And there is a relationship between level of governance and regional economic development. According to industrial governance status, we categorized five industries into Better, Worse, Steady and Fluctuant. The results suggest that the Public Utility sector belongs to Better, of which 63 sample companies have the mean value of 50.11, which is 1.15% higher than the whole mean value.

The Manufacturing Industry belongs to the Worse category, of which 629 sample companies' mean value is 48.71, 0.25% lower than the mean of the whole observed companies. The Service Industry is Steady, and Miscellaneous is Fluctuant.

Corporate governance has different performance levels between the industries because of competition, ownership structure, government supervision and market mechanisms. The competition in industries has a negative relationship with quality of corporate governance. The competition of listed companies in First Industry is most fierce, but the governance index is the lowest; the competition of companies in Public Utility is weakest, but the index is the highest. This phenomenon is probably caused by the environment of competition and government regulation. In the transition economy period, the market environment and system environment are not ideal for companies because the market is not perfect and regulations are not complete. An incomplete market and comparative lagging systems of regulations and rules compels companies to transfer running costs by related transactions, enlarging financial profit by capital operation rather than advancing their core competency by completing corporate governance structures and strengthening the functions of the board and supervisor committee. In the less competitive industries, the probability of transferring running costs by related transactions is greatly reduced. Meanwhile, because most Public Utility companies can affect the national economy and the people's livelihood, the government pays more attention to the stabilization of their development. So a reasonable mechanism is the key point to keep stable development. Observation suggests the Public Utility companies' indexes of shareholders, board, supervisors' committee and information disclosure are higher than other industries, but the governance indexes of management appointment and incentive and restraints are comparatively lower than other industries. It indicates that government has played an important role during the transition period.

The governance status of companies in the First Industry, Public Utility and Agriculture has significant correlation with regional distribution, especially for First Industry companies.

The P value from the test of independence for governance status between industries and regional distribution is 1.16 E^{-12}, so we consider that governance level of the First Industry has significant correlation with regional distribution. The correlation coefficients of governance level of companies in Public Utility and Agriculture industries and regional distribution are 0.1984 and 0.2666 respectively, which passes the test of independence. The correlation coefficients of governance level of companies in Miscellaneous and Service industries and regional distribution are 0.1579 and 0.1191; the correlations are insignificant. $CCGI^{NK}$ of companies in First Industry, Public Utility and Agriculture shows that the index of the eastern area is higher than that of the central area, and the index of the central area is higher than that of the western area. The phenomenon indicates that there is a certain relationship between level of governance and regional economic development. The governance status in developed eastern areas is better than western areas. But it is not in evidence in the Miscellaneous and Service companies.

Ownership and quality of corporate governance

The factors that influence or decide the governance status of listed companies are various; they not only contain market elements such as capital market, managers market and product market, outside environment factors such as the policy and rules of the government, laws of the country and the culture, but also contain many inside factors such as the operation of meetings of shareholders, the ownership structure of the listed companies, the structure and operation of the board, the behaviors of controlling shareholders, the participation of the supervisors' committee, the quality of the information disclosure, the appointment of the management, the incentives and restraints. Shareholders manage their interests by appointing directors to the board. So the board is the result of games with each power, and has a close relationship with the quality of the management governance. All the appointments, incentives and restraints of the management are the result of the right conditioning and check-and-balance of the board. The quality of the information disclosure also has correlation with the composition and operation of the board. The structure of the board depends on the structure of the ownership. So the ownership is the basic element that can decide the quality of corporate governance. In other words, the ownership structure decides the structure of corporate governance.

In order to manifest ownership's influence on the quality of corporate governance, and to explore the influence of state shareholders' "dominance of a single shareholder" character and the competition over the controlling rights of the company on the quality of corporate governance, we controlled listed companies' industrial nature and the time of going public, which could impact the corporate governance index.[1] Then, as Table 2.1 shows, we calculated the correlation coefficients of the corporate governance index and the shareholders' percentage of shares and there is negative relation. Although the correlation's degree is relatively low, the significance at 1% level means that the centralized ownership structure negatively influenced the complement of mechanisms of corporate governance. Data of the samples shows that the corporate governance index has a positive relationship with the second shareholder, the third shareholder, the fourth shareholder, the fifth shareholder, and the sum of the second shareholder to the fifth. It means that the competition of controlling rights can help to level up the quality of corporate governance. Data analysis suggests that the key point to level up the quality of corporate governance is to optimize the ownership structure and strengthen the competition of controlling rights of companies.

Table 2.1: The correlation of the percentage of major shareholders and the corporate governance index

Partial correlation	Percentage of the 1st	Percentage of the 2nd	Percentage of the 3rd	Percentage of the 4th	Percentage of the 5th	Percentage of the 2nd to the 5th
CCGI^{NK}	−0.098** (0.004)	0.0774* (0.024)	0.0845* (0.014)	0.0822* (0.017)	0.0754* (0.028)	0.09** (0.004)

* Significance at 5% level (2 tailed).   ** Significance at 1% level (2 tailed).

---

[1] We found that the time of going public has a negative relation to corporate governance index, and there are certain differences between industries.

The nature of the first shareholder has influence on the CCGI[NK] to some extent. When the listed companies are privately controlled, the quality of the corporate governance is better. The mean of this is 50.63, but the difference in the samples is significant for the standard deviation is 5.44. The mean value of the index of SOEs (state-owned enterprises) is 49.83 and the standard deviation is 5.26. By observing the ownership of listed companies, it is easy to find that the mean percentage point of first shareholders of SOE samples is 75.37%, the mean percentage point of second shareholders is 12.4%, and the mean percentage point of the second to the fifth shareholders is 24.63%. Meanwhile, the mean percentage point of first shareholders of private enterprise samples is 57.58%, the mean percentage point of second shareholders is 22.47%, and the mean percentage point of the second to the fifth shareholders is 42.42%. The shares held by shareholders clearly suggest that the ownership structure of private-owned companies is better and shareholders balance each other to some extent, while SOEs present the strong character of "one dominant shareholder" so that they cannot form the mechanisms of check-and-balance. On the six governance dimensions, private enterprises are better than SOEs on board governance quality, management, supervisors' committee and controlling shareholder behaviors, especially the quality of board governance. Because private enterprises have excellent boards, they performed better than SOEs on the appointment, incentive and restraints of management. And compared to the SOEs, private enterprises have better overseeing mechanisms.

Data samples also show that the governance status of colleges and institutions is the worst; their mean value is only 45.06. This is particularly so of the board index, for which the mean is 36.71; it is only higher than non-bank institution listed companies. Affected by the low score of the board index, the appointment, incentives and restraints mechanisms of management are only better than non-bank institution listed companies, too. But as the mean value achieved is 53.71, the governance quality of supervisor committees is the best of all kinds of listed companies. It indicates that the colleges and institutions place emphasis on overseeing and controlling functions of supervisor committees, but neglect improving the decisions and balance of the board, which is the core factor of corporate governance. From now on, the key for listed companies belonging to college and institution to enhance the quality of corporate governance is participating in the markets more, operating by market laws, strengthening the check-and-balance effect of the board, and playing the important role of boards on appointing, incentive and restraints of management.

The governance quality of foreign investment companies, for which the mean value is 49.43, is lower than private enterprises and higher than SOEs. And the standard deviation is 3.90, which suggests that there is little difference between the samples' governance status. Foreign investment companies do well in information disclosure but their boards do not take part in the corporate governance efficiently. This is mainly because the boards of the foreign investment companies are controlled by their parent companies; they cannot fulfill their duty completely.

Empirical analysis of corporate governance index and company performance

On the basis of literature researching the relationship of corporate governance and performance, we make out the criteria to measure company performance in the corporate governance empirical research and conduct the research on corporate governance and company performance.

Relative research on corporate governance and company performance

Scholars have not paid attention to the research of the relationship of corporate governance status and firm's performance until recent years. Black (1999) researched how corporate governance behavior influences firms' market value in Russia. By comparing the governance level of matured markets and rising markets, he argues that listed companies in the matured market have no obvious difference in governance status for the governance environment outside is relatively complete, so there is no significant relationship between governance level and a firm's performance. In the rising market, companies are greatly different in corporate governance and the corporate governance has a positive relationship with the performance because of the weakness in lawmaking and the incompletion of governance mechanisms. Klapper and Lover (2002) found that corporate governance influenced a firm's value and performance significantly. Newell and Wilson (2002) found, by studying six rising markets, that companies for which the governance status goes from the worst to the best can advance their values 10% to 20%. Durnev and Kim (2003), using the appraisal of CLSA as the quality of corporate governance, found that companies better in corporate governance have higher value. If a company increased 10 points in the governance score, its value may rise 10%. If a company has similar improvement in transparency, its value may rise 16%. CLSA's Asia branch proved that the status of corporate governance has a close relationship with ROE by studying the relationship between corporate governance and performance of listed companies in Asian rising markets. The mean ROE of all companies in the last five years is 388%, and that of the top 25% of companies in corporate governance evaluation is 930%.

There is little literature comprehensively analyzing the effect of Chinese listed companies' whole governance status on firms' performance. On the basis of the corporate governance index formed by the appraisal of Chinese listed companies, this book analyzes how the results of corporate governance factors affect firms' performance completely and systematically.

The measure of listed companies' performance

Most researchers abroad use Tobin's Q to measure performance because it can reflect the added value resulting from corporate governance. In recent years, foreign researchers prefer to use a new performance index EVA, as it measures a firm's performance on the side of value added. So it is propitious to connect with the incentive of managers, build up the conception of value creating, and relate to the demand of the capital market directly. But considering the principle of the cost and the benefit, it is not practical to use the EVA index, mainly because the obtaining of the cost of capital is difficult. The aim of corporate governance is to avoid listed company risk, protect stakeholders' rights, and promote the achievement of maximum stakeholders rights by setting up good structures and mechanisms of corporate governance. In order to measure the effect of corporate governance, besides considering the improvement of performance caused by corporate governance, we also should consider corporate governance's contribution to the rise in the market value of a listed company, such as strengthening the attraction of investment, increasing the ability of listed company development, efficiently limiting a listed company's operating risk, and increasing the level of a company's finance.

Based on the analysis above, this book will measure firms' performance on five dimensions, which are: company's market value, profitability, growing ability, capital stock expanding ability, and the financial safety in the future. In order to reflect the influence of corporate governance levels on performance, we controlled the variables that can affect the Tobin's Q and firm's performance; they are company size, the competition of industries, the proportion of first shareholder's holding and the nature of the first shareholder, the degree of the contest of controlling rights[2], ratio of debts to assets, and the ratio of floating shares. The controlled variables are listed in Table 2.2.

Table 2.2:   Controlled variables

Names	Variables	Meanings
Ln(Asset)	The natural logarithm of the asset	Influence of company's scale on the performance
Leverage	Debt to asset ratio	Influence of capital structure
Top1	The first shareholder's proportion	Influence of the first shareholder's proportion

---

[2]   We classify the character of the first big shareholder into nine types: venture enterprise, administrative companies of state-owned property, state-owned or state-owned and dominated companies, university and scientific research organizations, government, nongovernmental management, collective, non-financial organizations, and others. For each dummy variable, if it belongs to the type of shareholder, we evaluate 1, if not, 0. The variable "the proportion of the second shareholder to the fifth" is the controlled variable.

Table 2.2:   Controlled variables *(cont'd)*

Names	Variables	Meanings
top1_sq	Square of top 1	Influence of the square of the first shareholder's proportion
S	The sum of proportion of the second shareholder to the fifth	Influence of the intension of contending for inner domination rights
Indus$_i$	Nature of the industries	Influence of industry competition
Top1_chrc$_j$	Characteristics of the first shareholder	Influence of character of the first big shareholder
Rof	Ratio of floating shares	Influence of circulating share ratio

The correlation of corporate governance and the firm's performance

In order to reflect the relationship of the corporate governance index and the firm's performance accurately, we grouped all the listed companies by the scores of the corporate governance index. According to all the sample companies' means of CCGI^{NK}, they are divided into five groups. Compared to the standard group for which CCGI^{NK} scores are above 60, the results show that a company's corporate governance status has a close relationship to a firm's performance. The data indicates that the CCGI^{NK} mean value of the first one-quarter highest CCGI^{NK} companies is 55.03, and the mean of the last one-quarter of companies is 42.89, which is 12.14% lower than the former, so the difference is obvious. The ROE of the first one-quarter CCGI^{NK} companies is 4.79 times that of the last one-quarter companies, and POP 1.27 times, EPS 5.43 times, and NAPS 1.14 times. Table 2.3 shows the figures. Table 2.4 shows the descriptive statistics of the corporate governance index and performance.

Table 2.3: Regional comparison between corporate governance and performance

Index		EPS	NAPS	RONA	ROMS	ISOM
$CCGI^{NK}$ *Means* (GI_1)		0.1312	2.4320	0.5958	5.40	15.13
$CCGI^{NK}$ *above 60* (GI_2)		0.4077	3.5177	0.5908	11.59	44.97
$CCGI^{NK}$ *50-60* (GI_3)		0.1614	2.2947	0.6523	7.03	12.32
$CCGI^{NK}$ *40-50* (GI_4)		0.1164	2.6554	0.3572	4.38	18.46
$CCGI^{NK}$ *30-40* (GI_5)		−0.2619	1.6198	2.6000	16.17	16.33
$CCGI^{NK}$ *20-30* (GI_6)		0.1020	2.0650	0.1875	4.94	22.48
Interval	$GI_2 - GI_1$	0.2765	1.0857	−0.0050	6.19	29.84
	$GI_2 - GI_3$	0.2463	1.2230	−0.0615	4.56	32.65
	$GI_2 - GI_4$	0.2913	0.8623	0.2336	7.21	26.51
	$GI_2 - GI_5$	0.6696	1.8979	−2.0092	27.76	28.64
	$GI_2 - GI_6$	0.3057	1.4527	0.4033	6.65	22.49

Table 2.4: Descriptive statistics of corporate governance index and performance

Factors	Variables	Names	Means
Governance status	Corporate governance index	$CCGI^{NK}$	49.622%
Profitability	Profit ratio of main	ROM	19.35%
	Returns of net assets	ROA	6.8375%
	Earnings per share	EPS	0.1825
Growth ability	Increasing ratio of main earnings	ISOM	24%
Capital stock expanding ability	Funds of per share	FOS	1.4069
	Net assets per share	NAPS	2.669
Financial security	Bankruptcy forecasting	Z	2.4043
Market value	Market price per share	SMP	7.72
	60% for Tobin's Q	q_6	1.4694
	70% for Tobin's Q	q_7	1.5886
	80% for Tobin's Q	q_8	1.7074

Resource: Database of the Corporate Governance Research Center of Nankai University.

Controlling the factors analyzed above, the basic model of $CCGI^{NK}$ and performance is as follows:

$$P = \beta_0 + \beta_1 CCGI^{HK} + \beta_2 Ln(\text{Asset}) + \beta_3 Leverage + \beta_4 TOP_1 +$$

$$\beta_5 TOP1\_sq + \beta_6 S + \sum_{i=1}^{4} \beta_7 Indus_i + \sum_{j=1}^{8} \beta_8 Top1\_chrc + \varepsilon$$

In the equation above, P stands for the performance.

This model is a basic model about $CCGI^{NK}$ and performance index. When we do research on the relationship of $CCGI^{NK}$ and each performance, the model should be adjusted in accordance with the factors affecting the performance. Limited by space, this book does not list all the models of the relationship of $CCGI^{NK}$ and performance (for results please refer to Table 2.5 to Table 2.7).

Table 2.5 indicates that listed companies' financial security in the future has a positive relation with $CCGI^{NK}$, and the correlation

Table 2.5: Regression result of corporate goverance index and financial safety in future and the profitability

Index	Financial security	EPS	POP
(Constant)	−5.091 (0.425)	−1.144 (0.095)	6.078 (0.861)
CCGI^NK	1.626 (0.019)	0.261 (0.0394)	37.042 (0.062)
S	4.037 (0.543)	–	–
Leverage	−0.696 (0.048)	–	2.01 (0.292)
Sig. F Change	0.291	0.250	0.669
R²	0.053	0.025	0.158
Adj. R²	0.035	0.004	−0.004
Partial correlations	0.045 (0.019)	0.0295 (0.0394)	0.0646 (0.062)
D-W	1.938	1.967	2.002

Note: P values are noted in the brackets.

coefficient is 0.045, and the significance level is 0.019.[3] It suggests that good corporate governance structure and mechanisms are propitious for avoiding the financial risk and increasing financial safety to some extent. A company's ratio of debts to assets has a negative relationship with the financial safety in the future, at 5% significance level, suggesting that the higher the ratio of debts to assets, the higher the financial risks. The most important method to increase the financial safety is to increase the quality of corporate governance and decrease the ratio of debts to assets at the same time. By observing the relationship between listed companies' earning abilities and CCGI[NK], we found that EPS has a positive relation with CCGI[NK] at the 5% significance level and the correlation coefficient is 0.0295. The main business revenue also has a positive relation with CCGI[NK], the coefficient is 0.0646 and the significance level is 10%. All of the above show that good corporate governance structure and mechanisms could promote a company's profitability.

Table 2.6 is the regression result of CCGI[NK] and growth and stock expanding ability. The data does not show significant relationship between the quality of corporate governance and a company's growing ability[4], but the CCGI[NK] has significant relationship with NAPS of listed companies' stock expanding ability. The result means that the companies in good governance quality lean to equity financing, and it suggests listed companies which are good in governance structure and mechanism can easily finance by equity financing from the capital market.

The data in Table 2.7 shows that CCGI[NK] does not have significant relationship with price per share, Q_6, Q_7 and Q_8.[5] We think it is because the capital market in China is developing,

---

[3] Correlation coefficient here is partial correlation coefficients of dependent variables and dummy variables when controlling factors such as asset size, capital structure, characteristics of first shareholder, proportion of the first shareholder, proportion of the second shareholder to the fifth, the ratio of floating shares, and industries.

[4] Here we are using the index of current growing potential; as the hystereses of corporate governance influence the corporate performance, it's more reasonable to use the index of future growing potential.

[5] Considering the capital market in China is an immature one, we take discount for Tobin's Q and use Q_6, Q_7, Q_8 as indexes to reflect corporation value caused by corporate governance.

Table 2.6: The regression results of CCGI^{NK} with growth ability and stock expanding ability

Index	ISOM	After-tax profit margin	FOS	NAPS
(Constant)	529.439 (0.245)	−2,541.77 (0.033)	0.918 (0.283)	0.773 (0.679)
CCGI^{NK}	−177.87 (0.471)	610.472 (0.351)	−0.543 (0.537)	0.868 (0.094)
TOP1_sq	−129.608 (0.702)	−	−	−
S	−76.465 (0.871)	−	−	−
Sig. F Change	0.880	0.462	0.246	0.326
R^2	0.021	0.030	0.021	0.032
Adj. R^2	−0.010	0.000	0.002	0.006
Partial correlations	−0.025 (0.471)	0.032 (0.351)	−0.0214 (0.537)	0.295 (0.094)
D-W	2.042	2.006	2.126	1.979

Table 2.7: The regression result of corporate governance and firms' market value

Indexes	Price per share	Q_6	Q_7	Q_8
(Constant)	6.934 (0.155)	−0.9 (0.629)	−1.047 (0.60)	−1.193 (0.575)
CCGI^{NK}	4.118 (0.113)	0.056 (0.955)	0.039 (0.971)	0.024 (0.983)
Top1_sq	−2.591 (0.477)	1.76 (0.362)	1.42 (0.338)	1.646 (0.298)
Top1	−103.881 (0.323)	97.923 (0.401)	97.779 (0.401)	96.881 (0.406)
S	−3.166 (0.532)	1.194 (0.389)	2.078 (0.314)	2.393 (0.277)
Sig. F Change	0.012	0.738	0.718	0.701
R^2	0.05	0.028	0.029	0.290
Adj. R^2	0.022	−0.07	−0.06	−0.006
Partial correlations	0.055 (0.133)	0.002 (0.955)	0.01 (0.971)	0.001 (0.983)
D-W	1.970	1.854	1.852	1.85

the market degree is low. The sample shows that the holdings of the first shareholder have a negative relation with price per share at an insignificant level. It means "one dominant shareholder" has a negative influence on a company's market price to some extent. The sum proportion of the second shareholder to the fifth, the variable reflecting the competition of controlling rights, has an insignificant positive relationship with Tobin's Q, which suggests that the competition of controlling rights is good to increase a firm's value. The fiercer the competition of controlling rights is, the higher the firm's value is.

Conclusion

The result of applicative research on the corporate governance evaluation system shows the following:

(1) The construction of modern corporation mechanisms improved corporate governance status greatly, but the listed companies still have many problems with governance structure and structure mechanisms. Monitoring and controlling measures carried out by related departments has positive effects on ruling behaviors of listed companies' controlling shareholders as the behavior of controlling shareholders is controlled, but controlling shareholders have rights beyond their corporate power and can take advantage of the resources they control to entrench minority shareholders' rights such as transferring properties of a listed company. As the core section, the board made some achievements on construction of board regulations, but there are still problems in the running mechanisms. So the function of the board's decisions and balance check need to be strengthened. Acting as another important section, the supervisor committee's function is comparatively complete while the operating effect of it is weak. The rules construction of management of listed companies has made some improvement. Particularly the companies that are perspicuous in property rights have better governance status. But there are still some popular problems for them, such as the level of incentive and executive ensuring of management is relatively low. The monitoring and restraints of administrations and outside mechanisms promoted the

building up of information disclosure, and companies have made great progress. But the reality and integrity of the information disclosure still need to be improved. Presently the attendance of stakeholders in corporate governance is weak, because there is no complete mechanism for stakeholders to take part in the corporate governance activities and stakeholders as minority shareholders are aggrieved severely.

(2) Companies belonging to Public Utility, the weakest competition industry, have the best governance status, while companies belonging to the First Industry, the fiercest industry, have the worst governance status. It indicates that the quality of corporate governance has a relationship to the competition environment and government governance. The appointment, incentive and restraint of management of listed companies which belong to the Public Utility are weaker than companies of other industries. The situation means the incentive and restraint of management of that kind of company is influenced by the government's behavior rather than the competition of markets, which is not good for the improvement of a company's performance and competitive power. Thus we must comprehend the actions of government in corporate governance.

Competition is the key factor for winning because it can propel companies to disclose their information and perfect the governance mechanisms inside. And the listed companies that have incomplete governance mechanisms will be eliminated finally. But the actual situations of Chinese listed companies show that companies in the fiercely competitive industries do not depend on completing governance structures and mechanisms to increase their competition power, but depend on the irrational ways of related transactions and transferring costs. This phenomenon breaches the law of fair play and is not good for corporations' development in the long term. The best way to build up a company's long-term competitive advantage is to construct perfect governance structures and mechanisms. Thus the effective way is strengthening corporate governance and using feasible corporate governance schemes to decrease a company's unreasonable behaviors.

(3) Corporate governance status is positively related to financial security. In order to reduce financial risk and improve

financial security, scientific decision-making and supervisory or balance mechanisms should be introduced. As we know, the scientific decision-making mechanism can reduce the financial risk resulting from a bad decision, while the supervisory and balance mechanism could reduce more factors leading to financial insecurity, such as financial fraud. Thus the influence of corporate governance on financial security is mainly through scientific design and consequently the principal–agent relationship development based on property rights. In China the general shareholder meeting authorizes the board to make critical decisions. The board, which represents the shareholders, authorizes the managers to perform daily management. Accordingly a scientific decision-making process forms.

The analysis of the logistic relationship of corporate governance suggests that the key point to increase the safety of corporation finance and decrease the financial risk is to set up a series of mechanisms of scientific decisions and balancing, which is to say to build up completely corporate governance structures and mechanisms. The weak relationship between listed companies' corporate governance and financial safety shows that in order to increase listed companies' financial safety, companies should complete the corporate governance structure and governance mechanism. In the meantime, the logistic relationship of corporate governance and financial safety presented above also suggests that matching corporate governance and management is the key to decreasing financial risk.

(4) Corporate governance is a comprehensive system, and the quality of corporate governance is the result of insider factors and outsider environments. As to the insider factors, the ownership structure is a basic element to determine the quality of corporate governance. The "one dominant shareholder" of state-owned shares is not good for the improvement of corporate governance structures and governance mechanisms. And even the same ownership structure can cause different governance effects. The ownership of Chinese listed companies cannot change their ownership structures in a short time at present, thus the improvement of institutional design to ameliorate the behavior of controlling shareholders, the effect of governance

on the board, supervisor committees and management, the quality of the information disclosure, and the attendance of stakeholders are key points. As to the outsider environments, the perfection of the laws and regulations and the formation of market mechanisms are the safeguards of leveling up the quality of corporate governance completely.

CHAPTER

Research on Evaluation and Index of the Controlling Shareholders' Behavior

The controlling shareholders, the specific resource investors of the corporation, will face the firm's special risks—the costs minority shareholders need not pay—as they invest more resources in the corporation and their properties connect with the corporation's future more closely. But the complexity of the transition period in China decided the complexity of the behaviors of listed companies' controlling shareholders. Their target is not based on the comparison of the income and the cost, but the considering of the overall rights of the whole group. Thus, the analysis of the behavior of Chinese listed companies' controlling shareholders should extend the scope of controlling rights from the subsidiary companies of listed companies to the controlling shareholders and the whole group of other related companies for the sake of reflecting the controlling shareholders' domination of the resources of the whole group. The control benefit not only appears as cash flow rights, but also appears as a way of tunnelling further. The claims of "control right—cash flow right" paves the way for our analyzing factors affecting the behavior of the controlling shareholders of Chinese listed companies.

Reviews on the evaluation of controlling shareholders' behavior

The risk of specific resource has not become the barrier to the property concentration that Demsetz and Lehn (1985) found if the firm's certain risk was higher; the property was more concentrated by the study on America's 500 largest companies. The reason promoting investors become the controlling shareholders is that when they owned plenty of shares, they could get more cash flow returns. What's more, controlling shareholders could get particular returns which were obtained by controlling a company's resources. Thus controlling shareholders' target is obtaining cash flow returns and particular returns.

It is commonly considered that ownership's dispersal weakened the incentives of shareholders to monitor companies' behavior, so it created conditions for managers to control the companies. "In fact, as to shareholders, the stimulation is not the relative shares but the absolute amount," (Armen A. Alchian, 1986), the absolute amount means the cash flow taken by controlling shareholders. So even if under the situation of dispersed ownership structure, the major shareholders still have incentive to monitor a firm's managers. They supervise managers mainly by influencing the specific resource owners' agents, the directors.

As to minority shareholders, controlling shareholders' behaviors have strong externalities. Controlling shareholders undertake most costs brought by managers' poor decisions decreasing a firm's value (Demsetz and Lehn, 1985). Thus they have the stimulus to monitor the managers and take all the costs of monitoring behaviors, while the minority shareholders can share the returns and be "free riders." It is the positive externalities of controlling shareholders. When controlling shareholders have strong motivation for gaining particular returns relying on their controlling status and occupy a company's resources, they will enjoy the returns by themselves, but the costs will be shared by all the shareholders. The circumstance provides negative externalities to minority shareholders.

Many scholars use cash flow rights to measure controlling shareholders' positive externalities. When controlling shareholders own more cash flow rights, any behaviors damaging a company's interests could produce more loss for themselves. Thus if controlling shareholders have more cash flow rights, their interests are more in accordance with the company's interests, and they have more incentive to increase a company's value. The result of a study by La Porta et al (1998) demonstrates that if controlling shareholders have more cash flow rights, company values are higher. Claessens (2000) shows that the higher the degree of departure on controlling rights and cash flow rights, the more incentive controlling shareholders have to hurt minority shareholders' interests and firm value. This is because when shareholders have more controlling rights, they are more able to expropriate and transfer company resources, and less cash flow rights reduce the expropriation costs. So the degree of deviation of controlling rights and cash flow rights can weigh the intensity of controlling shareholders' negative externalities.

Taiwanese scholars Ye, Li and Ke (2002) used data of 251 companies listed in Taiwan from 1997 and 1998 as a sample to conduct empirical studies about the influence of departure on controlling rights and cash flow rights to firm value. The result also supports the conclusions above.

Character of the controlling shareholders' behavior of Chinese listed companies

Because of the effect of mechanisms during the transition period, the behaviors of controlling shareholders in Chinese listed companies is always beyond the companies' corporate boundary. For example, on the support of government policies, most state-owned enterprises adopt listing subsidiary companies of the corporations in order to reach the listing criterion, and embezzled the capital of public companies by the control power.

Shareholders' equal treatment

Following the principle of "majority capital," controlling shareholders are always dominating the shareholder meeting. They increase minority shareholders' participation costs, control minority shareholders' attendance, and hamper them getting enough information in time by limiting the process and attending qualification of the shareholders' meeting. By measuring the attendance and standard of shareholder meetings we can judge whether the controlling shareholders have interfered with the shareholder meeting.

The systematic inducement of negative externalities of controlling shareholders' behaviors

During the process of SOEs' shareholding reform, listed companies and their controlling shareholders experienced "capital confusion" because of the factors of IPOs (initial public offering) (Shi, 1998). This phenomenon blurred the corporation property boundary of listed companies, created conditions for controlling shareholders abusing of listed companies' resources, and expropriate minority shareholders' rights. Listed companies' independence to their controlling shareholders can reflect the degree of system inducement of aggrieved behaviors to minority shareholders.

The restriction mechanisms of the negative external effect of controlling shareholders

Completing or innovating the legal mechanisms of minority shareholder rights protection has been the focus of the modification and reformation of companies law all over the world for years. Many countries protect minority shareholders' rights mainly via strengthening minority shareholders summoning and suggestion rights at shareholder meetings, which can restrain controlling shareholders' rights. Chinese company law and stock law specify shareholders' rights in great detail, but the majority of them are following the "most capital" principle, so the minority shareholders rights still don't get enough consideration. The China Listed Company Governance Norms enacted by CSRC and SETC give some principles on protection of shareholders and the equal treatment of all shareholders which make helpful supplements for the company law. But there is still a long distance from Listed Company Governance Norms to· forming effective mechanisms for minority shareholders' rights protection. Whether the mechanisms of minority shareholders' rights protection are complete and are implemented efficiently can measure if the effective mechanisms of restricting the behaviors of controlling shareholders and decreasing the negative externalities are accomplished.

The negative externalities of controlling shareholders' behaviors

Listed companies' controlling shareholders maximize group interests by manipulating sources of subsidiary companies and related companies. The coordination and complementation between companies can increase the whole group's competitive power. But presently, Chinese listed companies have the problem of abusing group resources, which puts up strong externalities on the operation. It expropriates minority shareholders' rights and hampers the development of group companies. Appraising the status that controlling shareholders abuse a group's resources can reflect their degree of negative externalities directly.

Evaluation index of controlling shareholders' behavior

Based on the analysis of the behavior of the controlling shareholders, the index of controlling shareholders' behavior of Chinese listed companies contains four aspects, detailed in Table 3.1.

Table 3.1: Evaluation system of Chinese listed companies' controlling shareholders

Level 1 index	Level 2 index	Level 3 index	Target directions	Evaluation criterion
Behaviors of controlling shareholders	Related party transaction	1. Competition among same business	Evaluate the state of horizontal trade competition between listed companies and majority stockholders or other related parties	Listed companies and majority stockholders or other related parties belong to different industry
		2. Price foundation	Judge the normative norm of the related party transactions by the price foundation of the transactions	Whether have a formal analysis report on related party transaction pricing

Table 3.1:   Evaluation system of Chinese listed companies' controlling shareholders *(cont'd)*

Level 1 index	Level 2 index	Level 3 index	Target directions	Evaluation criterion
Behaviors of controlling shareholders	Related party transaction	3. Funds embezzlement	Measure the externality of the behaviors of controlling shareholders through whether majority stockholders embezzle the capital of companies	Embezzlement of companies' capital is nonexistent
		4. Loan guarantee	Measure the externality of the behaviors of controlling shareholders through whether the companies provide loan guarantee for majority stockholders or other related parties.	Loan guarantee is not nonexistent
	Independence of listed companies	5. Staff's personal independence	Measure whether listed companies and controlling shareholders have relationships with personnel	Independent
		6. Business independence	Measure whether listed companies and controlling shareholders have relationships on business	Independent
		7. Financial affairs independence	Measure whether listed companies and controlling shareholders have relationships on finance	Independent
		8. Capital and property independence	Measure whether listed companies and controlling shareholders have relationships on assets	Independent

Table 3.1: Evaluation system of Chinese listed companies' controlling shareholders *(cont'd)*

Level 1 index	Level 2 index	Level 3 index	Target directions	Evaluation criterion
Behaviors of controlling shareholders	Shareholder meeting status	9. Stockholder meeting participation	Measure the state that stockholder has a hand in stockholder plenary session	As far as possible stockholders have a hand in
		10. Shareholders meeting norm	Measure the stockholder's plenary session order; evaluate the state that stockholder has a hand in stockholder plenary session	Stockholder keeps the minutes integrated at the plenary session
	Minority shareholders rights protection	11. Provisional stockholder's proposal state of plenary session	Measure whether the rights of minority shareholders are protected	Being

The index of related party transaction

In this section we use four indexes—whether controlling shareholders and listed companies have same business competition, whether the related party transaction's price foundation can be controlled by controlling shareholders, whether controlling shareholders embezzle listed companies' capital freely, and whether listed companies provide loan guarantee for controlling shareholders and other related companies—to reflect the status of related party transactions by controlling shareholders.

The index of listed companies' independence

The status is evaluated from personnel, business, financial affairs, capital and other aspects. Firstly, we evaluate the status of personnel independence by indexes of whether listed companies' directors take part-time jobs in controlling shareholders' companies, whether using offices with controlling shareholders communally and whether controlling shareholders have denied or hampered listed companies' employees' appointment. Secondly, we judge business independence by indexes of the proportion of raw material purchased by controlling shareholders accounting for the total amount. Thirdly, we use whether companies' financial departments are led or guided by controlling shareholders and whether listed companies set up independent bank accounts to judge the status of financial independence. Fourthly, we examine the capital independence by whether listed companies rent auxiliary production systems, equipment, land, industrial property and know-how from controlling shareholders and other related companies.

The index of shareholder meeting status

This section reflects the participation and norm of shareholders' meetings by designing two indexes: the share proportion of attending shareholders at each meeting in last three years, and whether the record of shareholders meetings is complete.

The index of minority shareholders' protection

This section examines the implementation of laws, regulations and principles about the protection of minority shareholders, and whether listed companies formed effective mechanisms to protect minority shareholders' rights. Here we use shareholders and supervisors who own above 5% voting rights singly or jointly have put forward temporary proposals, and whether the board brought the proposal to agenda.

Descriptive statistics of evaluation of controlling shareholders' behavior

The general status of behaviors of controlling shareholders

We obtained 931 samples which are from listed companies of Shenzhen and Shanghai stock exchanges. The index of controlling shareholders' behavior ($CCGI^{NK}_1$) exhibits normal distribution; the maximum is 83.33, the minimum is 10.40, the mean value is 53.70 and the standard deviation is 10.95%. The controlling shareholder index of sample companies is relatively low, and belongs to the rank of $CCGI^{NK}_1 V$. And there are obviously differences between the controlling shareholder indexes of sample companies.

According to the scores of the controlling shareholder index, no one reached the rank of $CCGI^{NK}_1I$, and only two companies achieved the rank of $CCGI^{NK}_1II$, accounting for 0.22% of the whole sample; 46 companies reached $CCGI^{NK}_1III$, accounting for 4.96% of the sample; and 213 companies reached $CCGI^{NK}_1IV$, accounting for 22.98% of the sample. Others are under the rank of $CCGI^{NK}_1V$, taking the amount of 71.84%. The statistical result suggests that controlling shareholders' behavior of Chinese listed companies has strongly negative externalities.

The status of related party transactions

The index of related party transactions has a mean of 53.74 and a median of 54.01. The maximum is 98, the minimum is 3.1, and the standard deviation reaches the high value of 25.27%. The whole index of shareholders' behavior is low, belonging to $CCGI_1^{NK}V$, and the difference of the samples is great. Among the samples, 58.02% of controlling shareholders have competition with their controlled companies; companies whose profits obtained by related party transactions account for over 50% of the whole profits accounts for 61.3%; in 23.48% of companies the controlling shareholders occupies company capital illegally. And 40.37% of companies provide guarantees for the controlling shareholder and related parties, and in 20% of companies of that kind the chairman of the board and the manager and some directors have the right of passing the guarantee decision. The transaction index shows that the controlling shareholders in Chinese listed companies have a strong trend of "abusing related party transactions." On the one hand, some listed companies play earnings management in order to "keep the shell." On the other hand, they get illegal earnings by "tunnelling behavior." Presently controlling shareholders of Chinese listed companies have the behavior of abusing group resources by related party transactions. The negative externalities of the operation expropriate minority shareholders rights and are not good for the whole group's development in the long term.

The independence of listed companies

The China Listed Company Governance Norms specified clearly that listed companies should keep independence and enhanced the monitoring of companies. The measure serves to prevent major shareholders who take advantage of the confusion of listed companies from transfering resources, and to increase the independence of Chinese listed companies. The highest index of independence is 94, the lowest is 30.8, the mean is 78.02, and the standard deviation is 16.7%. The data shows that the index of independence is relatively high, belonging to the rank of $CCGI^{NK}_1III$. From the status reflected by the independence index, most listed companies can keep the independence of assets and finance. Among the samples, 71.83% have independent financial departments that are not led by controlling shareholders' financial administrations. Companies that have independent manufacturing and operation system which they need not rent from their controlling shareholders account for 79.66%. But listed companies are closely related with controlling shareholders on the aspect of employees and business. For example, in 41.46% of companies the chairman of the board does not take a part-time position in the controlling shareholders' companies, and the companies which can purchase raw materials and sell production by themselves make up 38.64% of the companies. All of that indicates the relationship between listed companies and controlling shareholders tends to be secret.

The status of shareholders' meeting

The shareholders' meeting index of samples has the maximum of 100, minimum of 21.56, mean value of 63.91, and a standard deviation of 20.05%. The total index belongs to the rank of $CCGI^{NK}_1IV$, and the difference within it is great. Although the total index reaches $CCGI^{NK}_1IV$ and some companies' index achieves $CCGI^{NK}_1I$, the high score is mainly a result of the sub-factor index, the standardization of shareholders' meetings—whether the record of shareholders' meetings is complete—which is strongly subjective. Among the samples, 93.57% of companies answered "complete." This index is not quite reasonable but we have not found a better one to replace it. An investigation about another sub-index which reflects the attendance at the shareholders' meeting found that the companies whose mean share proportion of attending shareholders for each meeting in last three years exceeds 70% only accounts for 3.78%; those under 40% achieve 51.24%. This index suggests that the shareholders' participation in Chinese listed companies' shareholders' meetings is quite low, and many problems—which include the process of holding the meeting and the qualification of the delegates—are not good for the minority shareholders. These problems give controlling shareholders enough opportunity to control the important decisions and close off the information.

The status of minority shareholders' protection

The highest of the minority shareholders' protection index is 63, the lowest is 0.12, and the standard deviation is 14.09%. And the mean value is a surprisingly low 7.19. In the tested samples, companies whose shareholders and supervisors who own above 10% voting rights singly or jointly and have put forward temporary proposals only account for 2.15%. And companies in which the board brought the proposal to the agenda merely account for 18.34%. The index of minority shareholders' protection indicates that Chinese listed companies have not built up effective mechanisms to restrict controlling shareholders, have not carried out the regulations to protect minority shareholders rights, and have not formed the atmosphere for minority shareholders to take part in the shareholders' meeting.

The construction of the system of minority shareholders' protection is underway. This factor has decisive influence on the low index of minority shareholders' protection. The mechanisms for controlling shareholders have not been set up for the lack of minority shareholders' rights protection. In relation to institutional inducement, controlling shareholders still have the motivation of tunnelling illegal income because of the concealed relations between controlling shareholders and listed companies. In relation to shareholders' equal treatment, controlling shareholders dominate the process and qualification of shareholder meetings, and minority shareholders are restricted in obtaining the latest information and cannot express their purpose.

The industry comparative analysis of shareholders' behavior index

We use common industrial category criterion for dividing sample companies into five industries to analyze the status of the shareholders' behavior index. In 2002, shareholders' behavior indexes of Chinese listed companies have different characteristics between industries. The mean controlling shareholders' behavior index of Public Utility companies is 56.76, which is the highest among the five industries, 3.02 percentage points higher than the mean value of the total sample and 2.74 percentage points higher than other industry averages. The mean values of the shareholders' behavior index of other industries are: Manufacturing Industry companies 53.68, Miscellaneous companies 53.71, Agricultural companies 53.69, Service companies 53.05. The mean indexes of the four industries have the same trend, while the service companies are a little lower than the others. Seeing from the difference of the sub-factor index, the minority rights protection index and independence of the company index of Public Utility companies are lower than Miscellaneous and Agriculture respectively, and these two factors have little difference with other industries. The related party transaction index and independence index of Manufacturing Industry and Service companies are both lower than those of other industries. The data narrated above suggests that the competition between the industries, ownership structure, governance of the government and the outsider market mechanisms cause corporate governance differences between the industries. Among all the factors, the competition of industries has a reverse relation with the behavior of the controlling shareholders.

Among the five industries, the shareholders' behavior index of Public Utility companies is the highest, probably because of the competition environment and the government's controlling. Their performance in the minority rights protection index and independence of the company index is weaker than that of shareholders' meeting index and related party transaction index. The shareholder behavior indexes of Service and Manufacturing Industry companies are appreciably lower than others. Because China is getting rid of the deflation and turning to flourish gradually, Service and Manufacturing Industry companies face fierce market competition, they are severely influenced by the competitive pressure, the lack of capital and the outsider market mechanisms, so the controlling shareholders of listed companies have strongly negative externalities on the operating level. The related party transaction index and independence index of Service and Manufacturing Industry companies are lower than those of other industries, proving the phenomenon. The competition of industries has a reverse relationship with the behavior of the controlling shareholders—the fiercer the industrial competition the more externalities of controlling shareholders in listed companies.

The comparative analysis of different kinds of controlling shareholders' behavior index

Presently, the state-owned controlling shareholders of Chinese listed companies can be categorized into three kinds: companies controlled by government or administration of state-owned property, administrative company of state-owned property, and state-owned and dominated company. They represent three formations of state-owned property agencies. Scholars compare each formation's superiority by measuring each kind of companies' performance directly. In fact, different controlling shareholders have different economic attributions, different idiosyncratic resources and different targets, so they manifest different behaviors.

Observing from the total index, government or administration of state-owned property is the lowest kind in the state-owned controlling shareholders (mean value is 44.02). Thus when the government dominates listed companies directly, minority shareholders may experience greater negative externalities, which—mainly because of the independence of this kind of listed company—are lower than others obviously. It can be concluded from the sub-indexes of institutional inducement, the low scores of companies controlled by government or administration of state-owned property is mainly because the listed companies that are controlled by government or administration of state-owned property are severely lacking independence on employments and finance. And the government or administration of state-owned property prefer to interfere with the human resource management and financial management of the listed companies.

The dependence of business has become a prevalent phenomenon to the listed companies (mean value is only 23). The second is state-owned and dominated companies (mean value is 46.82) for which relevant factors are also mainly from the independence of listed companies. But the difference from companies controlled by government or administration of state-owned property is that the causes deciding the low scores of the indexes are the capital independence of listed companies. And this proved our deduction that listed companies existed in "asset confusion" with their parent companies. The highest one is companies controlled by administrative company of state-owned property (mean value is 48.52). Although the total index is better than the other two kinds, there are still limitations on minority shareholders' rights protection and related party transactions. The three sub-indexes of minority shareholders' rights protection are all lower than those of others, thus completion and perfection the mechanisms of minority shareholders' rights protection are key to increasing the corporate governance level of companies controlled by administrative companies of state-owned property. On the aspect of a firm's operation, companies controlled by administrative companies of state-owned property are positioned at a middle level of other two kinds of companies. But we can observe an interesting phenomenon from the index of related party transactions, which is that while the operation index of companies controlled by government and administration of state-owned property is quite high, the "loan guarantee" and "pricing norm" are at low levels. This indicates that when government and administration of state-owned property controls listed companies, they prefer to offer guarantee for related companies with listed companies' capital, and make unfair transactions between listed companies and other related companies by administrative instructions.

The total index of joint venture enterprises is the highest (mean is 56.55), and the second is the private corporations (mean is 48.99). Joint venture enterprises are better at independence of companies and related party transactions, but the minority shareholders protection status is at a low level while private companies are good at it. The controlling shareholders of private companies pay more attention to the protection of minority shareholders and other stakeholders but their related party transactions are not as well controlled as joint venture enterprises. Not only do the economic attribution and target tropism of controlling shareholders determine their behaviors, the heterogeneity of industry competition also decides their behaviors. Even if the controlling shareholders are of the same nature, their controlling behaviors are still different. This conclusion can offer empirical sustentation for pattern selection of state-owned capital administrating. The controlling shareholders who have strongly negative externalities are not only state-owned companies' shareholders, but also including shareholders of private and joint-venture companies. Thus we conclude that the tunnelling behavior is not state-owned companies' shareholders' particular behavior.

Empirical research on the relationship between the index controlling shareholders' behavior and company performance

When choosing the performance variables of controlling shareholders, we use the performance indexes that can reflect a firm's value and the growing ability of the company. So in this book, we choose Tobin's Q and EPS as the performance variables of controlling shareholders' behavior. Acting as the company's primary subject, controlling shareholders affect the value and the growing ability of the company directly. EPS is the acknowledged accounting index measuring running performance and profitability, and it can reflect the company's actual value.

Choosing variables of the controlling shareholders' performance
Tobin's Q, the ratio of a company's market value (which comprises share market value and the bond market value) to asset replacement value, is a forward-looking performance index. Tobin's Q can reflect a company's intangible assets, value in the future and the growing ability. Moreover, the data for calculating Tobin's Q is sourced from market data which is

disclosed passively, making it difficult for managers to manage in earnings management. Thus Tobin's Q can make up for the limitations of accounting indexes representing historical data only and through which managers can easily perform earnings management. The studies of Montgomery and Wernerfelt (1988), McFarland (1988), Megna and Klock (1993), Lang and Stulz (1994), and Bharadwaj (1999) have indicated that using Tobin's Q as a performance index is better than accounting indexes. Meanwhile, the using of Tobin's Q does not need to be adjusted by the companies' risk levels.

Based on the above analysis, we have chosen Tobin's Q as one of the measures to assess listed company performance. Considering the non-floating shares of Chinese listed companies, we adjust Tobin's Q. We compute the prices of non-floating shares as 40%, 30%, and 20% of the floating shares' prices and define them as TQ_6, TQ_7 and TQ_8. Adjusted Tobin's Q probably overestimates a company's actual performance; but if four measures can result in the same conclusions, the conclusions must be robust. We use the method of Chun and Pruitt (1994) to compute Tobin's Q. Considering other important factors that affect the performance, there must be some controlled variables added into the models. For the sake of controlling the variables' influence on the performance and increasing the validity of the models, we choose four controlled variables:

1. The dummy variable of asset size. Take the logarithm of a company's total book value at the end of the year as the dummy variable of asset size to control the asset scale's influence on the performance.
2. The dummy variable of industry. Classify the sample companies into five industries by the common standard, to control the difference of companies in different industries by the dummy variable of industries. In order to avoid multi-collinearity, we make this dummy variable contain four values.
3. The dummy variable of capital structure. The debt to asset ratio, which is the financial leverage, was used to control the influence of capital structure on the performance.

4. The dummy variable of first dominant shareholder. Because Chinese listed companies have the character of "one dominant shareholder," the dummy variable of first dominant shareholder was used to control the influence of the ownership.

Table 3.2: Variables list of shareholders' behavior appraisal

Name of variable	Symbol of variable	Indexes of sub-factors	Symbol of variable
Controlling shareholders' behavior index	$CCGI^{NK}_{1}$	Competition among same business	$CCGI^{NK}_{111}$
Related party transaction index	$CCGI^{NK}_{11}$	Price foundation	$CCGI^{NK}_{112}$
Controlling variable of company's scale	C	Funds embezzlement	$CCGI^{NK}_{113}$
Controlling variable of capital structure	V	Loan guarantee	$CCGI^{NK}_{114}$
Company's independence index	$CCGI^{NK}_{12}$	Staff's personal independence	$CCGI^{NK}_{121}$
Dummy variable of industry	$Indus$	Business independence	$CCGI^{NK}_{122}$
Dummy variable of top one shareholder's nature	C_{1j}	Financial affairs independence	$CCGI^{NK}_{123}$
Shareholder's meeting index	$CCGI^{NK}_{l3}$	Capital and property independence	$CCGI^{NK}_{124}$
Minority shareholders' rights protection index	$CCGI^{NK}_{14}$	Stockholder meeting participation	$CCGI^{NK}_{131}$
Voting rights collection	$CCGI^{NK}_{141}$	Shareholders meeting norm	$CCGI^{NK}_{132}$
Accumulative voting rights	$CCGI^{NK}_{143}$	Temporary shareholder meeting	$CCGI^{NK}_{142}$

Regression analysis of controlling shareholders' behavior and firm's performance

The former descriptive analysis has supplied essential materials for the validity test of the controlling shareholders' behavior index. In this section we will make more validity tests by the method of regression analysis. Our research took the cross-sectional data of 2001–02, thus we take the cross-sectional data analyzing method which is commonly used in economics and finance.

The test contains two sections: one is testing the relationship between the controlling shareholders' behavior index and company performance, the other is testing the relationship between sub-factors and the performance. We use fixed effect models to do the first test, which is to say take the controlling shareholders' behavior as a "treatment variable." Under the circumstance of controlled other factors, if the "treatment variable" is significant it will prove that controlling shareholders' behaviors do affect the performance. And the sign and value of the treatment variable's coefficient reflect the direction and degree of the influence of controlling shareholders' behavior to firms' value. The regression models are as follows:

$$Y_i = \beta_0 + \beta_1 CCGI^{NK}_1 + \beta_2 C + \beta_3 V + \beta_4 \sum_{i=1}^{4} Indus_i + \beta_5 \sum_{j=1}^{8} Top1\_chrc_j + \varepsilon \qquad \text{.............(I)}$$

$$Y_i = \beta_0 + \beta_1 CCGI^{NK}_i + \beta_2 C + \beta_3 V + \beta_4 \sum_{i=1}^{4} Indus_i + \beta_5 \sum_{j=1}^{8} Top1\_chrc_j + \varepsilon \qquad \text{............. (II)}$$

$$Y_i = \beta_0 + \beta_1 CCGI^{NK}_{ij} + \beta_2 C + \beta_3 V + \beta_4 \sum_{i=1}^{4} Indus_i + \beta_5 \sum_{j=1}^{8} Top1\_chrc_j + \varepsilon \qquad \text{............. (III)}$$

In the equations above: Y_i represents a company's performance, which is EPS and Tobin's Q respectively in each model. Y is for Model (I_1), Model (II_1) and Model (III_1) when it is

EPS, while Y is for Model (I_2), Model (II_2) and Model (III_3) when it is Tobin's Q. $CCGI^{NK}_1$ is controlling shareholders' behavior index, $CCGI^{NK}_i$ is the factor index of controlling shareholders' behavior index, $CCGI^{NK}_{ij}$ is the sub-factor index of controlling shareholders' behavior index, C represents the controlled variable of company's size, V is the controlled variable of capital structure, I_i is the dummy variable of industries, C_{1j} represents the nature of the first shareholder which has nine kinds. In order to avoid multi-collinearity, we designed eight dummy variables. The regression analysis results of the six models—Model (I_1), Model (II_1), Model (III_1), Model (I_2), Model (II_2) and Model (III_2)—are listed in Table 3.3.

It can be concluded from the results of Model (I_1) and Model (I_2) in Table 3.3 that the controlling shareholders' behavior index has significant positive relation with the EPS at the 10% significance level, and also has positive relation with the Tobin's Q. It suggests the design of the controlling shareholders' behavior index in this book is reasonable and effective. In the companies which are high in the controlling shareholders' behavior index, minority shareholders' rights can be protected efficiently, and their interests can be reflected by meetings of shareholders. Thus these companies pay more attention to minority and other stakeholders' rights and they are able to achieve continuous long-term development. Meanwhile, the companies high in controlling shareholders' behavior index also have better independences, regular related party transactions, and weak "tunnelling behavior" and externalities. It means that such companies strengthen their competition power by increasing corporate governance, ensuring the scientific nature of decisions and effectiveness of the management. Thus the companies with better controlling shareholders' behavior indexes should have better performance.

The regression results of the shareholders' behavior index show that in the Model (II_1) of the index, shareholders' meeting status has significant positive relation with EPS at 1% significance level and the coefficient is 0.304. In the Model (II_2) the index of shareholders' meeting status has a certain positive relation with Tobin's Q, which means that the index of shareholders' meeting status plays an important role the positive relationship

Table 3.3:   Shareholders' behavior index

Variables	EPS			Tobin's Q		
	(I_1)	(II_1)	(III_1)	(I_2)	(II_2)	(III_2)
(Const)	−0.331 (1.208)	1.811*** (4.664)	−0.387 (−0.902)	1.811*** (4.664)	9.762*** (11.590)	7.437*** (10.630)
$CCGI^{NK}_1$	0.264* (1.715)		−	0.0147 (1.128)	−	−
$CCGI^{NK}_{11}$	−	0.057 (0.993)	−	−	0.016 (1.126)	−
$CCGI^{NK}_{12}$	−	−0.115 (−0.815)	−	−	0.335 (1.467)	−
$CCGI^{NK}_{13}$	−	0.304*** (3.389)	−	−	0.272 (0.863)	−
$CCGI^{NK}_{14}$	−	0.147 (1.166)		−	0.365 (1.094)	−
$CCGI^{NK}_{111}$	−	−	0.0405 (1.026)	−	−	0.122 (0.463)
$CCGI^{NK}_{112}$	−	−	0.0846* (1.7558)	−	−	0.150 (0.756)
$CCGI^{NK}_{113}$	−	−	−0.0517 (−1.401)	−	−	−0.114 (−0.086)
$CCGI^{NK}_{114}$	−	−	0.0974*** (3.689)	−	−	0.312*** (2.105)
$CCGI^{NK}_{121}$	−	−	−0.112 (−1.272)	−	−	0.356 (1.117)
$CCGI^{NK}_{122}$	−	−	0.115* (1.862)	−	−	0.116 (0.620)
$CCGI^{NK}_{123}$	−	−	0.115 (1.462)	−	−	0.257 0.518
$CCGI^{NK}_{124}$	−	−	−0.127 (−1.543)	−	−	0.0794 (0.265)
$CCGI^{NK}_{131}$	−	−	0.167* (1.862)	−	−	0.175 (0.257)
$CCGI^{NK}_{132}$	−	−	0.243*** (3.075)	−	−	0.189 (0.663)
$CCGI^{NK}_{141}$	−	−	−0.084 (−0.05)	−	−	0.0806 (0.108)

Table 3.3: Shareholders' behavior index *(cont'd)*

	EPS			Tobin's Q		
$CCGI^{NK}_{142}$	–	–	0.044 (0.345)	–	–	0.214 0.463
$CCGI^{NK}_{143}$	–	–	0.067 (1.241)	–	–	0.0828 0.415
Adj_R^2	0.031	0.056	0.0743	0.048	0.063	0.053
F	2.970	2.756	2.626	2.722	2.363	2.563
D-W	1.988	1.991	2.023	1.870	2.012	2.011

Note: ***, **, * mean significance at 1%, 5%, 10% level respectively.

between the controlling shareholders' behavior index and the performance, and reflects that the companies which have excellent performances and values can operate the insider controlling mechanisms of shareholder meetings well and ensure the scientific nature of decisions and effectiveness of the management. The minority shareholders' rights protection and related party transaction indexes have insignificant positive relation with companies' performance and value indexes. It proves that companies with excellent performances and values are regular in related party transactions, thinking much of the rights of minority shareholders and other stakeholders, and pursue persistent development. The independence indexes of companies have a positive relation with Tobin's Q but it is insignificant, and have negative relation with EPS, the companies' performance index. It indicates that valued companies should be better at independence, but the independence status of Chinese listed companies is not ideal presently because companies' performances are made via earnings management.

The regression results of Model (III$_1$) and Model (III$_2$) suggest that the price foundation, loan guarantee, business independence, shareholder meeting participation and norm of listed companies' related party transactions have positive relations with the performance index EPS, at the significance of 10%, 5%, 10%, 10%, and 5% respectively. Loan guarantee index has significant positive relation with Tobin's Q, the companies' value index.

The regression results above show that the price foundation and loan guarantee of listed companies' related party transactions which affect the standardization of related party transactions directly are the important factors influencing the related party transaction index. The relationships of the independence factor index with the performance and value index resulting from Model (III$_1$) and Model (III$_2$) further prove that Chinese listed companies achieve performance through earnings management, but the companies which are better in independence have high values, and all the indexes of shareholders' meeting factors have positive relations with company performance.

The regression results above show that the controlling shareholders' behavior index we designed can reflect the relationship of controlling shareholders' behavior and companies' performance objectively.

Conclusions

The research results of the evaluation and index of the controlling shareholders' behavior conclude that:

(1) The overall index of controlling shareholder's behaviors that have strongly negative externalities in China is relatively low, controlling shareholders' relation with listed companies are becoming "intangible" from "tangible," and they still have the motivation of entrenching illegal earnings. The controlling shareholders continue abusing related party transactions. Meanwhile the controlling of the process and qualification of the shareholders' meeting by controlling shareholders means the minority shareholders can hardly get enough information in time and fully express their interests. The reasons are the lack of protection in the institutional system for protecting minority shareholders' rights and the lack of mechanisms to limit controlling shareholders' behavior.

(2) It is not only controlling shareholders in SOEs that have strongly negative externalities; the controlling shareholders indexes of private companies and joint venture companies are also at a low level. It can be concluded that the "tunnelling

behavior" is not a special characteristic of SOEs' controlling shareholders.

We can see from the two conclusions above that resolving the "agency problem" between the controlling shareholders and minority shareholders should not only depend on decreasing the proportion of state-owned shares and floating the state-owned shares, and it should also pay great attention on improving the construction and completion of minority shareholders' rights protection and making an effective governance mechanism in listed companies.

(3) The economic attribution and target choosing of the controlling shareholders determined their behaviors. Even if they are all SOEs' shareholders, the negative externalities of their behaviors are different. The negative externalities of "companies controlled by government or administration of state-owned property" is higher than that of "state-owned and dominated company," which is higher than that of "companies controlled by administrative company of state-owned property;" this finding will give empirical support for the selection of state properties' administration. Under the existing framework designing a contingent governance scheme for controlling shareholders' behavior is an effective way. Therefore, the controlling shareholders' intervention in the employee and finance areas of "government or administration of state-owned property" companies should be monitored and controlled; the "capital confusion" problem of the listed companies and their parent companies in the state-owned and dominated companies need to be resolved; and companies controlled by administrative companies of state-owned properties must pay more attention to the completion and perfection of minority shareholders' protection.

(4) Shareholders' behavior positively correlated to performance. Good results in shareholders' meetings, related party transactions and minority shareholders' protection all affect companies' performance positively; the shareholders' meeting governance index has an especially positive relationship with performance. However, the major shareholders of Chinese listed companies restrained performance greatly.

CHAPTER

Research on Evaluation and Index of Directorates Governance

Evaluation of directorates governance is one of the core factors of the evaluation of corporate governance. On the basis of some conclusions from Chinese and foreign research, we set some correlative indexes of directorates governance for analyzing the relationship between directors' governance and company performance of Chinese listed companies in different aspects. We reach a conclusion that there exists an inverse U-shape relationship between directors' governance and company performance, and find evidence of the existence of a substitution effect among directors' governance mechanisms. The policy implications of this conclusion are in the following conditions of directorates governance. The key to our directorates governance reformation is introducing strategic investors and improving the mechanisms of board committees and internal governance. Problems include lack of external governance mechanisms, weak majority shareholders, insufficient regulations of internal directors, and inadequate incentive effects.

Literature review on evaluation of directorates governance

Directorates governance is at the core of corporate governance. A directorate is the legal entity of corporate property rights, and it executes decision-making functions and evaluation and regulation functions for executives. So an efficient directorate is consistent with the corporate development and benefits of shareholders. Fama (1980) indicated the directorate as the supreme control system in a company, and companies with effective directorates have better management performance than companies with ineffective directorates.

Analysis of directorate quality and governance

Directorate quality connects with the operation of the directorate, the performance of the directorate, and the benefits of shareholders. The company law of America declares that directorates in public companies administer their own affairs. This law also gives directorates some formal rights based on a unified standard which reflects shareholders' benefits, such as to evaluate management creation and performance, distribute compensation, and punish managers (Fama and Jensen, 1983). Some masters of organization theory indicate that the board can make operation decisions as long as it has capabilities in evaluating management innovation (Mizruchi, 1983). Economists also point out that the directorate is the major factor in large companies' corporate governance structure. Shareholders' benefits will be hindered if managers lack a restraint system during governance (Fama and Jensen, 1983). Agency theory indicates that directorates have a wide range of rights in employment, dismissal and pay compensation to advanced managers, so they can protect the investors and thus be an important factor in corporate governance (Williamson, 1984). Directorates governance is becoming the focus of corporate governance. In 1997, *Commercial Weekly* organized a group consisting of stock analysts, pension fund managers and experts in corporate governance to investigate 50 companies' directorate quality. They found that directorate quality is the determinant index of companies' future performance and share return.

An investigation by the Russell Reynolds Commission in 1997 found that institutional investors direct most of their attention to directorate quality as the key evaluating factor. According to an investigation by McKinsey & Company in 2000, more than 80% of investors would pay more than a 20%

price premium for companies with the same profit but a strong directorate. Inefficient directorates could lead to many problems, even being merged. After the Asian financial crisis, about 75% of investors pay the same or more attention to directorate quality rather than financial problems. How to increase the efficiency of directorates governance is the key factor to increase the efficiency of corporate governance.

Some analysts have conducted empirical research into directorates governance from different aspects. At first, it was only research on relativity between the monomial factor of directorates and management performance. Most of the empirical research is on the relativity between independence of directorates and management performance, and the composition of directorates and management performance, especially in the field of discussing whether there exists a premium directorate structure. Lipton and Lorsch (1992) conducted comparative research between the size of a board and management performance through empirical analysis, and reached the conclusion that the best size of a board is seven or eight people. After this, Yermack (1996) used 500 large American public companies' data from 1984 to 1991 (published in *Forbes*), and found through empirical analysis a negative relationship between the size of boards and management performance.

In relation to the composition of the board, Hermalin and Weisbach (1988) find some association between the percentage of external directors and CEO and management performance. When the CEO is going to retire, the percentage of external directors will decrease; and when the CEO takes a post not long ago, the percentage of external directors will increase. Also, the percentage of external directors and the corporate performance have a negative relationship. Mishra and Nielsen (1999) take bank-owned corporations as a sample for research on bank performance, independence of the board, and CEO's sensitivity to compensation. This research indicates that when taking size, growth opportunity (measured by the ratio of every share's market value and book value), and the percentage of board ownership as the control variable, there is a negative relationship between the independence of the board and the CEO's sensitivity to compensation, which showed the positive aspect of independent directors. When the bank-owned corporations have a bad firm performance, independent directors fully use compensation contact to ensure managers and shareholders have the same benefits. This research proves that independent directors are effective in such conditions.

Randall Morck, Andrei Shleifer and Robert Vishiny (1988) report a non-linear relationship between firm performance (Tobin's Q) and the percentage of external board ownership through empirical research. Pearce and Zahra (1992) analyze the relativity between firm performance and board composition, which is measured by size and the percentage of external directors. They conclude that environment, strategy and former performance can affect the board composition. The board will enlarge its size and external directors when facing high uncertainty, diversification, large financial leverage and poor former performance. What is more important, the research argues that there is a positive relationship between former board composition and financial performance.

Kenneth J. Rediker and Anju Seth (1996) figured out all the mechanisms used in directorates governance to settle the conflicts of shareholders and managers. A specific mechanism's function may be affected by other mechanisms which are operated synchronously in the corporation; that is, there should be a substitution effect among monitoring mechanisms carried out by external directors, external major shareholders and internal directors, and incentive mechanisms carried out by managers. And then Daily and Dalton et al (1998) conducted research based on 977 companies and reached a conclusion that there is no significant association between board composition and financial performance. Further research indicates that the index selection of company size, financial performance, and diversification of board composition may have a certain effect on the relationship between board composition and firm performance.

Research on evaluation of directorates governance

In order to review some integrated factors for directorates governance, some research centers from other countries have conducted research on the issue. National Association of Corporate Directors (NACD) claims that the most important and difficult two questions in directorates governance are the construction of directors' abilities and a perfect system for evaluating directorates governance. So the key factors for evaluating directorates governance are as follows: controlling rights of independent directors, evaluating procedures and objectives for directors, trustworthy and private procedures, and transparency. The desired effects of evaluation are distinguishing the rights between directorates and managers, enhancing mutual benefit among directors, and improving directorate quality.

The evaluation index system for corporate governance of American company Standard & Poor's is accepted by markets. This system—which is measured by composition and operation of directorates—consists of directorates' composition, ability, efficiency, external directors' independence and ability, compensation, and the right to appoint and remove. For example, the composition of directorates should ensure all shareholders' benefits are fairly treated, and depend on the size and board committee of the directorate.

Commercial Weekly is passionate about the evaluation of directorate quality. It chose the best and worst directorates in 2002 based on 16 indexes, which included independence, directors' quality, board ownership, and operation quality. The evaluating factor of Deminor Corp. in Europe is directorates' structure and functions, which consists of the relationship among independent directors, chairman and CEO, voting, compensation, and operation of the board committee. Credit Lyonnais Securities Asia made an evaluation of corporate governance through 495 listed companies in 25 developing countries in 2002, considering the factors of independence and responsibility. Most foreign evaluations of directorates governance are based on well-established legal systems and mature mechanisms, and draw conclusions from different emphases. But listed companies in China are facing an imperfect market, so these are not applicable in China. Some also claim that with a perfect market and close governance level, there is no significant association between listed companies' corporate governance and firm performance (Ishi and Metrik, 2001). On the contrary, in imperfect markets there is significant positive relationship between corporate governance and firm performance (Klapper and Lover, 2002).

Although directorates of Chinese listed companies are operating according to relative laws and regulations, the quality is low due to the imperfect laws, especially the "domination of a single shareholder" factor. CSRC established the code of corporate governance for China's listed companies, based on corporation law. There are more than 30 detailed rules to regulate directorates and directors, which indicates that directorates of Chinese listed companies have many complicated problems to be solved. Owing to this specific period for Chinese listed companies, most evaluations on them are confined to directorate size and composition and firm performance through empirical analysis (Kong Yongxiang, 2000; Li Yougen, 2001).

Although some researchers try to bring directorates into evaluation of corporate governance (Fei Wuwei, 2001; Wu Shukun, 2002), there is always a lack of systematic indexes and effective tests. It would have great practical relevance to establish Chinese listed companies' directorates governance indexes based on foreign evaluation experience and the Chinese environment, such as laws, regulations and systems. These indexes could fully reflect Chinese corporate governance conditions, make empirical analysis on the relationship between directorates governance and firm performance, and find factors which affect directorates governance in order to perfect directorates governance and improve firm performance.

Evaluation index of directorates governance of Chinese listed companies

In order to conduct empirical research on the relativity between directorates governance and firm performance, we must make judgments on the condition of directorates governance. So we designed a set of directorates governance indexes (a part of the corporate governance evaluation system) based on Chinese listed companies' conditions and features and content of Standard & Poor's regarding directorates governance. We referred to confirmation of evaluation indexes and methods as the primary content.

Confirmation of directorates governance evaluation indexes

The directorates governance evaluation index consists of directors' behavior, directorates operation, directors' compensation, directorates organization and independent director system. This section designs a set of evaluation indexes and standards as "China's listed companies' directorates governance evaluation system," which is based on effective operation and scientific decision-making. Directorates should carry out proxy rights for general meetings of shareholders. We designed the directorates governance evaluation system of Chinese listed companies based on 16 aspects and five dimensionalities, which are rights and responsibilities of directors, directorates operation, directorates organization, directors' compensation and independent director system (see Table 4.1).

Table 4.1:   Directorates governance evaluation system

Main factor	Sub-factor layer	Specification
Directors' rights and obligations ($CCGI^{NK}_{21}$)	Nomination ($CCGI^{NK}_{211}$), Compensation ($CCGI^{NK}_{212}$), Training ($CCGI^{NK}_{213}$), Self-examination ($CCGI^{NK}_{214}$)	Indicate assiduity and dependability obligations of directors
Directorates operation efficiency ($CCGI^{NK}_{22}$)	Size ($CCGI^{NK}_{221}$), Composition ($CCGI^{NK}_{222}$), Time of meeting ($CCGI^{NK}_{223}$)	Indicate function and effect of directorates
Directorates organization ($CCGI^{NK}_{23}$)	Leader composition ($CCGI^{NK}_{231}$), Appointment of committee ($CCGI^{NK}_{232}$), Operation of committee ($CCGI^{NK}_{233}$)	Indicate efficiency and independence of directorates
Directors' compensation ($CCGI^{NK}_{24}$)	Compensation ($CCGI^{NK}_{241}$), Form of compensation ($CCGI^{NK}_{242}$), Evaluation of performance ($CCGI^{NK}_{243}$)	Weigh compensation and its incentive and restraint condition of directorates
Independent director system ($CCGI^{NK}_{25}$)	Percentage of independent directors ($CCGI^{NK}_{251}$), Incentive of independent directors ($CCGI^{NK}_{252}$), Independence ($CCGI^{NK}_{253}$)	Indicate constitution of independent director system

Directors' rights and obligations

Directors have specific legal status with their own rights and obligations. Directors' obligations include assiduity and dependability. Assiduity obligations require directors to take responsibility for their position, such as attending meetings and paying attention to the management of the corporation. Dependability obligations require directors to carry out their functions for value-maximizing and not damaging corporation value. An effective board can regulate directors' behavior through nomination, including training and self-examination.

Directorates operational efficiency

A directorate is a decision-making institution selected by shareholders' congress and it consists of individual directors. Its function is making strategies for corporate management and regulating managers; this includes size, composition and efficiency of meetings.

Directorates organization

Directorates efficiency is dependent on the quality of internal diversity and cooperation, and committees play an important role in this. The appointment of a committee is good for diversity and cooperation of directorates. Thus all sorts of committees comprise the important index to evaluate the independence of directorates, and they need relative indexes to evaluate their own operation.

Directors' compensation

Directors' compensation consists of material and mental incentives. In order to carry out incentives for directors, it is necessary to establish a directorates efficiency evaluation system which consists of compensation, form of compensation and evaluation of performance.

Independent director system

Under the ownership structure of "domination of a single shareholder," the establishment of an independent director system can ensure independence of directorates, scientific decision-making and efficiency of directorates. An independent director system is an important evaluation index in corporate governance and includes percentage of independent directors, incentive of independent directors and independence.

Confirmation of evaluation standards

Confirmation of directorates governance evaluation depends on the basis and objectives of indexes. We design these indexes based on practical operation in order to help investors make decisions, governments perform monitoring functions, and companies to make self-examinations and credit restraints. According to theoretic and empirical research and practical characteristics, we confirm evaluation standards based on relevant laws, regulations and rules, such as *The Company Law of the People's Republic of China, Securities Law of the People's Republic of China, Shanghai Stock Exchange Guidelines for Corporate Governance of Listed Companies,* and *Guidance for Independent Director System of Listed Companies.* This evaluation system is based on these standards and uses a 100-mark system; the highest total possible score is 100 and the lowest total possible score is 0. Then we design objectives, guidance and index levels (main and sub-factor) according to their own weights.

Confirmation of importance coefficient of evaluation index

In the design progress of the directorates governance evaluation system of Chinese listed companies, we employed both subjective and objective evaluation, as well as layered disposal methods to compile the board governance index, and for more details, we utilized subjective evaluation for both destination and main code layers, with objective evaluation for the indicator layer. In particular, based on the observations the objective evaluation method confirms the weight coefficients, and also takes the present characteristics of China's listed companies' governance environment into consideration, thus the layered analysis method has been introduced to confirm the weigh coefficients of the indicators through a multiple layers appraisal system. In this book, we use objective methods and subjective methods to evaluate the weight of each representative layer, and adopt marking methods to analyse each layer, and then obtain judgment matrixes about correlative main (or subdivided) factors' weightiness coefficients. Our judgment matrixes and layers' coherence ratio have passed the relevant test. And the general layer rank, main (or subdivided) factors' weightiness coefficient in board governance appraisal system obtains gratifying coherence.

Our specialty is setting index models based on the conditions of Chinese listed companies and evaluation systems of foreign mature capital markets. This section sets multi-tier index systems, and some of them have contact with other evaluation indexes of corporate governance. They bring the directorates governance evaluation index into the corporate governance evaluation system, and it becomes an evaluation index system with Chinese characteristics.

Descriptive statistics of directorates governance of Chinese listed companies

We take Chinese listed companies in 2002 as our research sample. Data was obtained from the questionnaires (with a recall ratio of 92%) from the Corporate Governance Research Center of Nankai University, listed companies that disclosed their annual reports in 2002, questionnaires from our own team, and so on. We have 35,000 data points with elimination of some outliers, and the final available sample is 931 companies.

General specification of conditions of directorates governance

The China directorates corporate governance index ($CCGI^{NK}_2$) has a basically normal distribution. Mean of $CCGI^{NK}_2$ is 43.40 and maximum and minimum are 74.51 and 1.56 respectively, which reflects a poor condition of directorates governance and belongs to $CCGI^{NK}_2VI$. There are only seven companies in all samples that meet $CCGI^{NK}_2III$, with no $CCGI^{NK}_2I$ or $CCGI^{NK}_2II$, and 73.68% are $CCGI^{NK}_2VI$. According to the five main factors of directorates governance, mean of $CCGI^{NK}_{21}$ is 34.24, falling into $CCGI^{NK}_2VI$, and standard deviation of $CCGI^{NK}_{21}$ is 23.48% with a high dispersion; mean of $CCGI^{NK}_{22}$ is 59.17, falling into $CCGI^{NK}_2V$, and standard deviation of $CCGI^{NK}_{22}$ is 18.74% as the best governance condition; mean of $CCGI^{NK}_{23}$ is 42.19 and standard deviation of $CCGI^{NK}_{23}$ is 31.94%, with lack of internal controlling organs; mean of $CCGI^{NK}_{24}$ is 41.32 and standard deviation of $CCGI^{NK}_{24}$ is 22.50%, with absence of incentive and restraint mechanisms in most companies; mean of $CCGI^{NK}_{25}$ is 53.59 with a high directorates governance. Standard deviation of $CCGI^{NK}_2$ of all the sample companies is 10.37% with a low dispersion, although there is a high dispersion of sub-factors, such as the standard deviation of $CCGI^{NK}_{21}$ is 23.48% and $CCGI^{NK}_{25}$ is 33.94%.

The China directorates governance index is low with a low dispersion as a whole, but there is a high dispersion of sub-factors. It is illustrated that Chinese listed companies still lack effective directorates governance mechanisms. There is a low standard deviation in different industries and different departments in the same industry. Maximum mean is Miscellaneous corporations at 44.59; minimum mean is First Industry corporations at 42.97. The same factor index is highly stable in all industries although there are some differences in means. In contrast, there are many differences in means and dispersions of sub-factor indexes. In the field of directorates governance, $CCGI^{NK}_2$ has a low dispersion in the same industry but a high dispersion in sub-factor indexes. It indicates that different industries are at different levels of directorates governance, while tending to be common in the same industry. There is a high dispersion in sub-factor indexes stemming from the industry itself.

Detailed specifications of conditions of directorates governance

Taking all the five main factors as a whole, we can find that $CCGI^{NK}_{23}$ and $CCGI^{NK}_{25}$ are better, with more than 60% falling into $CCGI^{NK}_2IV$; in the sub-factors of directorates operation efficiency, indexes of board size and external director are better, with means 99.68 and 61.00; means of source of directors and nomination are 35.75 and 22.43 respectively, which are lower. Although most companies comply with the laws and regulations, the operation system still needs improvement. The worst condition is directors' rights and obligations; 73.04% are $CCGI^{NK}_2VI$. Mean of its sub-factor "chairman's external investment" is 16.64, which shows the inefficiency of board decision-making. Due to the absence of an effective governance mechanism, directorates governance of Chinese listed companies has many serious problems. Boards cannot carry out the function of decision-making. This indicates that the key to corporate governance reformation should be the establishment of corporate governance systems.

Analysis on directorates governance index classified by the nature of domination of a single shareholder

The nature of the controlling shareholder should affect directorates governance significantly. Based on the different natures of controlling shareholders, we sort all means of directorates governance indexes from maximum to minimum as follows: private company; state-owned company; state-owned property management company; government; collective company; joint ventures; universities and colleges; scientific research institution; and other institutions. When a private company acts as controlling shareholder, the maximum mean of directorates governance index can reach 45.59; when universities, colleges and scientific research institutions act as controlling shareholder, minimum mean of directorates governance index is only 36.71. What is different from our usual point is when a foreign company acts as controlling shareholder, there would be a low mean of directorates governance index. This is because some practical geographical factors make it difficult for them to participate in directorates governance. It suggests that we should attract local investors besides introducing foreign strategy investors.

According to directors' rights and obligations, when a private company and a collective company act as controlling shareholder, the mean is high; according to directorates operation efficiency, when a private company, universities, colleges, scientific research institutions and other institutions act as controlling shareholder, the mean is high; according to directorates organization, when a private company and state-owned property management company act as controlling shareholder, the mean is high; according to directors' compensation, when a state-owned company, state-owned property management company and government act as controlling shareholder, the mean is high; according to independent director systems, when a private company and collective company act as controlling shareholder, the mean is high. Different controlling shareholders have different influences on directorates governance. Private companies perform better in many fields.

Empirical research on the relationship between directorates governance and corporate performance

Variable employed

Due to the core effect of the directorate in corporate governance, it can influence current and future firm performance through effective strategy and controlling. Return on Net Assets (RONA) is a common index to evaluate firm performance, but we designed an integrated index that consists of earning capacity, capital stock expansion and growth to reflect capacity of corporations for future development. We take RONA and firm performance (FP) as dependent variables to reflect efficiency of corporate governance, and directorates governance index $CCGI^{NK}$, directors' rights and obligations $CCGI^{NK}_{21}$, directorates operation efficiency $CCGI^{NK}_{22}$, directorates organization $CCGI^{NK}_{23}$, directors' compensation $CCGI^{NK}_{24}$, and independent director system $CCGI^{NK}_{25}$ as independent variables for regression analysis. During the process of regression, we bring 12 control variables I_i ($i = 1, 2, \ldots, 12$) into the model because of the industry effect on firm performance and growth. Due to the influence of controlling shareholders on directorates governance, we bring another two control variables HS_1 and HS_2 into the model based on the percentage of shares of domination of a single shareholder and the top five shareholders.

Formal model and regression results

We designed a univariate quadratic regression model (I) because we find a non-linear relationship between firm performance and $CCGI^{NK}_2$ through a scatter chart; we designed a multiple linear regression model for the relationship between firm performance and sub-factors of directorates governance (II).

$$RONA(FP) = C + \beta_1\, CCGI^{NK}_2 + \beta_2\, (CCGI^{NK}_2)^2 + \beta_3\, HS_1 + \beta_4\, HS_2 + \alpha_i\Sigma i + \varepsilon \dots\dots\dots\dots\dots\dots\dots\dots\dots\dots\dots(I)$$

$$RONA(FP) = C + \beta_1\, CCGI^{NK}_{21} + \beta_2\, CCGI^{NK}_{22} + \beta_3\, CCGI^{NK}_{23} + \beta_4\, CCGI^{NK}_{24} + \beta_5\, CCGI^{NK}_{25} + \beta_6\, HS_1 + \beta_7\, HS_2 + \alpha_i\Sigma Ii + \varepsilon \dots\dots\dots\dots\dots\dots\dots\dots\dots (II)$$

In the above models, C, β_1, β_2, β_3, β_4, β_5, α_i and so on are relative coefficients. For our sample research data, we use econometrics software Eviews 3.1 for simulations. Table 4.2 shows the regression results of (I).

Table 4.2 shows two major results: there is a non-linear inverse U-shape relationship between RONA and $CCGI^{NK}_2$ variables with significance at 10%; there is a weak non-linear inverse U-shape relationship between firm performance and $CCGI^{NK}_2$ variables with significance at 10%.

There is an inverse U-shape relationship between firm performance and $CCGI^{NK}_2$, which is consistent with our hypothesis. Because of the positive relationship, good directorates governance will improve current and future firm performance, but poor directorates governance will impose pressure on future

Table 4.2:   Regression results of RONA, FP and $CCGI^{NK}_2$

Regression results	RONA		FP	
	Coefficient	Prob.	Coefficient	Prob.
C	−16.52	0.09	0.58	0.00
$CCGI^{NK}_2$	98.20	0.05	0.25	0.03
$(CCGI^{NK}_2)^2$	−107.32	0.02	−0.30	0.07
$R\text{-}squared$	0.11		0.08	

improvement. The effect of the directorate is crucial not only in a poor firm performance period but also in a mature period which needs an effective governance mechanism, including directorates operation.

These models have a low degree of fit. We arrived at some possible reasons: first, some variables which may be affecting firm performance need to be eliminated; second, there is a long time lag of a directorate's effect from decision-making and controlling influence. According to Jensen, a directorate's behavior is passive to a certain extent. The descendent firm performance will compel a directorate to improve its operation even if it would work in a few years. Due to the shortage of data, the long relationship between FP and $CCGI^{NK}_2$ still needs more empirical research.

We look backward for (II) and get regression results with significance only for $CCGI^{NK}_{23}$, $CCGI^{NK}_{24}$ and $CCGI^{NK}_{25}$. Other factors neither improve obviously the degree of fit nor significance. Table 4.3 shows regression results of RONA, FP and $CCGI^{NK}_{23}$, $CCGI^{NK}_{24}$ and $CCGI^{NK}_{25}$.

We can get some conclusions from Table 4.3: first, there is a negative relationship between RONA and $CCGI^{NK}_{23}$, and a positive relationship between RONA and $CCGI^{NK}_{25}$, both with significance at 5%; secondly, there is a weak negative relationship between firm performance and $CCGI^{NK}_{23}$ and $CCGI^{NK}_{24}$, and a weak positive relationship between firm performance and $CCGI^{NK}_{25}$, with significance at 10%, 5%, and 5% respectively.

Table 4.3: Regression results of RONA, FP and $CCGI^{NK}_{23}$, $CCGI^{NK}_{24}$, $CCGI^{NK}_{25}$

Regression results	RONA		FP	
	Coefficient	Prob.	Coefficient	Prob.
C	−4.25	0.07	0.79	0.00
CCGI$^{NK}_{23}$	−14.31	0.00	−0.24	0.06
CCGI$^{NK}_{24}$	−9.08	0.02	−0.13	0.03
CCGI$^{NK}_{25}$	15.92	0.01	0.16	0.04
R-squared	0.10		0.07	

Furthermore, these conclusions prove the causes of the inverse U-shape relationship between directorates governance and firm performance in (I) and (II). Firstly, there is no significant correlative relationship between $CCGI^{NK}_{21}$, $CCGI^{NK}_{22}$ and firm performance. Although directorates do better in legal operation and controlling, they still lack an effective operation system. As an incentive and restraint mechanism, the effect on directors of directorates compensation is limited. The independent director system is important to improve firm performance, and the appointment of committees will help companies' future development as a controlling system. Because firm performance reflects future capacity, the low coefficient of firm performance and $CCGI^{NK}_{23}$ and $CCGI^{NK}_{24}$ is relative to the functions of committees. The empirical findings are consistent with Kenneth J. Rediker and Anju Seth; different directorates governance mechanisms have a substitute effect. An independent director system plays a key role in improving directorates governance. Time lag and substitute effect are the root of the inverse U-shape relationship between directorates governance and firm performance.

Conclusions and policy suggestions

Directorates governance significantly affects firm performance in theory. We get the following findings from empirical research on the relationship between firm performance and directorates governance:

(1) There is an inverse U-shape relationship between firm performance and directorates governance. It is due to the particular Chinese situation. According to Kenneth J. Rediker and Anju Seth, all the mechanisms used in directorates governance are used to settle the conflicts of shareholders and managers. A special mechanism should be affected by other mechanisms used in corporations at the same time, such as monitoring mechanisms carried out by external directors, external major shareholders and internal directors, and incentive mechanisms carried out by managers. Now in China, an immature capital market leads to the absence of external directorates governance

mechanisms; state-controlled ownership leads to a hollow position, lack of strategic investors and weak governance of controlling shareholders.

Directorates governance lacks necessary objectivity and motivation because of weak supervision of internal directors and the incentive effect on manager shareholdings and insider control. Directorates governance becomes a passive behavior oriented to self-benefits, and is only adopted in circumstances of poor firm performance. So the key to reform of directorates governance is to enhance directorates' efficiency and internal governance systems and to introduce strategic investors (especially the private institutional investors) for the development of governance mechanisms of controlling shareholders. There is a limitation on our research because of the shortage of data and the relationship between directorates governance and firm performance, so the long relationship between them still needs more empirical research.

(2) Directorates governance has a high relativity with current RONA and low relativity with future RONA. As an incentive and restraint mechanism, directors' compensation systems are not significant or consistent with firm performance. Directorates have a strong controlling capacity in contrast with weak strategy-making capacity. Little firm performance of Chinese listed companies comes from directorates governance, which is the core of corporate governance. Thus, improvement of directorates governance and making it operate for corporation value-maximizing is the key to reform of directorates.

(3) Firm performance has a negative relationship with directorate organization and directors' compensation but a positive relationship with independent directors, all of them significant. Directorates do well in organization and poorly in operation systems. Directorates of Chinese listed companies still need improvement. Although most companies have carried out independent director systems and appointed committees, the latter does not work as efficiently as the former due to the lack of operation and incentive mechanisms. We should strengthen the establishment of operation systems of board committees.

(4) In relation to independent director systems, although in general they do well, they still have some deficiencies of

independence, strategy making and internal director control. It is essential to improve board committees to enhance control and restriction on internal directors. The lack of nomination systems of independent directors and the right to know leads to weak independence.

(5) Directorates governance is a system itself including internal and external governance mechanisms. Directorates of Chinese listed companies are under administration management with function transformations and advancement problems, especially state-owned companies. Because of the current weak external governance mechanisms, the key to improving efficiency of directorates governance is the establishment of effective internal operation systems. When the "hardware" of directorates governance is all ready, we should establish "software" which includes operation systems, directors' rights and obligations, compensation mechanisms and independent director systems.

The limitation of this research is that we only chose the cross-section data not time series data, so the stability of the research results needs further testing. Although the treatment of data follows expertise, there inevitably exists subjective factors which leads to measuring errors. Despite these issues, our conclusions are still meaningful for the directorates of Chinese listed companies.

CHAPTER

Research on Evaluation and Index of Supervisors' Committee Governance

The improvement of internal supervision mechanisms is the key to corporate governance and reduction in governance risk. Different market economy countries have significant differences in practice of internal supervision due to their differences in ways of economic development, social traditions, politics and legal mechanisms. Germany carries out a double-layer mechanism of separation of directorate and supervisors' committees, which possess more of a monitoring function. German corporations law regulates that all corporations should have a double-layer mechanism, including administrative and supervisors' committee in the directorate. The former is composed of executive managers responsible for daily affairs, and the latter is the controlling department responsible for nomination and appointment. Supervisor committees in Japan are different from the single-layer mechanisms of America and Britain and double-layer mechanism of Germany. In Japanese companies, directorates and supervisors' committees are both elected by the general meeting of shareholders, and the latter supervises the former. The particularity of establishment of supervisors' committees in Chinese corporate governance creates the particularity of the evaluation of supervisors' committees in the evaluation system of corporate governance.

Review of evaluation of supervisors' committee governance

Compared to other compositions of the evaluation index system of corporate governance, research on an evaluation index of supervisors' committees in China is a totally blank area, for the following reasons: first, the "single-layer mechanism" represented by America and Britain is the international mainstream, and its internal supervisory mechanism is carried out by an independent director system without a supervisors' committee. Although some internationally famous corporations such as Standard & Poor's, Deminor Corp. and Credit Lyonnais Securities Asia design their own evaluation systems of corporate governance, they do not come down to evaluation of supervisors' committee. Secondly, from the corporate governance aspect, Chinese corporate governance is close to the "double-layer mechanism" of the continental law system, which appoints separate directorates and supervisors' committees under the general meeting of shareholders. Supervisors' committees under the double-layer mechanism represented by Germany and Japan are consistent with weak capital markets and managers' controlling status, and are highly different from Chinese supervisors' committees. So the relevance of evaluation of supervisors' committees from single-layer-mechanism countries is limited.

In the process of evaluation of corporate governance of Chinese listed companies, some financial institutions (such as Haitong Securities and Dapeng Securities) do not take evaluation of supervisors' committees into account. Due to the scarcity of research on evaluation of supervisors' committees, we cannot estimate the effect of supervisors' committees on directorates and whether it is still important when we introduced the foreign independent director system. Above all, it is meaningful in theory and practice to design a system to evaluate supervisors' committees of Chinese listed companies based on international supervision experiences in a different corporate governance mode and the Chinese environment and reforms.

Evaluation index of supervisors' committee governance of Chinese listed companies

In Chinese listed companies, a supervisors' committee is the full-time supervisory organ and exercises the supervisory right as the representative of investors with responsibility for the general meetings of shareholders. Supervisors' committees can monitor the directorate and managers, management and financial affairs. In the supervisory process, a supervisors' committee can request the directorate and managers to correct actions exceeding their authority.

We take "effective supervision" as our objective and accord to its principles of positive, effective, independent, complete and objective operation to design the evaluation index system, which is completed with the independent director system. This system is also based on guarantee of supervisory capacity and operation efficiency of supervisors' committee:

1. *Guarantee of supervisory capacity.* It is the basic index for evaluation of supervisors' committees. Firstly, members of supervisors' committees should be independent of directorate and managers to ensure their independence; secondly, enthusiasm of members of supervisors' committees is one of the premises for effective supervision of supervisors' committees, and they should have compensation equaling their capacity and devotion; thirdly, there should be enough external supervisors in supervisors' committees to enhance supervision; finally, members of supervisors' committees should not take a part-time position which would go against their independence. As a whole, we consider non-staff nomination of supervisors, full-time extent of supervisor, working days guarantee of external supervisor, and compensation of external supervisors as the evaluation index of guarantee of supervisory capacity (see Table 5.1).

2. *Operation efficiency of supervisors' committee.* This is the main evaluation index of supervisors' committees. Listed

companies are interest groups with abundant financial resources. They need supervisors with professional knowledge and experience in law, finance and accounting, and capacity to communicate with shareholders, employees and other stakeholders. To ensure efficiency, firstly the size of a supervisors' committee ought to be effective to achieve a rational arrangement for above supervisors. Secondly, the composition of members of a supervisors' committee ought to be effective to determine the efficiency and responsibility of it. The members of a supervisors' committee should ensure the committee has enough experience, capacity and professional background to supervise the directorate, managers and corporate finance independently. Thirdly, the supervisors' committee exercises the right of supervision effectively. A supervisors' committee has the right to request proposals referred by directors, managers and financial principals, and correct the falseness of financial reports and irregularities of managers. It also could call a temporary general meeting of shareholders when necessary. Finally, meetings of supervisors' committees—including time, attendance and completeness of record—ought to be effective. Above all, we designed conditions of calling in the temporary general meeting of shareholders in the most recent three years, efficiency of the size and structure of the supervisors' committee, efficiency of meetings of the supervisors' committee, efficiency of how the supervisors' committee exercises the right of supervision, and completeness of supervising records made by the supervisors' committee as the evaluation index of operation efficiency of a supervisors' committee (see Table 5.1).

Table 5.1: Evaluation index system of supervisors' committees of Chinese listed companies

Main factor	Sub-factor layer	Specification	Evaluation standard
Guarantee of supervisory capacity $CCGI^{NK}_{31}$	1. Non-staff nomination of supervisor	The inspection of non-staff nomination of supervisor is highly important to the efficiency of supervision	The non-staff nominator of supervisor could stand for shareholders' benefits
	2. Full-time extent of supervisor	It is the key to the independence of supervisors' committee whether the chairman takes a part-time job in the corporation and the type and nature of the part-time job	The chairman of supervisors' committee could have a position not relative to directorate or managers in order to keep independence
	3. Working days guarantee of external supervisor	A definite percentage of working days is the basic guarantee of the efficiency of external supervisors	The working days of external supervisors could not be below a definite extent
	4. Compensation of external supervisor	The inspection of mean and quantity of compensation external directors get from corporation is important for supervisors' working quality and independence	The compensation of external directors ought to be based on their fulfillment of responsibility

Table 5.1: Evaluation index system of supervisors' committees of Chinese listed companies *(cont'd)*

Main factor	Sub-factor layer	Specification	Evaluation standard
Operation efficiency of supervisors' committee CCGI$^{NK}_{32}$	5. Conditions of calling in the temporary general meeting of shareholders in most recent three years	Inspect supervisors' committee whether exercise the right on some topics	Corporation law gives supervisors' committee the right to "call in the temporary general meeting of shareholders"; furthermore, corporation article could give it the right to "call in the general meeting of shareholders independently"
	6. Efficiency of the size and structure of supervisors' committee	Inspect the foundation of supervisors' committee to fulfill the function	Ensure supervisors' committee have enough experience, capacity and professional background to supervise directorate, managers and corporate finance independently
	7. Efficiency of meetings of supervisors' committee	Inspect supervisors' committee's ability to fulfill the function	Supervisors' committee should hold conference periodically and guarantee the supervisors' attendance

Table 5.1: Evaluation index system of supervisors' committees of Chinese listed companies *(cont'd)*

Main factor	Sub-factor layer	Specification	Evaluation standard
Operation efficiency of supervisors' committee CCGI$^{NK}_{32}$	8. Efficiency of how supervisors' committee exercises the right of supervision	Inspect supervisors' committee's ability to fulfill the function of supervising directorate, directors and managers	Supervisors' committee has the right to request relative directors, managers and financial principals to attend meetings and receive inquiries
	9. Completeness of supervising records made by supervisors' committee	The supervising and inspecting records are the important basis to evaluate directors and managers	All supervising records ought to be kept completely

Descriptive statistics of supervisors' committee governance of Chinese listed companies

The essence of corporate governance is a series of arrangements about contact systems whose core is the balance of power. Different system environments, industry backgrounds and corporation natures would have important effects on supervisors' committee governance. Based on the above index system and different system characteristics, we analyzed supervisors' committee governance of 931 Chinese listed companies, which is reflected by the China supervisors' committee governance index (CCGI$^{NK}_{3}$).

General specification of index of supervisors' committee governance

General analysis of evaluation index of supervisors' committee governance

China's supervisors' committee governance index ($CCGI^{NK}_3$) has a basically normal distribution, but index of guarantee of supervisory capacity and operation efficiency of supervisors' committee have an anomalistic distribution. The mean of $CCGI^{NK}_3$ is 48.64 and maximum and minimum are 77.7 and 11.9 respectively, which reflects a poor condition of supervisors' committee governance. The mean of $CCGI^{NK}_{31}$ is 49.75 and maximum, minimum and median are 95.88, 4.11 and 50.67 respectively; the mean of $CCGI^{NK}_{32}$ is 45.91 and maximum, minimum and median are 78.75, 15.71 and 46.97 respectively. Standard deviation of $CCGI^{NK}_{31}$ is 20.65% and $CCGI^{NK}_{32}$ is 9.252%, both with a high dispersion. Most $CCGI^{NK}_{32}$ values are less than $CCGI^{NK}_{32}$, which indicates that we need to enhance operation efficiency in an improved supervisors' committee.

Divided by Corporate Governance Index of Nankai University

Considering all 931 sample companies, 1.07% belong to $CCGI^{NK}_3III$, 11.49% belong to $CCGI^{NK}_3IV$, 30.50% belong to $CCGI^{NK}_3V$, and 56.94% belong to $CCGI^{NK}_3VI$, without $CCGI^{NK}_3II$, which reflects a poor condition of supervisors' committee governance. Furthermore, there is little difference in $CCGI^{NK}_3$ among the same rank companies and a huge difference between $CCGI^{NK}_{31}$ and $CCGI^{NK}_{32}$. Standard deviation has a positive trend from $CCGI^{NK}_3III$ to $CCGI^{NK}_3VI$. The main reason for the high standard deviation between $CCGI^{NK}_{31}$ and $CCGI^{NK}_{32}$ in the same rank companies may be the difference in industry and nature.

Divided by different industries

According to different competition, governmental regulation, external market mechanisms and business type, we divided the 931 listed companies into Manufacturing, Agriculture, Public Industry, Tertiary Industry and Miscellaneous for analysis. There is a significant difference among $CCGI^{NK}_3$, $CCGI^{NK}_{31}$ and $CCGI^{NK}_{32}$

in different industries. $CCGI^{NK}_3$ of Public Industry is the best, Manufacturing is the worst. This is due to the government's excessive participation in public industries such as electronics and energy. This participation takes governmental regulation into supervisors' committee governance and improves the guarantee of supervisory capacity and operation efficiency of supervisors' committee. Manufacturing companies are in a competitive industry and most of them are state-owned corporations. Because of the Owners' Absence of State Property, "insider control under administration"—which stems from government participation— is prevalent, and thus leads to the low efficiency of operation of supervisors' committee. It indicates that government's proper participation could improve supervisors' committee governance in transformation.

Divided by nature of corporation

We divided the 931 sample companies into 705 state-owned companies and 146 private companies, excluding companies and institutions whose controlling shareholders are universities, colleges, scientific research institutions and other non-bank capital institutions. We made descriptive statistics for them. The dividing standard is the nature of controlling shareholder: private companies and collective companies are private companies; state-owned companies, state-owned property management companies and government companies are state-owned companies.

According to the conditions of supervisors' committee governance, a private company is better than a state-owned company; according to the guarantee of supervisory capacity, all the companies have significant differences both in private companies and state-owned companies, and private companies have a weak predominance; according to the operation efficiency of supervisors' committee, there is no evident difference between private companies and state-owned companies. In addition, a private company can establish a supervisors' committee system at the beginning under corporation law, so it is more competitive in the non-staff nomination of supervisors, full-time extent of supervisors, working days guarantee of external supervisors and compensation of external supervisors than a state-owned company.

Detailed specification of conditions of supervisors' committee governance

The specifications of conditions of supervisors' committee governance include nine aspects as follows.

(1) Non-staff nomination of supervisor

The non-staff nomination of supervisor would stand for most shareholders' benefit. From the sample data, the non-staff nomination of supervisor mainly consists of nominations from percentage of ownership, directorate, chairman of supervisors' committee and controlling shareholders. Non-staff nominations of supervisors of Chinese listed companies mostly come from a controlling shareholder, which is not good for the enforcement of the supervisors' committee system.

(2) Full-time extent of supervisor

The part-time aspect of the chairman is the key to the independence of supervisors' committees. A supervisors' committee has the full supervisory right authorized by the general meeting of shareholders. As the company law of the People's Republic of China does not regulate whether the chairman of a supervisors' committee is permitted to take a position in the Party (the Communist Party of China) Committee, the chairman of the directorate often takes a position in the Party Committee. So if the chairman of the supervisors' committee also takes a position in the Party Committee, their subordinate relationship would make it difficult to be independent. In order to maintain independence, the chairman of the supervisors' committee could take a position not relative to the directorates and managers in the Party Committee—68.61% of chairmen of supervisors' committees take positions such as general secretary in the Party Committee, chairman of the Labor Union, and secretary of Discipline Inspection Commission across all sample companies. It indicates that the chairman of the supervisors' committee taking positions in the party committee is very popular in China.

(3) Working days guarantee of external supervisor

A definite percentage of working days is the basic guarantee of the efficiency of external supervisors. According to all sample companies, the mean of working days of external supervisors is 19.36 and maximum and minimum are 1 full year and 0 day, respectively. As to working days, 76.92% of companies have a mean of 0 to 20; 13.68% of companies have a mean of 21 to 40; 6.13% of companies have a mean of 41 to 60; and 3.28% of companies have a mean above 60.

(4) Compensation of external supervisors

The compensation of external supervisors ought to be based on their fulfillment of responsibilities. A seasonal compensation structure would enhance efficiency of decision-making and working positivism—20.79% of sample companies pay low compensation to external supervisors.

(5) Conditions for calling in the temporary general meeting of shareholders in most recent three years

Corporation law gives supervisors' committees the right to "call in the temporary general meeting of shareholders"; furthermore, corporation articles could give the right to "call in the general meeting of shareholders independently". Through the investigation of supervisors' committees exercising the right to "call in the temporary general meeting of shareholders", we can judge whether supervisors' committees exercise their right properly: supervisors' committees in 0.92% of sample companies have exercised their rights properly.

(6) Efficiency of the size and structure of supervisors' committee

In theory and practice, an effective size of a supervisors' committee is the guarantee of supervision, and a reasonable composition of a supervisors' committee is the guarantee of effective supervision on top management and reflection of all shareholders' benefits. Considering all sample companies, the mean of size is 4.35 people, which is more than 3—the minimum requirement regulated by the company law—and maximum and minimum are 11 and 2 respectively. According to the source of supervisors, most of them come from inside, with a lack of employees and independent supervisors, which is unfavorable for the supervisory balance.

(7) Efficiency of meetings of supervisors' committee

Supervisors' committees should hold conferences periodically and guarantee the supervisors' attendance. Supervisors' committees would submit written explanations to the CSRC and circulate a bulletin if the meeting could not convene. Considering all sample companies, the mean of the times of meetings of supervisors' committees is 9.93 and the maximum, minimum and median are 24, 3 and 9 times per year respectively.

(8) Efficiency of supervisors' committee exercising the right of supervision

A supervisors' committee has the right to request directors, managers and financial principals to attend meetings and receive inquiries. With regards to the question "Would the supervisors' committee have the right to reject proposals of directorate?", 99.46% of companies responded "yes" and 0.54% responded "no"; with regards to "Whether there were deceits in corporate financial reports and then the deceits have been corrected", and "Whether the directors and general managers have conducted illegal actions which then also have been corrected?", 99.45% and 99.34% of companies responded "no" respectively. Overall, the condition of supervisors' committee governance is not satisfied.

(9) Completeness of supervising records made by supervisors' committee

The supervising and inspecting records are an important basis to evaluate directors and managers. Complete supervising records are propitious to evaluate top management. From our research,

94.08% of sample companies have complete supervising records and 5.92% do not.

Empirical research on the relationship between supervisors' committee governance and company performance

Based on different system characteristics and corporation natures, we analyze supervisors' committee governance of 931 Chinese listed companies, which is reflected by the China supervisors' committee governance index ($CCGI^{NK}_3$).

Regression analysis of supervisors' committee governance and financial warning coefficient

In view of the effect of supervisors' committees on corporation operation, it has a weak influence on performance indexes such as earnings per share and return on net worth. We take supervisors' committee governance index and performance indexes such as earnings per share, Tobin's Q and return on net worth for regression analysis, and find a low goodness of fit (R^2 is very close to 0, or even is 0 and cannot make T-test or F-test). On the contrary, the efficiency of supervisors' committees could affect financial security during operation. We use the Z-Score Model designed by Altman—this computation model consists of five financial rates, and the formula is:

$$Z = 1.2 \times A + 1.4 \times B + 3.3 \times C + 0.6 \times D + 1.0 \times E$$

A = Working capital / Total assets
B = Retained earning / Total assets
C = Earnings before interest and income tax (EBIT) / Total assets
D = Equity / Liability
E = Sales / Assets

We designed dependent and independent variables for regression analysis. Furthermore, we take the financial warning coefficient as the dependent variable to predict financial security and reflect risk operation results, and take the evaluation index of supervisors' committee ($CCGI^{NK}_3$), guarantee of supervisory capacity ($CCGI^{NK}_{31}$) and operation efficiency of supervisors' committee ($CCGI^{NK}_{32}$) as the independent variables.

In order to reflect the effect of supervisors' committee governance on financial security, we use the natural logarithm of industry difference, nature of controlling shareholder, and sales to investigate the industrial regulation level, nature of controlling shareholder, and economy of scale in the model. We also bring industry and nature of controlling shareholder dummy variables into the regression equation and get (I), (II) and (III):

$$Z = \beta_0 + \beta_1 CCGI^{HK}_3 + \beta_2 Ln(sales) + \sum_{i=1}^{4} a_i indus_i +$$
$$\sum_{j=1}^{8} \lambda_j Top\_chrc_j + \varepsilon \qquad\qquad \text{............(I)}$$

$$Z = \beta_0 + \beta_1 CCGI^{HK}_\omega + \beta_2 Ln(sales) + \sum_{i=1}^{4} a_i indus_i +$$
$$\sum_{j=1}^{8} \lambda_j Top\_chrc_j + \varepsilon \qquad\qquad \text{............. (II)}$$

$$Z = \beta_0 + \beta_1 CCGI^{HK}_{31} + \beta_2 CCGI^{HK}_{32} + \beta_3 Ln(sales) +$$
$$\sum_{i=1}^{4} a_i indus_i + \sum_{j=1}^{8} \lambda_j Top\_chrc_j + \varepsilon \qquad \text{............ (III)}$$

Z is the financial warning coefficient; $CCGI^{NK}_\omega$, ($\omega = 1, 2$), $\omega = 1$ stands for guarantee of supervisory capacity and $\omega = 2$ stands for operation efficiency of supervisors' committee; $Ln(sales)$ is the natural logarithm of sales; $Indus_i$ is a dummy variable that stands for different industries (Manufacturing, Agriculture, Public Industry, Tertiary Industry and Miscellaneous; we only use four of them to avoid multicollinearity). If $Indus_i$ belongs to its own industry, we use 1; on the contrary is 0; $Top1\_chrc_j$ is a dummy variable that stands for nature of controlling shareholders with nine factors (private company; state-owned company; state-owned property management company; government; collective company; foreign capital company; universities and colleges;

Table 5.2: Regression results of supervisors' committee governance to financial warning coefficient

Financial warning coefficient (Z)				
Variable	Model (I)	Model (II)-1	Model (II)-2	Model (III)
$CCGI^{NK}_3$	3.407** (2.238)	–	–	–
$CCGI^{NK}_{31}$	–	2.069** (2.484)	–	2.039** (2.335)
$CCGI^{NK}_{32}$	–	–	1.556 (0.848)	0.225 (0.117)
Ln(sales)	–0.0852 (–0.672)	–0.0684 (–0.539)	–0.0101 (–0.792)	–0.0697 (–0.546)
Intercede	1.971 (1.208)	2.393 (1.561)	3.02** (1.842)	2.317** (1.393)
R^2	0.017	0.018	0.012	0.018
F	1.096	1.180	0.786	1.101
D-W	1.988	1.98	1.991	1.981

Notes: ***, ** and * separately indicate significance at 1%, 5% and 10% respectively; result of T-test is in brackets; due to the massive control variables of industry and controlling shareholder, we did not bring them into the regression results.

scientific research institutions; and other institutions—we only use eight of them to avoid multi-collinearity). If $Top1\_chrc_j$ belongs to its own shareholder, we use 1; on the contrary is 0. We make a regression analysis, and the regression results of model (I), (II) and (III) can be found in Table 5.2.

From the regression results, there is a positive relationship between evaluation index of supervisors' committee governance ($CCGI^{NK}_3$), guarantee of supervisory capacity ($CCGI^{NK}_{31}$), operation efficiency of supervisors' committee ($CCGI^{NK}_{32}$) and financial warning coefficient. Evaluation index of supervisors' committee ($CCGI^{NK}_3$) and guarantee of supervisory capacity ($CCGI^{NK}_{31}$) have a statistical significance in the model, which indicates that efficient supervision of supervisors' committee is propitious to financial security. These models have a low R^2 of goodness of fit, possibly due to the inadequate corporate governance during transformation. According to model (III), there is no statistical significance between operation efficiency of supervisors' committee ($CCGI^{NK}_{32}$) and financial warning coefficient, but the intercede has a high significance at 5% which shows that other uncontrollable factors affect the model. On the contrary, although there is not significant negative relationship between the natural logarithm of sales and Z, it also reflects the positive relationship between size and poor financial security of Chinese listed companies.

Regression analysis of supervisors' committee governance and stockholding ratio of top five shareholders

Controlling shareholders controlling the general meeting of shareholders is a common phenomenon in transforming economic countries. The nature of a supervisors' committee is an institution for discussing affairs which is controlled by the directorate. In order to test the effect of stockholding ratio of controlling shareholders on supervisors' committee governance, we designed a regression model based on stockholding ratio of the top five shareholders and supervisors' committee governance:

$$CCGI^{HK}_3 = \beta_0 + \beta_1 TOP_i + \sum_{i=1}^{4} a_i indus_i + \sum_{j=1}^{8} \lambda_j TOP1\_chrc_j + \varepsilon \dots (IV)$$

$$CCGI^{HK}_\omega = \beta_0 + \beta_1 TOP_i + \sum_{i=1}^{4} a_i indus_i + \sum_{j=1}^{8} \lambda_j TOP1\_chrc_j + \varepsilon \dots (V)$$

The means of $CCGI^{NK}_3$, $CCGI^{NK}_{31}$ and $CCGI^{NK}_{32}$ are the same as model (I), (II) and (III); $Top_i (i=1,2,3,4,5)$ stands for the stockholding ratio of the top one to five controlling shareholders (we use only four of them to avoid multicollinearity). We take the stockholding ratio of the top one to five controlling shareholders as an independent variable and supervisors' committee governance as a dependent variable for regression analysis. The regression results can be found in tables 5.3, 5.4 and 5.5. The regression coefficient movement of governance index and top one to five shareholders can be found in figure 5.1.

Table 5.3:   Regression results of stockholding ratio of top five shareholders to supervisors' committee governance

Evaluation index of supervisors' committee governance $CCGI^{NK}_3$					
Variable	**Model (IV)-1**	**Model (IV)-2**	**Model (IV)-3**	**Model (IV)-4**	**Model (IV)-5**
Top_1	−0.103*** (−5.505)	−	−	−	−
Top_2	−	0.127*** (4.231)	−	−	−
Top_3	−	−	−0.297*** (4.881)	−	−
Top_4	−	−	−	0.439*** (4.498)	−
Top_5	−	−	−	−	0.530*** (3.773)
$Indus_4$	0.068*** (4.590)	0.069*** (4.631)	0.07*** (4.779)	0.073*** (4.991)	0.076*** (5.151)
$Top_1\_chrc_1$	−0.041*** (−2.791)	−0.037** (−2.552)	−0.04*** (−2.757)	−0.04*** (−2.727)	−0.039*** (−2.658)
$Top_1\_chrc_2$	−0.049*** (−3.26)	−0.046*** (−3.024)	−0.049 (−3.256)	−0.049*** (−3.329)	−0.048*** (−3.141)
$Top_1\_chrc_7$	0.021* (1.680)	0.03** (2.410)	0.027** (2.124)	0.029** (2.319)	0.033*** (2.628)
Intercede	0.549*** (34.792)	0.452*** (71.968)	0.455*** (79.322)	0.457*** (81.205)	0.459*** (81.996)
R^2	0.094	0.081	0.087	0.084	0.077
F	6.775***	5.757***	6.243***	5.948***	5.457***
D-W	2.093	2.084	2.110	2.131	2.126

Notes: ***, ** and * separately indicate significance at 1%, 5% and 10% respectively; result of T-test is in brackets; due to the massive control variables of industry and controlling shareholder, we did not bring them into the regression results.

Table 5.4: Regression results of stockholding ratio of top five shareholders to guarantee of supervisory capacity

	Guarantee of supervisory capacity $CCGI^{NK}_{31}$				
Variable	Model (V)-1	Model (V)-2	Model (V)-3	Model (V)-4	Model (V)-5
Top_1	−0.231*** (−6.903)	−	−	−	−
Top_2	−	0.3503*** (5.557)	−	−	−
Top_3	−	−	0.649*** (5.66)	−	−
Top_4	−	−	−	0.92*** (5.221)	−
Top_5	−	−	−	−	1.136*** (4.547)
$Indus_4$	0.105*** (3.935)	0.107*** (3.962)	0.112*** (4.177)	0.117*** (4.372)	0.076*** (5.151)
$Top_1\_chrc_1$	−0.048* (−1.824)	−0.041 (−1.540)	−0.047* (−1.765)	−0.046* (−1.715)	−0.044* (−1.652)
$Top_1\_chrc_2$	−0.077*** (−2.82)	−0.069** (−2.533)	−0.077*** (−2.795)	−0.076*** (−2.758)	−0.073*** (−2.656)
$Top_1\_chrc_7$	0.06*** (2.616)	0.078*** (3.461)	0.073*** (3.232)	0.079*** (3.508)	0.086*** (3.828)
Intercede	0.660*** (23.085)	0.438*** (38.407)	0.448*** (42.901)	0.453*** (44.158)	0.457*** (44.737)
R^2	0.116	0.099	0.103	0.096	0.089
F	8.571***	7.190***	7.481***	6.891***	6.348***
D-W	2.096	2.091	2.011	2.131	2.127

Notes: ***, ** and * separately indicate significance at 1%, 5% and 10% respectively; result of T-test is in brackets; due to the massive control variables of industry and controlling shareholder, we did not bring them into the regression results.

Table 5.5: Regression results of stockholding ratio of top five shareholders to guarantee of supervisory capacity

	Guarantee of supervisory capacity $CCGI^{NK}_{32}$				
Variable	**Model (V)-6**	**Model (V)-7**	**Model (V)-8**	**Model (V)-9**	**Model (V)-10**
Top_1	−0.016 (−0.986)	−	−	−	−
Top_2	−	0.01 (0.382)	−	−	−
Top_3	−	−	0.062 (0.795)	−	−
Top_4	−	−	−	0.112 (1.336)	−
Top_5	−	−	−	−	0.107 (0.906)
$Indus_4$	0.043*** (3.408)	0.0433*** (3.460)	0.043*** (3.427)	0.0431*** (3.462)	0.043*** (3.531)
$Top_1\_chrc_1$	−0.048* (−1.824)	−0.035*** (−2.830)	−0.034*** (−2.901)	−0.036* (−2.914)	−0.034*** (−2.877)
$Top_1\_chrc_2$	−0.03** (−2.385)	−0.0298 (−2.338)	−0.031** (−2.409)	−0.031** (−2.425)	−0.03* (−2.383)
$Top_1\_chrc_7$	−0.005 (−0.424)	−0.002 (−0.205)	−0.047 (−0.447)	−0.005 (−0.473)	−0.034 (−0.323)
Intercede	0.475*** (35.423)	0.461*** (87.001)	0.46*** (94.739)	0.46*** (96.72)	0.461*** (97.728)
R^2	0.038	0.037	0.039	0.039	0.038
F	2.588***	0.037***	2.627***	2.660***	2.576***
D-W	2.070	2.070	2.073	2.078	2.076

Notes: ***, ** and * separately indicate significance at 1%, 5% and 10% respectively; result of T-test is in brackets; due to the massive control variables of industry and controlling shareholder, we did not bring them into the regression results.

Figure 5.1: Regression coefficient movement of governance index and top one to five shareholders

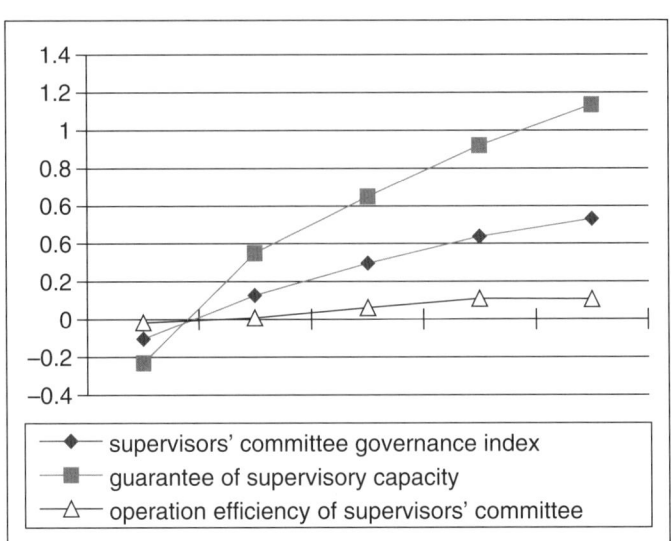

From the regression analysis results, we can reach some conclusions:

(1) There is significant negative relationship between Top_1 and $CCGI^{NK}_3$, and a weak negative relationship between Top_1 and U_1. This means that there is a negative relationship between the stockholding ratio of controlling shareholders and supervisors' committee governance. The main reasons are: firstly, based on their controlling status, controlling shareholders elect their own "trusted supervisor" through the general meeting of shareholders, for their own benefits. The electing standard is to make sure the supervisor is an "obedient supervisor"; being a "capable supervisor" is only the second requirement. It provides poor capacity of supervisors at the beginning of the establishment of the supervisors' committee. Secondly, according to the status of directors and supervisors, they are different agents belonging to the same trustee. So, when directors and managers harm the corporation's benefit for their own benefits, the supervisor would not exercise supervisory rights efficiently. Due to the above two reasons, supervisors' committees would be ineffective under the control of controlling shareholders.

(2) There is a positive relationship between Top_2, Top_3, Top_4, Top_5 and $CCGI^{NK}_3$. In models (IV) and (V), the regression coefficients of Top_2 to Top_5 with their independent variables have an increasing trend which can be found in figure 5.1. It indicates that the increase of stockholding ratio of the top two to five would have a good effect on supervisors' committee governance. The main reason is the establishment of a competitive ownership structure which can come to equilibrium through negotiation, games and personnel arrangement based on individual benefit.

(3) Supervisors' committee governance in utility companies is better than in manufacturing companies.

(4) The nature of the controlling shareholders affects supervisors' committee governance significantly. Private companies are excellent in supervisors' committee governance and guarantee of supervisory capacity but poor in operation efficiency of supervisors' committee due to imperfect operation mechanisms. State-owned companies, state-owned property management companies and government companies are state-owned companies poor in supervisors' committee governance, guarantee of supervisory capacity, and operation efficiency of supervisors' committee, which tests the conclusion of descriptive statistics.

Conclusions and policy suggestions

We conducted empirical research based on the evaluation index system of supervisors' committee governance and related data of Chinese listed companies: we summarize here some characteristics of it in transformation:

(1) Supervisors' committee governance of Chinese listed companies is still at a low level. The Chinese supervisors' committee governance index ($CCGI^{NK}_3$) has a basically normal distribution with a relatively higher guarantee of supervisory capacity than operation efficiency of supervisors' committee. There are big differences among sample companies. One of the reasons is the low guarantee of supervisory capacity, such as the chairman of supervisors' committee gets a position in party,

nonstandard nomination of supervisors, and low compensation of external supervisors. The other reason is the low operation efficiency of supervisors' committees, such as unreasonable structure and inefficient meetings. So the key to improve supervisors' committee governance is to settle the "hollow position" problem which includes mechanism and structure.

(2) There is a positive relationship between supervisors' committee governance and firm performance. It indicates that as the legal supervisory institution, supervisors' committees are very important in Chinese transformation. The low level of supervisors' committee governance in practice is not caused by the mechanism but the operation, such as unreasonable ownership and "domination of a single shareholder".

(3) The nature and stockholding ratio of controlling shareholders significantly affects supervisors' committee governance. A private company is better in the guarantee of supervisory capacity than a state-owned company. There is a negative relationship between operation efficiency of supervisors' committee and the stockholding ratio of the top one shareholder, and a positive relationship between operation efficiency of supervisors' committee and the stockholding ratio of the top two to five shareholders. In order to settle the "hollow position", we must improve ownership structures and introduce strategic investors to establish a monopolistic competition structure which can enhance balance and competition.

(4) We could introduce independent supervisors who are social experts but not employees. Independent supervisors do not hold shares or have a relationship with controlling shareholders. Their rights and obligations are the same as other supervisors. The aim is to establish an independent supervisors system to make supervisors independent and break them away from controlling shareholders and directorates.

CHAPTER 6

Research on Evaluation and Index of Top Management Governance

Management mentioned in this research means the top executives, including general manager, vice-general manager, three chiefs (chief accountant, chief economist, chief engineer) and secretary of the board. The development of the company is directly decided by their work effectiveness. However, whether work effectiveness is good or not is decided by the quality of incentive and restriction mechanisms. Evaluation of top management is aimed at ensuring decision-making is scientific and in the long-term interests of the company, and for making scientific evaluation of managerial incentive and restriction status. It can offer objective information about top management to those inside the company, and to outside institutions and individuals. So the index of top management governance is an important part of the index of corporate governance.

Practices on evaluation of top management governance at home and abroad

The internationally famous evaluation systems of corporate governance have adopted some evaluation indexes about top management governance.

The corporate evaluation index (2001) launched by Standard & Poor's set the evaluation index of disclosure conditions of managerial ownership in information disclosure, and the appointment, compensation structure, and appointment process of top management, replacing process, the relationship between management and directorates, and so on, in the governance structure of directorates.

The more than 70 indexes of evaluation systems of corporate governance launched by Deminor—which is favored by European institutional investors—pay more attention to the use of corporate options and the relationship between board chairman, CEO, and so on.

The evaluation system of CLSA (2001) emphasizes evaluation of management restrictions (for example, higher shareholding for stimulating management), whether the evaluation on equity and capital cost is appropriate, whether they distribute the spare cash to shareholders, and so on.

ISS just makes the evaluation on compensation structure and shareholding ratio of management.

ICLG and ICRA both make the evaluation on management structure.

Thailand evaluation and information service company (2001) makes the evaluation on company inside control, and DVFA (2000) also refers to some content about corporate management.

The evaluation system of listed companies launched by Haitong security research institution refers to the content as follows: top management ought to obtain correlation with corporate performance and appropriate compensation; the company ought to establish relative performance evaluation and selecting mechanisms; top management ought to establish expedient communicating channels; and how to keep managerial stability.

Black et al (2003) consider whether the CEO and board chairman can be the same person, in the corporate governance evaluation system established in the process of evaluation on the governance situation of Korean public companies.

The Taiwan corporate governance evaluation system established by Ye Yinghua (2002) has evaluated the situation of the largest shareholder being appointed CEO.

The evaluation system of Governance Metrics International in America has taken the factor of top management's compensation.

The practice of top management governance evaluation at home and abroad indicates that evaluation of top management in their evaluation system is insufficient; moreover, they haven't taken it as an independent governance aspect to make a general evaluation, but it appeared separately in each part of the whole evaluation system. In view of the significant effect of Chinese listed companies' specific transitional and emerging economies background and top management operation performance, we take evaluation of top management as an important dimension of which to make systemic evaluation in order to promote development and deepening evaluation of corporate governance theory. In the evaluation system of CCGI^{NK}, we evaluate three dimensions: appointment and removal mechanism, execution guarantee, and incentive and restriction mechanism.

Evaluation index of top management governance

When the team set up the evaluation system of top management governance of Chinese listed companies, a new conception of the corporate governance core is established from governance structure to governance mechanism, based on a new conception of "governance inside and outside" and "scientific decision-making", taking the restriction of "inner person controlling" and integrating the specific background of Chinese transitional and emerging economies.

Theoretic foundation that constructs the whole sketch of evaluation system of top management

In the academic field, research on the problem of corporate governance has continued for several years. Property rights, super property rights, and others appear in succession. The key problem traditional corporate governance theory wants to solve is the agency problem—the condition of ownership and operation rights being separated, which results in management idleness and misuse of authority, and needs the establishment of a set of mutual restriction mechanisms decreasing the risk and cost to agency to solve. This also means effective restriction on rights and stimulation through the establishment of high-quality corporate governance structures. It contains property rights thinking essentially; the owners of corporate property rights that possess spare profit have more motivation to improve the corporate performance endlessly, and it can realize the purpose through property rights transformation. However, in the opinion of super property rights theory, property rights transformation is just a measure of a transforming mechanism; only the competition and governance mechanisms have significant effect on the realization of corporate objectives.

The appearance of new economic circumstances brings new demands to corporate governance, ceaselessly varying exterior markets and technological innovation make the complication of decision-making increase greatly, and decision-making errors increase in the new conditions. Sometimes they are fatal for the companies, but the traditional governance structure is good medicine for them. The purpose of corporate governance is to ensure effective and normal operation, and ensure protection and satisfaction of all kinds of stakeholders, but not imposing restraints. Scientific decision-making is not only the core of corporate management but also the core of corporate governance. The emphasis of corporate governance has transformed from the establishment of corporate governance structures to the perfection of governance mechanisms and from restriction on rights to scientific decision-making. So evaluation of top management of Chinese listed companies spreads around the designing and evaluating of mechanisms of governance and how to ensure scientific decision-making.

New conception about the evaluation situation of top management governance

The setting of structures and mechanisms of corporate governance not only needs to consider the problem of "no diligence," but also needs to consider the problem of "no competence." Corporate governance based on the conception of scientific decision-making not only needs a full and effective corporate governance structure, but also several specific governance mechanisms beyond the governance structure, including inner supervision mechanisms and outer governance mechanisms. The index of evaluation of top management governance is a kind of inner evaluation system aiming at the problem of top management governance. The selection of the index and confirming of criteria are both advantageous to advance the outer market mechanisms and realization of the objective of scientific decision-making.

Strong administration of appointment and removal is the specific characteristic of Chinese listed companies and a negative factor obstructing continuous development. Rational policies and mechanisms of appointment and removal are significant in finding the corporate governance hindrance forming in the process of top management's appointment and removal, promoting marketization and legalization of mechanisms of appointment and removal of top management, and solving the initial problem of top management governance. The method of top management's selection and engagement, degree of administration, and separation of two kinds of rights of CEO and board chairman are set up from the perspective of evaluation of "administration model" and improvement of governance of "market model."

Masterstroke through the evaluation system of top management governance: restrict "insider control"

"Insiders' control" is an important issue of Chinese corporate governance—its significance lies in the absence of restriction mechanisms. To improve the transformation of corporate governance structures, there ought to be a discussion of the problem of agency and insiders' control to let more people realize the significance of problem (Zhou Xiaochuan, 2001). The phenomenon of "insiders' control" in the course of transitional and emerging economies of China is more remarkable in the Chinese listed companies, and the management may ignore minority shareholders' opinions as the representation of national share. At the same time they also may ignore large shareholders' opinions as insiders. Consequently the management may damage the interests of minority shareholders and the nation. The main reasons lie in: (1) popularity of the phenomenon of CEO and board chairman's plurality; (2) management accounting for a majority of directorate seats or controlled by a minority representing large shareholders results in the invalidation of shareholder meetings and directorate; (3) until now the shareholding system reform in China is only of the increment capital, which means only the increment capital has liquidity. However, state-owned and corporate shares which account for a large proportion cannot flow, and the function of management supervising and incentive of relative corporate governance is small. On the condition of non-supervising inside and outside, it cannot guarantee independent and perfect operation decision-making. Incidents such as the veracious investing of large shareholders of the Kangsai group, window dressing of Zhengzhou Baiwen, and falsification of Monkey King Group then appear.

Early in the 1930s, in western market economy countries corporate top management had motivations and behaviors to encroach on the interests of owners, and corporate governance structure was perfected in the course of keeping away insiders' control. According to this meaning, restriction on insiders' control has become a masterstroke of design of evaluation index systems of top management. This includes a significant evaluation index of insiders' control and sets up a relative index in the mechanism of balancing of insiders' control.

Set up all-sided index system of incentive and restriction mechanism

Incentive and restriction mechanisms belong to the relative maturation field in the research of top management governance, and compensation incentive relative theory of them is most often referred to. Compensation incentive and restriction mechanism, control rights incentive and restriction mechanism, and equity incentive and restriction mechanism are the three main aspects, to evaluate.

(1) Design index from multi-perspective of top management's compensation gross, structure and the relationship between

compensation and corporate performance, and evaluate compensation incentive and restriction degree from two points of views of intensity and dynamic characteristic. Regarding this the majority of evaluation systems set up a similar index, but as a result of compensation levels and form of management of different countries having a different directional effect on corporate governance situations and performance, aiming at this kind of index there are different index criteria and index values based on different empirical research situations.

(2) Equity incentive is very important in the international capital market and regarding the listed company imperfection of equity incentive mechanism predicates imperfection of the corporate governance mechanism. Corporate managerial ownership governance is advantageous for forming long-term and cogent incentives and restrictions, and promoting their endeavors to maximize long-term corporate benefit. Evaluating a single factor of managerial ownership (equity quantity, liquidity, shaping way) helps to promote good governance in the market mechanism which Chinese listed companies need to adapt. However, because of no liquidity of the majority of capital stocks of current Chinese listed companies, the validity of equity incentive and restriction mechanisms will come as a big discount to the share price.

(3) In the course of transition from "administration style" to "economy style," control rights incentive and restriction mechanism has significant practical value. Control rights incentive and restriction mechanism is carried out by control rights income and control rights return. Operation control rights make operators possess positions of privilege, share non-pecuniary compensation, and bring them normal compensation. Decision-making control rights give operators corporate control rights returns, which is a kind of affirmation, respect and protection for the operators' human resources property rights. As far as it goes, in Chinese listed companies control rights restrictions are more meaningful than incentives.

Speaking of evaluation, a sub-system of top management governance evaluation index consists of three dimensions.

Appointment and removal

Much research indicates that strong administrative characteristics of appointment and removal is a disadvantage factor which blocks Chinese listed companies' continuous development. A scientific appointment and removal mechanism is vital for selection of excellent management and continuous and healthy corporate development. In the evaluation system of top management governance of $CCGI^{NK}$, we establish four sub-indexes to corporate appointment and removal mechanism—that is, selection and nomination method of general management (directorate should adopt open and transparent processes to select, appoint and restrict the rights of dominant shareholders moderately to ensure fairness of process and enough competition); other top supervisors' selection and nomination method; top management administrative degree (whether they are appointed by organization department and own administration level); and setting status of CEO and board chairman positions.

Execution guarantee

Top management are the ones in charge of a corporation's daily operation; whether their decisions are carried out effectively and they are able to pass the correct information to directorates in time are vital for them to fulfill their responsibilities. This includes many aspects of evaluation, such as corporate leading structure, control process of management's daily operation, management interior control degree, and top management's plurality in shareholders' firm or related firm.

Incentive and restriction mechanism

Top management's compensation level, compensation structure, relative degree of compensation, and corporate performance can reflect valid and dynamic characteristics of corporate incentive at top management. Firstly, we design the index from a multi-perspective such as top management's gross compensation, structure, and the relationship between compensation and corporate performance, and make an evaluation of the degree of compensation incentive and restriction from intensity and dynamic characteristics of these perspectives; secondly, we build a degree index of equity incentive. Corporate managerial ownership is in favor of forming long-term and cogent incentives and restrictions, and promoting their endeavors for corporate long-term benefit maximization. Evaluation of the single factor of managerial ownership (equity quantity, liquidity, shaping method) increases this aspect of weight; thirdly, we have designed an index which reflects control rights incentive effect, which achieves expectant function through moderate control rights which makes management possess position privilege and non-pecuniary compensation—otherwise, control rights are advantageous for carrying out demands of top management (such as self-value's realization), which finally form managerial incentives.

Please refer to Table 6.1 about a particular evaluation index of top management.

Table 6.1:   Evaluation index system of top management governance

Principal level	Sub-element-level factor	Brief illustration
Appointment and removal mechanism $(CCGI^{NK}_{41})$	Selection and engagement method of general manager $(CCGI^{NK}_{411})$, selection and engagement method of other supervisors $(CCGI^{NK}_{412})$, top management's administrative degree $(CCGI^{NK}_{413})$, two position status of CEO and board chairman $(CCGI^{NK}_{414})$	Evaluation of independence and managerial appointment and removal mechanism
Guarantee of operation $(CCGI^{NK}_{42})$	Decision-making support $(CCGI^{NK}_{421})$, operation control $(CCGI^{NK}_{422})$, double position $(CCGI^{NK}_{423})$, insiders' control $(CCGI^{NK}_{424})$, CEO position setting $(CCGI^{NK}_{425})$	Evaluation of support guarantee, operation control, exterior relationship, interior restriction, etc.
Incentive and restriction mechanism $(CCGI^{NK}_{43})$	Compensation level $(CCGI^{NK}_{431})$, compensation structure $(CCGI^{NK}_{432})$, compensation dynamic incentive $(CCGI^{NK}_{433})$, stock ownership proportion $(CCGI^{NK}_{434})$, equity liquidity $(CCGI^{NK}_{435})$, stock ownership method $(CCGI^{NK}_{436})$, decision-making report mechanism $(CCGI^{NK}_{437})$, non-pecuniary compensation $(CCGI^{NK}_{438})$	Evaluation of incentive and restriction status of compensation, stock ownership and dominant stock ownership

Refer to Zhang Guoping research on "2003, evaluation and index of top management governance", Vol.3, pp. 4–12, about particular illustrations of evaluation index of top management.

Descriptive statistics of top management governance of Chinese listed companies

The whole status of Chinese listed company top management governance

The index of sample corporate top management governance is a normal distribution. Maximum, minimum and mean are 77.74, 11.98 and 47.44 respectively, which is at the level of $CCGI^{NK}_4$VI. Speaking of the three principal-level factors, mean and standard deviation of sample corporate top management governance appointment and removal mechanism index are 63.07 and 10.26% respectively, which is at the level of $CCGI^{NK}_{41}$IV; mean of incentive and restriction mechanism of top management governance ($CCGI^{NK}_{43}$)—for which deviation and deviation degree are highest—is 33.02, which is at the lower level of $CCGI^{NK}_{41}$IV. Maximum, minimum and deviation are 93.33, 2.50 and 12.01% respectively. Mean of guarantee index of operation of top management governance is 61.77 and deviation is 7.98%, which is at the level of $CCGI^{NK}_{41}$IV. It is obvious that the average situation of corporate top management governance is not very good as a whole, incentive and restriction mechanism is weakest, and the difference is quite big among the companies.

The index of 931 companies' corporate top management governance does not reach the level of $CCGI^{NK}_4$I or $CCGI^{NK}_4$II—the maximum is only at the level of $CCGI^{NK}_4$III, and only one arrives at this level. There are 60 companies reaching at the level of $CCGI^{NK}_4$IV, which account for 6.44%, 337 companies arriving at the level of $CCGI^{NK}_4$V, which account for 36.19%, and 539 companies above the half of index of corporate top management governance of listed companies at the level of $CCGI^{NK}_4$IV, which account for 57.25%. Index level of managerial appointment and removal mechanism is relatively high, and centralized degree is low. Eight of the sample are at the level of $CCGI^{NK}_4$I, 22 of the sample are at the level of CCG_4I^{NK}II, most of the sample are at the level of $CCGI^{NK}_4$III accounting for 37.06%, 76 of the sample are at the level of $CCGI^{NK}_4$VI accounting for 8.16%, and 269 and 212 of the sample are respectively at the levels of $CCGI^{NK}_4$IV and $CCGI^{NK}_4$V.

Sign aberrance of index of guarantee of operation of sample corporate top management is lowest; interval accounting for 54.89% is beyond the level of $CCGI^{NK}_4IV$, 4 and 25 of the sample are respectively at the levels of $CCGI^{NK}_4I$ and $CCGI^{NK}_4II$, only 29 of the sample are at the level of $CCGI^{NK}_4VI$; 20.19% and 18.69% respectively are at the levels of $CCGI^{NK}_4III$ and $CCGI^{NK}_4V$. Incentive and restriction status of the sample is the worst; 1, 2 and 1 of the sample are respectively at the levels of $CCGI^{NK}_4I$, $CCGI^{NK}_4II$ and $CCGI^{NK}_4III$, 2.36% and 6.77% are respectively at the level of $CCGI^{NK}_4IV$ and $CCGI^{NK}_4V$, and those of the sample above the level of $CCGI^{NK}_4V$ account for less than 10%.

Comparative analysis of index of Chinese listed company top management governance

Comparing the index characteristics of top management governance by industry and dominant shareholder characteristics, the results are as follows.

The industry classification we adopt is referred to as listed company industry classification as published by the China Securities Regulatory Commission (2001), which lists distribution situations of top management governance of Chinese listed companies in 13 industries. Regarding $CCGI^{NK}_4$, the mean of Real Estate is largest at 50.46; Tertiary Industry and Broadcasting and Press come in at 50.42 and 49.46 respectively. Financing and Insurance is poorest at 45.15. Mining, and Electricity, Gas and Water are respectively the last but one/two, at 45.82 and 46.10, which illustrates the average level of these industries is poor, but the latter's standard deviation of the index of top management governance is the largest of all the industries—that is, 10.36%—and the difference among companies is quite large and there are some good companies in the industry. Financing and Insurance's standard deviation is quite small at only 4.93%, which indicates that the whole top management governance situation is quite bad, perhaps because of specific industry characteristics. As viewed from the individual company, the companies that have good governance conditions come from Manufacturing, for which the largest index score is 71.60. However, several companies' scores in IT and Manufacturing are also low. The governance conditions of top management show polarization in Manufacturing. The index situation above indicates there is serious deficiency in some Chinese listed companies.

Regarding the appointment and removal mechanism, IT is best with a mean of 67.41, and Tertiary Industry and Real Estate are next, which their averages respectively 66.84 and 64.40. This indicates that in these industries there are fewer problems, which is in favor of excellent management selection. Financing and Insurance's situation is not optimistic—only scoring 47.50—and its deviation is quite large at 15.28%. Governance situations among the companies are not at the same level, which indicates that the appointment and removal mechanism is scientific in some companies.

Regarding the dimension of guarantee of operation ($CCGI^{NK}_{42}$), there is not much difference—the ratio in the highest group and lowest group differs only by 5.14%. The best industry is IT, which gets 63.19, while Broadcasting and Press and Real Estate are second and third respectively. The mean value of guarantee of operation of Tertiary Industry is lowest, at 58.05; Electricity, Gas and Water is the last but one and gets 60.82; and Financing and Insurance is the last but two and gets 61.16.

Regarding incentive and restriction mechanism, the whole state of listed companies' governance is quite bad; the Broadcasting and Press industry has the mean of only 36.88, though it is the maximum one. The Mining industry is worst, with its score at 27.39. Electricity, Gas and Water and Financing and Insurance have not got ideal performance, with 31.05 and 29.70 respectively. Only in the IT and Manufacturing industries—the best companies' index of incentive and restriction mechanism—go beyond 65, with 93.3 and 85.0 respectively. This illustrates that incentive and restriction of listed companies' top management isn't perfect, and the aspects of the alignment of compensation level, structure, dynamic incentive and control rights and so on still need to be improved. On the one hand, this is related to the imperfect development of the Chinese security market; on the other hand, part of the incentive measure is restricted by the laws and rules at present. However, through mechanism innovation, there is still sufficient room to establish an effective incentive mechanism such as that for companies getting high scores.

Real Estate, which has the most top management average states, has a high score in appointment and removal mechanism, guarantee of operation, and incentive and restriction mechanism. The general score of Tertiary Industry is situated second, but two dimensions are relatively bad. It illustrates that though in the Tertiary Industry the general level is relatively good, the establishment of top management governance mechanism is out of line and does not have balanced development. The general score of agriculture, forestry, stockbreeding and fishery is situated third, while the sub-element-level index of it is listed out of the first three, which indicates that each part of top management governance is balanced and overmatches the average level. The general score of IT ranks in middling place, but the aspect of appointment and removal mechanism of IT is excellent, which gets maximum of all the industries and shows the management governance characteristic of this industry.

Comparative analysis of index of top management governance according to dominant shareholder characteristic

Among the nine kinds of dominant shareholder characteristics, the ratio of index of top management in the highest group and lowest group differs only 6.839%; the synthesis index of top management governance of the dominant shareholder of private, collective and foreign investment are 49.73, 49.38 and 49.05 respectively. It is well-known that the property rights of these three kinds is quite transparent, which illustrates that the clarity of property rights is advantageous to improving the management governance, enhancing the relationship between management and stakeholders, and increasing the incentive and restriction effect. Shareholders whose synthesis index of top management is quite bad are non-bank financial institutions, colleges, academic institutes and public utilities, and government, state-owned asset management departments and other government departments, for which the scores are 44.50, 47.13 and 47.51 respectively. This indicates that when the dominant shareholders are in these three kinds, it is not optimistic for the status of top management governance. Perhaps it is because there is a remarkable difference between the objectives of the dominant shareholders and the corporate objective itself. Furthermore, dominant shareholders for which the synthesis index of top management governance is the highest are state-owned or state-controlled companies, and the worst score of top management of private and collective large shareholders is close to zero. It indicates that there exists big differences among the companies.

Regarding the dominant shareholders' characteristic, the dominant shareholders which are private, foreign investment, and college, academic institutes and other public utilities do very well, and their scores are 69.29, 66.02 and 65.23 respectively, which illustrates that these companies have rational mechanisms in the aspects of selection of CEO and other supervisors; non-bank financial institutions and state-owned asset management department as largest shareholder got lower scores—only 56.67 and 58.99 respectively—which illustrates these companies need to be improved and consummated. Comparing the scores of each element of top management governance, it can be seen that general scores of state-owned asset management department are below the level of middling, and the score of appointment and removal mechanism is the lowest in the whole evaluation of top management governance, which illustrates that this kind of company may pay more attention to the construction and consummation of selection and engagement. Top management governance general index of the firms whose largest shareholder is college, academic institute or other public utility is low, while the score at the aspect of appointment and removal mechanism is at the front, which indicates a weak point of top management governance of this kind of company lies in incentive and restriction and guarantee of operation.

The firms with state-controlled enterprises (SOEs), private, and collective as largest shareholder are situated as the first three; that is, 62.00, 61.97 and 61.91. They perform best in the aspect of guarantee of operation, but are fifth in their evaluation of appointment and removal mechanism, and sixth in their evaluation of incentive and restriction mechanism—areas that they need to improve on. Private and collective perform well, situated second and third respectively. The firms with non-bank financial institutions and government, state-owned asset management department and other government department as largest shareholder are situated last for guarantee of operation, at 58.33 and 60.34 respectively. The worst mean value and the best mean value differ by 3.67% and the gap in three sub-element levels is the lowest, which indicates difference of largest shareholders' characteristic has little influence on the mechanism construction of guarantee of operation of top management governance. The appointment and removal mechanism is most affected, and the best mean value and the worst differ by 12.63%. The firms with largest shareholder of government, state-owned asset management department, other government department, college, academic institute and other public utility are influenced by the history and tradition factor, with these companies' shareholders intervening and exerting control. This has a negative influence on top management's daily operation and mechanisms, which results in the low score at this aspect.

Regarding the score of incentive and restriction mechanism, the firms with collective, state-owned asset management company and private as largest shareholder do very well, with 34.55, 34.29 and 33.41 respectively. However, the whole level is relatively low and the highest average value is beyond 40, which indicates there is a very long way to go at the construction of the incentive and restriction mechanism. Comparatively, performance of collective is relatively good, and mean value of the firms with non-bank financial institution, college, academic institute and public utility as largest shareholder are lower—only 28.33 and 30.38. Firms with private as largest shareholder are a little worse than firms with collective as largest shareholder at the aspect of mechanism construction of incentive and restriction, while at the aspects of appointment and removal mechanism and guarantee of operation they do better than collective. The firms with college, academic institute and other public utility as largest shareholder are behind at the aspect of synthesis index of top management governance evaluation; at three sub-element levels the worst is construction of incentive and restriction mechanism. Average scores of three sub-element level firms with non-bank financial institution as largest shareholder are situated last, which indicates this kind of company requires improvement at each aspect of top management governance. The score of firms with foreign investment as largest shareholder are above the middling level, which indicates foreign investors pay more attention to the problem of top management governance and achieve primary improvement.

Empirical research on the relationship between top management governance and company performances

In this text we employ three agency variables to express the company performance; that is, earnings per share (EPS), cash flow per share (CFPS) and net asset per share (NAPS).

Selection and definition of agency variables between top management governance and company performances

We select EPS because it can reflect a listed company's final results. However, as we know, profit confirmation of income statement is based on the accrual system which doesn't care whether cash has been received and when it can be received. This kind of accounting system allows a listed company to adjust and manipulate profit easily, or it can be said that it offers top management of a listed company much space for retained earnings management. Thereby, we adopt CFPS as a validation index. Whether a company possesses sufficient cash is vital. It not only relates to capability of dividend payment and repayment, but also survival and development. The cash amount confirmation of a cash flow statement is based on a receipt and payment system. However, in a receipt and payment system, income and profit are changed for cash and have higher reliability. And operation cash flow is most important of all cash flow, which is the synthetic reflection on the capability of the company for creating value. At the same time, in virtue of analyzing the cash flow, we can verify whether there is a steady relation between index of top management governance and corporate performance. So we select CFPS as the second agency variable of corporate governance.

In addition, NAPS reflects asset par value per share, which is the start of confirmation of corporate market value for investors. The higher the NAPS, the more the shareholders own; the lower the NAPS, the less the shareholders own. Generally, companies operating well have higher NAPS (the higher, the better), while companies operating badly have lower NAPS. So we choose NAPS as the third agency variable of corporate governance.

Relative analysis between top management governance and corporate governance

Table 6.2 lists each level factor of top management governance, corporate performance index and coefficient correlation between top management governance and corporate governance. From the table, we can see that in the principle-level factor of top management evaluation there is significant correlation when both appointment and removal mechanism are beyond 1%. Regarding sub-element-level, administrative degree as sub-element-level factor of appointment and removal mechanism presents significant positive correlation with EPS at the significance level of $p = 1\%$; at the same time, EPS is significantly relative with operation control, compensation level, dynamic incentive of compensation and percentage of management shares—its coefficient correlations are respectively 0.137, 0.156, 0.102 and 0.104 at the significance level of $p = 1\%$. It indicates there is quite a significant correlation between EPS and index of top management governance, and improvement of top management governance means better corporate performance. In other words, if the companies want to improve corporate performance, they must improve the status of top management governance. It is the same as Black (2001, 2003) and the research conclusions on Russia's and Korea's markets.

From Table 6.2, we can also find that CFPS has significant positive correlation with $CCGI^{NK}_{4}$—coefficient correlation is 0.071 at the significance level of $p = 5\%$. It indicates the improvement of top management governance level is advantageous to the increase of CFPS to improve the capability of corporate value creation. In addition, CFPS shows significant positive correlation with management holding share proportion and equity liquidity. In addition, we have found that CFPS is significantly related to operation control, dynamic incentive of compensation and management holding share proportion at the significance level of $p = 5\%$.

Regression analysis between index of top management governance and corporate governance

To test the relationship between index of top management governance and corporate governance, we construct eight regression models.

When *DEPVAR* means EPS, it represents (I), (II) and (III):

$$DEPVAR = \beta_0 + \beta_1 CCGI^{NK}{}_4 + \sum_{i=1}^{12} \alpha_i Indus_i + \beta_2 Ln(Asset) + \beta_3 Levera + \varepsilon$$

$$DEPVAR = \beta_0 + \beta_1 CCGI^{NK}{}_{41} + \beta_2 CCGI^{NK}{}_{42} + \beta_3 CCGI^{NK}{}_{43} + \sum_{i=1}^{12} \alpha_i Indus_i + \beta_4 Ln(Asset) + \beta_5 Levera + \varepsilon$$

$$DEPVAR = \beta_0 + \beta_1 CCGI^{NK}{}_{431} + \beta_2 CCGI^{NK}{}_{432} + \beta_3 CCGI^{NK}{}_{433} + \beta_4 CCGI^{NK}{}_{434} + \beta_5 CCGI^{NK}{}_{437} + \beta_6 CCGI^{NK}{}_{438} + \sum_{i=1}^{12} \alpha_i Indus_i + \beta_7 Ln(Asset) + \beta_8 Levera + \varepsilon$$

When *DEPVAR* means NAPS, it represents (V), (VI) and (VII):

$$EPS = \beta_0 + \beta_1 CCGI^{NK}{}_{411} + \beta_2 CCGI^{NK}{}_{412} + \beta_3 CCGI^{NK}{}_{413} + \ldots\ldots (IV)$$
$$\beta_4 CCGI^{NK}{}_{414} + \sum_{i=1}^{12} \alpha_i Indus_i + \beta_5 Ln(Asset) + \beta_6 Levera + \varepsilon$$

$$CFPS = \beta_0 + \beta_1 CCGI^{NK}_{411} + \beta_2 CCGI^{NK}_{412} + \beta_3 CCGI^{NK}_{413} +$$
$$\beta_4 CCGI^{NK}_{414} + \beta_5 CCGI^{NK}_{431} + \beta_6 CCGI^{NK}_{432} +$$
$$\beta_7 CCGI^{NK}_{433} + \beta_8 CCGI^{NK}_{434} + \beta_9 CCGI^{NK}_{437} +$$
$$\beta_{10} CCGI^{NK}_{438} + \sum_{i=1}^{12} \alpha_i Indus_i + \beta_{11} Ln(Asset) +$$
$$\beta_{12} Levera + \varepsilon$$

From the model (I) and model (V) of Table 6.3, we can see that the index of top management governance has significant positive correlation with EPS and NAPS at the significance level of p = 10% and 5% respectively, which illustrates index value of top management governance reflects value of EPS and NAPS directly. Speaking of the 931 samples' situation in 2002, when average value of index of top management governance increases by 0.1, EPS and NAPS will increase 0.0278 and 0.1044 respectively.

Seen from sub-element-level factor, in model (II) there is significant correlation between EPS and construction of appointment and removal mechanism, and its coefficient is 0.409 at the significance level of p = 5%, which reflects that construction of appointment and removal mechanism of listed companies exerts an important impact on corporate performance. Integrating the regressive result of model (I) and model (III), we find that speaking of EPS, construction of appointment and removal mechanism plays a very important role in the status of top management, while top management administrative degree and method of selection and engagement exert an important impact on appointment and removal mechanism, which is positive relative with EPS at the significance level of p = 5% and 15% respectively. Seen from model (VI), management shareholding proportion and compensation level of top management have significant relationship with EPS, however decision-making report mechanism shows significant negative correlation, which illustrates that speaking of our samples, the board granting director permission to examine and approve investment quotas has a bad influence on EPS. This is because the directorate system in China is under construction, and there isn't good experience with regard to investment authorization, so problems may be in grant proportionment or proceeding regulation.

The investment limitation granted by the directorate will have a disadvantageous influence on EPS. The reason may be that due to directorates of our country being in their early days, there is no successful experience at this kind of investment authorization, or it may be the problem of authorization proportion or regulating items.

Seen from model (VI), incentive and restriction mechanism and appointment and removal mechanism have significant correlation with NAPS. To speak in detail, NAPS will increase by 0.0577 and 0.056 respectively as their scores increase by 0.1 on average. In the model (VII), management shareholding proportion and dynamic incentive present positive correlation with NAPS—that is 10% and 20%—which indicates consummation of this aspect of governance status will benefit NAPS in order to establish the steady foundation for improving the corporate market value. Meanwhile, decision-making operation mechanism presents negative correlation with NAPS.

In the model (VII) of CFPS and index of top management governance's regression, compensation level, dynamic incentive and management shareholding proportion present significant positive correlation with CFPS at the significance level of $p = 5\%$, and regressive coefficient is 0.435, 0.405 and 0.696 respectively. Decision-making operation mechanism is not similar to several former models; it presents significant correlation at the significance level of $p = 15\%$, which indicates that scientific compensation of top management is a benefit to CFPS and the capability of value creation. Selection and engagement of top management, top management administrative degree and non-pecuniary compensation are all positively relative with CFPS. However, selection and engagement method of top management presents negative correlation with CFPS at the significance level of $p = 20\%$. It indicates that the relation between CFPS and selection and engagement method of top management from the model (III) is not steady, so this factor presents significant negative correlation with CFPS. This indicates the companies good in the mechanism construction have strong value creation capability, thereby to some extent it suggests there are lots of retained earnings in our country's listed companies.

In addition, seen from all regressive models, there exists significant relationship between LnAsset and corporate performance at the significance level of p = 5%, which indicates corporate asset scale exerts advanced impact on corporate performance; meanwhile, level has negative influence on corporate performance and we can find these phenomenon from (I) to (VIII). Regarding the 931 samples, level (2002) exerts negative impact on top management governance performance— the higher the level, the worse the corporate performance.

Conclusions and policy suggestions

Through the empirical research between index of top management governance of Chinese listed companies and corporate performance, we can make the following conclusions and policy suggestions.

Research conclusions

Research results on evaluation of top management show:

(1) General level of Chinese top management governance is relatively low, average value of index of top management governance is 47.44, and among the principle factors there exist quite large differences, which is represented that the appointment and removal mechanism and guarantee of operation's mean value are 63.07 and 61.77 respectively, however mean value of incentive and restriction mechanism is only 33.02. This indicates there exists larger deficiencies at the aspects of incentive and restriction mechanism construction of Chinese listed companies' top management governance. In order to stimulate the enthusiasm of Chinese listed companies' top management and exert their innovation, enhancing the incentive and restriction is vital, or else incentive deficiency of sufficient "insider control" will seriously restrain the healthy development of Chinese companies.

(2) Seen from the industry status, the three industries owning the highest mean value of index of top management are Real Estate, Tertiary Industry and Broadcasting and Press, at the average scores of 50.46, 50.42 and 49.46 respectively. The worst three industries are Financing and Insurance, Mining, and Electricity, Gas and Water, with average scores of 45.15, 45.82 and 46.10 respectively.

(3) Seen from the largest shareholders' characteristic, mean value of the index of top management governance of the firms with private, collective and foreign investment as largest shareholder rank highest, at 49.73, 49.38 and 49.05 respectively. The shareholders with the worst scores are non-bank financial institution, college, academic institute and public utility, government, state-owned asset management department and other government department, whose mean values are 44.5, 47.13 and 47.51 respectively.

(4) Selection and engagement of general manager exerts positive impact on EPS; however, it has negative correlation with CFPS, which indicates the firms with good performance don't necessarily have strong value creation. It indicates that there exists lots of retained earnings management phenomena in our country's listed companies.

(5) Corporate asset scale exerts advanced impact on corporate performance; level (2002) exerts negative impact on top management governance performance.

Policy suggestions

The general status of Chinese listed companies' top management governance is relatively bad. Comparing from appointment and removal mechanism, guarantee of operation and incentive and restriction mechanism, management incentive seems negligible, whose score only equals half of the former two parts' scores. Enhancing the incentive of top management is crucial to improving Chinese top management governance. Based on our research, at each aspect of top management incentive top management's administrative degree, compensation level, percentage of shares, compensation dynamic incentive and other factors exert more significant impact on corporate performance. Hence, in order to improve the level of top management governance, we ought to:

(1) Cancel the administrative position. Management's administrative title is a historically bequeathed problem, which will disperse the economical work objective of top management and is not a simon-pure characteristic management should possess.

(2) Improve the compensation level of top management. At present Chinese top managements' compensation cannot embody their important role in the process of corporate development, and deficient incentive phenomena are universal. Therefore, enterprises should open their minds to let the management who make great contributions receive considerable compensation and embody their value in order to realize two wins.

(3) Realize or increase dynamic incentive, long-term incentive and significant incentive. Design the compensation structure of top management scientifically and to embody the dynamic relationship among the compensation level, corporate performance and corporate value, to bring top management rich compensation at the same time as corporate performances are improved. Through the research we also found that an increase of percentage of shares is a benefit to the improvement of corporate performance. Hence, Chinese listed companies may also increase percentage of shares to stimulate their long-term operation behaviors. Though the condition of putting share options in practice in China is not mature, and there are lots of laws and market restrictions, we cannot be limited by share options. As long as we master this kind of thinking, we can set down some incentive plans creatively based on Chinese companies' specific conditions. In addition, the incentive of management at present is not significant, and this makes up the deficiency of significant mechanisms. However, as the operation scale enlarges and competition increases, this kind of non-mechanism risk will become bigger and bigger, so we try our best to make insignificant incentives significant.

Table 6.2:   Each variable Pearson coefficient correlation matrix

Variable	$CCGI^{NK}_{4}$	$CCGI^{NK}_{41}$	$CCGI^{NK}_{42}$	$CCGI^{NK}_{43}$	$CCGI^{NK}_{412}$	$CCGI^{NK}_{413}$	$CCGI^{NK}_{414}$	$CCGI^{NK}_{421}$	$CCGI^{NK}_{422}$	$CCGI^{NK}_{425}$	$CCGI^{NK}_{431}$	$CCGI^{NK}_{432}$	$CCGI^{NK}_{433}$	$CCGI^{NK}_{434}$	$CCGI^{NK}_{435}$	EPS	CFPS
$CCGI^{NK}_{41}$	0.396 (****)	1															
$CCGI^{NK}_{42}$	0.219 (****)	0.021	1														
$CCGI^{NK}_{43}$	0.860 (****)	0.025	-0.019	1													
$CCGI^{NK}_{411}$	0.288 (****)	0.670 (****)	0.014	0.049													
$CCGI^{NK}_{412}$	0.271 (****)	0.752 (****)	-0.019	0.024	1												
$CCGI^{NK}_{413}$	0.261 (****)	0.634 (****)	0.060	0.025	0.211 (****)	1											
$CCGI^{NK}_{414}$	0.071 (*)	0.205 (****)	0.063	-0.012	0.011	0.031	1										
$CCGI^{NK}_{421}$	0.132 (****)	-0.020	0.496 (****)	0.011	-0.030	0.020	0.034	1									
$CCGI^{NK}_{422}$	0.133 (****)	0.071	0.198 (****)	0.060	0.081 (*)	0.051	-0.019	0.017	1								
$CCGI^{NK}_{423}$	0.100 (****)	-0.022	0.449 (****)	-0.010	-0.026	0.050	0.013	-0.008	-0.020								
$CCGI^{NK}_{424}$	0.130 (****)	0.130 (****)	0.360 (****)	0.007	0.078 (*)	0.067 (*)	0.078 (*)	0.000	0.025								
$CCGI^{NK}_{425}$	0.168 (****)	0.069	0.187 (****)	0.114 (****)	0.072 (*)	0.037	0.000	-0.036	0.012	1							
$CCGI^{NK}_{431}$	0.429 (****)	0.060	0.082 (*)	0.459 (****)	0.032	0.043	-0.005	0.030	0.109 (****)	0.022	1						

Table 6.2: Each variable Pearson coefficient correlation matrix *(cont'd)*

Variable	$CCGI^{NK}_{41}$	$CCGI^{NK}_{42}$	$CCGI^{NK}_{43}$	$CCGI^{NK}_{412}$	$CCGI^{NK}_{413}$	$CCGI^{NK}_{414}$	$CCGI^{NK}_{421}$	$CCGI^{NK}_{422}$	$CCGI^{NK}_{425}$	$CCGI^{NK}_{431}$	$CCGI^{NK}_{432}$	$CCGI^{NK}_{433}$	$CCGI^{NK}_{434}$	$CCGI^{NK}_{435}$	EPS	CFPS
$CCGI^{MK}_{432}$	0.406 (****)	0.035	0.444 (****)	0.017	0.032	0.020	-0.006	0.005	0.111 (****)	0.220 (****)	1					
$CCGI^{MK}_{433}$	0.472 (****)	0.027	0.500 (****)	-0.038	0.031	0.010	0.086 (***)	0.051	0.109 (****)	0.087 (**)	0.146 (****)	1				
$CCGI^{MK}_{434}$	0.284 (****)	0.034	0.392 (****)	0.028	0.043	-0.054	0.003	0.023	0.036	0.035	0.105 (****)	-0.023	1			
$CCGI^{MK}_{437}$	0.480 (****)	-0.023	0.588 (****)	0.050	0.002	0.041	-0.006	0.004	0.015	0.015	0.013	0.024	0.006			
$CCGI^{MK}_{438}$	0.251 (****)	-0.065	0.272 (****)	0.027	0.027	-0.002	0.000	-0.047	0.070	0.000	0.067	-0.015	0.007			
$CCGI^{MK}_{435}$	0.618 (****)	-0.006	0.722 (****)	0.266	-0.064	0.339 (***)	0.035	(a)	-0.235	0.428 (**)	0.344 (**)	-0.021	0.671 (****)	1		
$CCGI^{MK}_{436}$	0.355 (**)	0.023	0.501 (****)	-0.044	0.018	0.056	-0.114		-0.655 (****)	0.032	0.274	0.010	0.322 (**)	0.421 (****)		
EPS	0.063	0.022	0.048	0.055	0.108 (****)	-0.016	0.020	0.137 (****)	-0.007	0.156 (****)	0.014	0.102 (****)	0.104 (****)	0.228	1	
CFPS	0.041	0.058	0.056	-0.030	-0.039	-0.001	0.026	0.024	-0.010	0.108 (*)	-0.003	0.083 (**)	0.088 (**)	0.316	0.368 (****)	1
NAPS	0.071 (**)	0.037	0.061	0.009	0.049	-0.018	-0.012	0.060	0.029	0.011	0.078	0.051	0.101 (****)	0.074 (**)	-0.013	0.515 (****)
LNAsset	0.006	0.089 (****)	0.004	-0.096 (****)	-0.049	-0.009	0.163 (****)	0.030	-0.013	0.094 (**)	0.039	0.084 (**)	0.055	-0.002	0.258 (****)	0.288 (****)
LEVER	-0.008	-0.022	-0.010	-0.039	0.004	0.005	-0.035	-0.012	-0.008	0.010	0.013	-0.023	0.080 (**)	-0.148	-0.289 (****)	-0.065

Note: ****, ***, **, * represent significance degree at the level of 1%, 5%, 10%, 15% respectively; limited by the space, we delete some irrelevant content.

Table 6.3:   Index of top management governance and ESP, NAPS and CFPS regressive result

	EPS			
Variable	Model (I)	Model (II)	Model (III)	Model (IV)
(Const)	−1.074 *** (−5.200)	−1.291*** (−5.676)	−1.342*** (−6.729)	−0.699*** (−2.368)
$CCGI^{NK}_{4}$	0.278 ** (1.941)	−	−	−
$CCGI^{NK}_{41}$	−	0.409*** (3.588)	−	−
$CCGI^{NK}_{42}$	−	−0.005 (−0.036)	−	−
$CCGI^{NK}_{43}$	−	0.116 (1.240)	−	−
$CCGI^{NK}_{411}$	−	−	0.132* (1.573)	−
$CCGI^{NK}_{412}$	−	−	0.013 (0.195)	−
$CCGI^{NK}_{413}$	−	−	0.251*** (3.707)	−
$CCGI^{NK}_{414}$	−	−	−0.085 (−0.638)	−
$CCGI^{NK}_{431}$	−	−	−	0.292*** (3.198)
$CCGI^{NK}_{432}$	−	−	−	0.068 (0.551)
$CCGI^{NK}_{433}$	−	−	−	0.031 (0.419)
$CCGI^{NK}_{434}$	−	−	−	0.199** (1.919)
$CCGI^{NK}_{437}$	−	−	−	−0.153*** (−2.771)
$CCGI^{NK}_{438}$	−	−	−	−0.141 (−1.123)
Indust dum	Yes	Yes	Yes	Yes
LNAsset	0.105 *** (7.781)	0.110*** (8.104)	0.111*** (8.142)	0.097*** (4.090)
Lerera	−0.377 *** (−8.900)	−0.371*** (−8.793)	−0.242*** (−5.572)	−0.929*** (−8.663)
Adj_R^2	0.173	0.184	0.159	0.299
F	12.705	11.927	8.582	6.998
D-W	1.931	1.933	1.975	2.052

Note: ****, ***, **, * represent significant degree at the level of 1%, 5%, 10%, 15% respectively; T label at each bracket; limited by the space, we delete some insignificant variables

Table 6.3: Index of top management governance and ESP, NAPS and CFPS regressive result *(cont'd)*

Variable	NAPS			CFPS
	Model (V)	Model (VI)	Model (VII)	Model (VIII)
(Const)	−3.769*** (−6.221)	−3.788*** (−5.553)	−2.533*** (−2.359)	−2.376 *** (−2.711)
$CCGI^{NK}_4$	1.044*** (2.088)	−	−	−
$CCGI^{NK}_{41}$	−	−	−	−
$CCGI^{NK}_{42}$	−	−0.236 (−0.490)	−	−
$CCGI^{NK}_{43}$	−	0.577** (1.786)	−	−
$CCGI^{NK}_{411}$	−	−	−	−
$CCGI^{NK}_{412}$	−	−	−	0.157 (0.676)
$CCGI^{NK}_{413}$	−	−	−	0.157 (0.675)
$CCGI^{NK}_{414}$	−	−	−	−0.041 (−0.124)
$CCGI^{NK}_{431}$	−	−	0.291 (0.872)	0.435 *** (2.271)
$CCGI^{NK}_{432}$	−	−	−0.069 (−0.155)	0.000 (0.001)
$CCGI^{NK}_{433}$	−	−	−	0.405 *** (2.520)
$CCGI^{NK}_{434}$	−	−	0.735** (1.946)	0.696 *** (3.332)
$CCGI^{NK}_{437}$	−	−	−	0.180 * (1.537)
$CCGI^{NK}_{438}$	−	−	0.120 (0.262)	0.221 (0.830)
Indust dum	Yes	Yes	Yes	Yes
LNAsset	0.593*** (12.920)	0.602*** (12.994)	0.517*** (6.177)	0.232 *** (4.485)
Lerera	−1.966*** (16.608)	−1.965 (−16.586)	−2.300*** (−11.752)	−
Adj_R²	0.370	0.371	0.413	0.348
F	35.694	31.299	11.589	3.306
D-W	1.805	1.804	2.011	2.151

Note: ****, ***, **, * represent significant degree at the level of 1%, 5%, 10%, 15% respectively; T label at each bracket; limited by the space, we delete some insignificant variables

CHAPTER

Research on Evaluation and Index of Information Disclosure

Information disclosure is defined as a system of law, for which the purpose is to defend the legal benefits of stakeholders, under which the corporation should disclose the information about the business achievements, financial situation and governance system completely, truthfully and in a timely way, in terms of the relevant regulations. Hence, the information users can judge the value of the company with this information. Information is characterized by externality, monopoly supply and asymmetry. Information users must refer to the accounting rules and information disclosure institution to attain the necessary information. According to the contract theory, the impetus of the information disclosure is from two main aspects; one is from the subscription, execution and supervision of the contract itself, and the other is from the effect of the market mechanism. The impetus from the contract will drive the corporation to provide all the information relative to the contract complement. If the signatories are numerous, the contract will probably be in vain because of the high cost.

As one section of the external regulation instrument, information disclosure can: provide evidence to the establishment of the corporate governance policy for government and securities regulatory authorities; help to enhance the efficiency of the resource allocation; reduce transaction costs; rebound to establish the ex post facto solution mechanism; shorten the isolation between the voluntary information disclosure from the listed company and the information demand of the investors; and improve the information quality. It can also help the investors to judge the integrity and authenticity of the information, and consequently advance the quality of the corporate governance. Where information chains lack the link of information disclosure evaluation, the information chains can't be integrated any more. It is both reasonable and feasible to appraise the information disclosure. The empirical analysis from John Kofi (2002) proved that compulsory information disclosure reduced the valuation variation. However, excessive external intervention will lead to the inefficiency of the resource allocation. Considering that, the evaluation of the information disclosure, a "moderate" external mechanism, is necessary to put into practice.

Review of evaluation of information disclosure

The literature concerning information disclosure consists of the quality research of information disclosure, the evaluation research of information disclosure, and the design of the evaluation system of the information disclosure.

Quality research of information disclosure

For a long time, much attention has been focused on the quality of financial information and the contents of disclosure. Quite a lot of research was done in this field by accounting professional organizations, regulatory authorities and academics.

Financial information disclosure

After the 1970s and 1980s discussion about relevance and reliability, research into financial qualitative information has drawn common attention to information transparency since the 1990s. In 1978, the Financial Accounting Standards Board (FASB) defined the function of financial statements as providing useful information for decision-making. In 1980, FASB announced financial accounting concept bulletin no. 2—"Qualitative features of accounting information"—putting forward two standards of qualitative information as relevance (timeliness) and reliability (truthfulness, verifiability and objectivity). It outlined a framework of qualitative information to meet the needs of users, but it didn't study authenticity as a separate concept. From the perspective of economics, Watts and Zimmerman summarized materiality of independent accounting principles and auditing principles to evaluate public companies in the Hesperian economic development history; moreover, they pointed out the agent issue existing in the information releasing process.

The role that financial intermediaries (such as investment banks and venture capital funds) play in solving the asymmetry between the primary market investors and listed companies has been analyzed theoretically by Booth and Smith (1986), Beatty and Ritter (1986), and Gale and Stiglitz (1989). The four quality characteristics—from the International Accounting Standards Committee (IASC, 1989) mentioned in "The frame of preparing and supplying financial reports"—are understandability, relevance (materiality), reliability (true reflection, substance over format, neutrality, prudence, completeness), and comparability. According to the "enterprise accounting principles" (1993) in China, the seven important characters of the quality of information are authenticity, relevance, comparability, consistency, timeliness, clarity, and materiality.

The U.S. Securities and Exchange Commission (SEC, 1996) issued a statement on the "core standards" by the International Accounting Standards Committee, putting forward the high quality standards of the core evaluation criteria. The high quality was defined as comparability, transparency and full disclosure. There are two key elements in the financial reports evaluation model: first, the quality of financial reporting mainly refers to transparency, comparability and full disclosure; second, pay more attention to the profitability information, such as comprehensive earnings, net income and core earnings, and emphasize the protection of investors, with particular attention to the manipulation of profits. Transparency of information quality requirements are high; there must be enough useful information content. Since 1997, Arthur Levitt repeatedly stressed comparability, transparency and full disclosure, and in 1998 he issued the "importance of high-quality accounting standards." On the description of characteristics about the quality of information, different from the statement of FASB, he took the protection of investors' interests as the goal, and the information was characterized by integrity, transparency, impartiality, comparability and adequate disclosure.

Commissioned by the United Nations Conference on Trade and Development Board (UNCTAD), M Zubaidur Rahman (1998) studied the subject of "The role of accounting disclosure in the East Asian financial crisis: lessons learned," and pointed out that insufficient disclosure of information in relation to the 1997 Asian financial crisis had a significant breadth and depth of negative impact. Based on six aspects of affiliated party loans, foreign currency debt, derivatives, branch information, contingent liabilities and the disclosure of bank financial reports, the research compared the information disclosure in Asian countries with IAS, and found the information disclosure in these countries is apparently lower than the requirements of IAS. The reasons for the failure of a financial institution mainly include high indebtedness, reliance on the private sector for foreign exchange, and lack of transparency and explanation (lack of accountability). Information disclosure was not fully reflected in the following ways: first, the debt had been hidden in the affiliated transactions and tables outside financing; second, the exchange risk from a large number of short-term foreign currency borrowings was not obvious at the micro level; third, the detailed information about the great risks assumed by the real estate branch agencies was not disclosed in the level of concentration; fourth, the contingent liability formed by the company or the parent company to provide security was not disclosed; fifth, no accounting for bad debts due to loans.

In 1999, a "Blue Ribbon Committee"—the establishment of which was funded by the New York Stock Exchange (NYSE) and National Association of Securities Dealers (NASD)—noted in its submitted research report that the external auditors and the board of audit inside the company should discuss the judgments given by the auditors, which are about the quality of accounting principles used to prepare the financial reports, and should not only be concerned about the admissibility of the accounting principles. The content of the discussion included financial information disclosure clarity, consistency, completeness, honest expression, verifiability and neutrality, accounting principles, and the basically estimated level of adventure or optimism. The U.S. audit profession conducted the study to assess the quality of financial reports. In fact, the Audit Standards Committee (ASB, 1999) did not fully accept the concept of FASB no. 2; instead, it reacted to the suggestions by Levitt and the Blue Ribbon Committee, including revising audit guidelines Notice No. 61 (SAS 61), which required auditors to evaluate a company's accounting measurement and disclosures in accordance with SEC regulations. The American Institute of Certified Public Accountants (AICPA, 2000) issued a notice (Practice Alert No. 2)—"The quality of the accounting principles guide discussed with the board of audit"—which was different from the FASB's conceptual framework to assess the quality of financial information; this notice instead requires truth and fairness, similar to the highest demand of the British accounting standards.

In Table 7.1, we can see the comparison of the financial information quality evaluation indexes from FASB, the Blue Ribbon Committee and the SEC.

Table 7.1:   Comparison of financial information quality evaluation indexes

FASB: Make policy useful		Blue Ribbon Committee, SEC: Protect investors' rights and interests, concern about earning management					
Relevance	Prediction value	Purpose of Blue Ribbon Committee	Clarity of the disclosure	AICPA: "improve enterprise's report"; American Audit Criterion Committee SAS 61	Clarity and completeness of the accounting information disclosure	SEC Model: Criteria used for assessing the International Accounting Principles	Transparency
	Feedback value		Accounting principles and basically estimate the degree of danger and optimism		Consistency and comparability of accounting policy		Comparability (make profits, etc.)
	Timeliness						
Dependability	Authenticity				Accounting information is accurate, verifiable and neutral		Full disclosure
	Verification						
	Neutrality						

Financial information pays much attention to accounting receipts and little attention to the value of enterprises, resources and wealth changes, core competencies report. The disclosed evaluations of financial information show two inadequate connects. First, the financial reporting system taking the current financial resources and the financial situation as the core and taking the historical cost and the accrual as a basis hardly meets the needs of the information users to understand corporate values, core competencies, resources and wealth changes, the future financial potential, and impact of the decision-making in the financial information; second, the dispute on the authenticity of information does not clarify its substantive meaning for a long time. Complete, accurate and timely disclosure of internal control and its operation in listed companies, stock structure and change is an important part of the information disclosure. Including the information of the corporate governance structure, non-financial information in the disclosure of information takes a prominent place; it must be disclosed and evaluated (Shi Ximin, 2001).

Extension of the content of information disclosure

The content of the information disclosure is expanding, which is not limited to financial information disclosure evaluation. Instead, non-financial information is used primarily to evaluate company performance, public policy, risk forecasting, and corporate governance effectiveness. The situation of corporate governance structure is an important part of the information disclosure, and the information disclosure of this part has already been an area of concern for market regulators; moreover, the investors also pay attention to the information disclosure of corporate governance. For example, LENS Investment Management Company, founded in 1992, from the financial assessment and corporate governance evaluation specially searched for the companies which are underestimated and can be enhanced through corporate governance, and then invested in these kinds of companies. The American Institute of Certified Public Accountants (AICPA, 1994) issued "Improving business reporting—A customer focus," which summarizes five types of information that users require, namely, the financial and non-financial data, analysis on financial and non-financial data by the management department, forecasting information, information of shareholders and management, and company background. In assessing the quality of financial information standards, in addition to the relevance and reliability, comparability of the information stood out, including comparability between enterprises, the coherence of each period, and statement consistency between projects.

Samuel A. Dipiazza (2002) pointed out management should follow six objectives when preparing the information reports: completeness, compliance (the audit opinion is the statement to evaluate company health problems), consistency, commentary (pointing out the risks, uncertainty factors), clarity, and communication. Quality of information disclosure is determined by the following factors: quarterly bulletin, the detail and clarity of the annual report, the access to the discussion results by company management and financial analysts, and the frequency of issuing information through the media.

In September 1998, Basel Committee Banking Supervision promulgated the study "Enhance the transparency of banks," and this pointed out that to be looking at the essence of the information, the information disclosure must provide timely, accurate, and relevant qualitative and quantitative information and full disclosure; what's more, the disclosure must be based on sound measurement principles. The information quality includes: comprehensiveness, relevance and timeliness, reliability, comparability, and materiality. Effective disclosure includes disclosing more information. With the information provided by a company, users can accurately judge the company's financial position, risk management strategies and practices, accounting policies, risk degree, business management and corporate governance. Public disclosure of information can facilitate the investors in accurately evaluating the financial position and performance, risk distribution and management of the banks, minimize the risk of moral hazard, promote sound management and fair competition and improve the efficiency of resource distribution. Market constraints provisions stress the balance of disclosing qualitative and quantitative information, and are divided by the type of risk; meanwhile, they still consider the impact of internal risk measurement methods on information disclosure. In "Corporate governance principles", the OECD (2004) made it clear that corporate governance should ensure that relevant information of company events is disclosed accurately and in a timely fashion.

Related research of information disclosure evaluation

The exploration of information disclosure evaluation is also under discussion. As the market environment is different, the coherent standards for the evaluation indicators system of information disclosure have not yet formed. Although the U.S. Securities and Exchange Commission (1996) didn't design the evaluation indicators system of the information disclosure directly, the evaluation criteria of the information quality raised by it possessed an important reference value. In 1998, Standard & Poor's took the lead in setting up a corporate governance services system, establishing a target system for financial transparency and information disclosure. In February 2001, Standard & Poor's put forward the "Standard & Poor's Company Transparency & Disclosure Survey"; subsequently, they proclaimed the "Standard & Poor's Corporate Governance Scores: Criteria, Methodology and Definitions" in July 2002. Durnev and Kim (2002) indicated Standard & Poor's evaluation indicators are just correspondingly effective, and financial information cannot be completely representative of the transparency of the company. Using the annual report to assess the transparency of information, it is impossible to evaluate the information that is not included in the annual report. Ye Yinhua (2002) also pointed out that Standard & Poor's only took the information in the annual report as the evaluation target, which means the information that did not appear in the annual and quarterly reports could not be evaluated; hence, there is an apparent lack of credibility.

In the survey report of "The Opacity Index" issued by PricewaterhouseCoopers (2001), "opacity" was defined as the lack of clear, accurate, formal, easily discernible and widely accepted practices in areas such as commercial economy, finance, and government regulation. Targeting 35 countries or areas, the survey report rated and classified the opacity index from five aspects of corruption, legal, financial policy, accounting standards and practices (including corporate governance and information disclosure), and government regulation.[1]

With regard to other relevant research, Demier and CLSA companies measured the corporate governance situation from the angles of corporate governance disclosure and the structure and function of the board. The evaluation of the information transparency in the corporate governance principles by CLSA Corporation (Lyonnais Securities) includes: to promulgate timely annual reports, to disclose the operating results quickly, to provide clear and substantial messages, and to focus on the transparency of information. As to the evaluation of published information on the company website, the relevant evaluation criteria are timeliness, clarity, information content, and so on. However, timely, clear and information content are all quite ambiguous concepts, and lack objectivity. Pei Wuwei (2001) also referred to the information disclosure and relative evaluation indicators in his study of corporate governance evaluation systems. Beijing Citylink International Financial Consultant launched the evaluation indicators for board governance of listed companies in China in 2002, involving information disclosure evaluation.

Related research of information disclosure evaluation indicators design

The situation of the corporate governance correlates closely with the information disclosure evaluation. The system of corporate governance evaluation indicators involved the information disclosure evaluation in varying degrees. Some scholars and intermediaries have studied the information disclosure evaluation indicators to a certain extent, providing the reference research ideas to the further research on the evaluation of the information disclosure systems. Because of the diverse market

---

[1] In that report, the opacity index in China is 87, and China was classified among countries with the lowest transparency. In a sub-survey "accounting standards and practices", the index of China ranked the second to the last.

environment, uniform criteria have not yet formed. From a technical viewpoint, the evaluation criteria of the information disclosure mainly consider three factors: timing, quality and quantity, which basically meet the requests for the form, content and scope of the information disclosure. As a regulator of securities trading, the Securities and Exchange Commission possesses its own evaluation criteria of the information quality, which takes on an important referenced significance.

On 14 October 2002, Standard & Poor's announced that the evaluation of the information transparency can be divided into three levels, with 98 indicators: first, the transparency of ownership and investor relations, with a total of 28 indicators; second, financial transparency and disclosure of information (information disclosure), with a total of 35 indicators; third, the disclosure degree of the board and management structure and process, with a total of 35 indicators. Some scholars propose different views of the Standard & Poor's evaluation system.

The twelve inquiry questions to measure the transparency index of the information disclosure designed by PricewaterhouseCoopers (2001) cover the following issues:

1. The consistency of accounting standards.
2. The ease of acquisition of private sector information for typical investors.
3. The degree of uncertainty relevant with the accounting standards.
4. The status that the private sector complies with accounting standards.
5. The status that government complies with accounting standards.
6. The status that state-owned enterprises comply with accounting standards.
7. The status that the central bank complies with the accounting standards.
8. The status that commercial banks are in compliance with accounting standards.
9. The frequency of banks providing regulatory departments with accurate information.

10. The ease of attaining company cash flow information.
11. The ease of acquiring the information of the company's current capital structure.
12. The ease of acquiring the information of the company's level of operating risk.

The index of information disclosure

Index design of information disclosure evaluation

The evaluation index of information disclosure of the listed companies in China contains four aspects. The first is financial information, including applied accounting standards, financial standing (financial position) of the company, and associated transactions. The second is audit information, including audit report from certified public accountant and interior control evaluation. Audit and information disclosure evaluate the legitimacy and independence of the audit relationship. The third is whether the disclosed information about corporate governance meets the relevant specifications. Although there is higher qualitative criterion at present, specific quantized standards are still deficient. The fourth is timeliness of the information disclosure. The company should set up a website so that investors can look up relevant information. But quantized standard is not mentioned either. In view of the contents of the existing assessment indicators, listed companies in China should act on the principle that disclosed information should be scientific, systematic and timely, based on the internationally acknowledged principles and code of corporation governance. They should learn from (borrow ideas from) American FASB 2nd concept Bulletin, the American Blue Ribbon Committee, the suggestions of AICPA and the 61st Auditing Standard Bulletin, the criteria of the SEC, accounting standards, the law and codes about listed companies in company law, securities law, and company accounting standard rules of implementation on information disclosure, and in a comprehensive way design the evaluation standard of information disclosure borrowing ideas of the existing research.

The components of information disclosure evaluation

The evaluation system of the information disclosure, whose core element is transparency of information, chooses authenticity ($CCGI^{NK}_{51}$), timeliness ($CCGI^{NK}_{52}$) and completeness ($CCGI^{NK}_{53}$) as its three indicators (the main factors), with 15 specific indexes (the sub-factors). Meanwhile, it established the relevant evaluation criteria, and was applied to analyze and appraise the information disclosure of the listed company in China. Finally, the index of information disclosure evaluation was formed.

Authenticity

Authenticity is defined that the description to the information should be consistent with the relevant phenomenon. Factual accuracy requires the information disclosed by the company to reflect the tendency of the facts and the economical activities, and can be tested by some criteria. However, the authenticity of the information is also relative and dynamic, which represents the history. Usually, it is impossible for external people to decide whether the data about the company is true or not only by the disclosed information. But referring to the historical records about the listed company and its correlative persons, they can appraise the authenticity of the information disclosure. On the perspective of the information transference, regulatory departments and intermediaries can collect, analyze and test the information, and it is feasible and reasonable to use this kind of testing to appraise the authenticity of the information disclosure.

The components of evaluation indexes on authenticity are as follows:

1. Whether the annual financial report received non-standard unqualified opinion or is condemned publicly ($CCGI^{NK}_{511}$).
2. Whether the accounting policy and accounting evaluation varied or not in the latest three years ($CCGI^{NK}_{512}$).
3. Whether the company changed the accountant office or not ($CCGI^{NK}_{513}$).

4. Whether the changed accountant office will ever be challenged or appealed ($CCGI^{NK}_{514}$).
5. Whether the accountant office which presides over the auditing of the annals supply other kinds of services to the company or not ($CCGI^{NK}_{515}$).
6. Whether the supervisory board ever found and corrected counterfeit information in the financial report or not ($CCGI^{NK}_{516}$).

Timeliness

The timeliness of the information means supplying the decision-maker with the information before it can influence the decision. The information should be timely as well as true. There are abuses in timeliness and dissymmetry because of the differences in the times when investors, supervision and regulation authorities, the general public and business interior management personnel grasp the information. To deal with it, the system of information disclosure requires company exchange, intensifying the transparency of the company, and reducing the difficulties of supervision and government. All of these are helpful to regulate the operating conduct of managers, and protect the benefits of investors. Analyzing from the standpoint of public investors, it can help the investors to make rational value judgments and decision-making if information is disclosed in time. To the listed company, disclosing the information in time can make the share price of the company adjust in time, ensure that the transaction is continuous and effective, and reduce the blindfold action in the market.

The components of evaluation indexes on timeliness include:

1. Whether the resolutions of the shareholders conference are disclosed in time or not ($CCGI^{NK}_{521}$).
2. Whether the resolutions by the board of directors are disclosed in time or not ($CCGI^{NK}_{522}$).
3. Whether the periodic reports in the latest three years are disclosed in time or not ($CCGI^{NK}_{523}$).

4. Whether the financing entrusting is disclosed in time or not ($CCGI^{NK}_{524}$).

Completeness

The completeness of the information disclosure requires the listed company to provide the complete information—that is to say, the company can't neglect or hide important information—so as to make the information users clearly aware about the corporate governance structure, financial situation, business achievements, cash flow, business risk and the degree of the risk, and so on. The completeness makes sure that the investors know well the company's panorama, the essential items and the results. Generally, the completeness consists of two aspects: format and content.

The components of evaluation indexes on completeness contain:

1. Whether the decisions of the shareholders conference are disclosed completely or not ($CCGI^{NK}_{531}$).
2. Whether the decisions by the board of directors are disclosed completely or not ($CCGI^{NK}_{532}$).
3. Whether the decisions by the supervisory board are disclosed completely or not ($CCGI^{NK}_{533}$).
4. Whether the periodic reports in the latest three years are disclosed completely or not ($CCGI^{NK}_{534}$).
5. Whether the financing entrusting is disclosed completely or not ($CCGI^{NK}_{535}$).

The evaluation indexes of the information disclosure about China-listed companies are shown in Table 7.2.

Table 7.2: Information disclosure evaluation system

The main factors ($CCGI^{NK}_5$)	The sub-factors	Instructions
Authenticity ($CCGI^{NK}_{51}$)	Whether the annual financial report received unstandardized unqualified opinion or is blamed publicly; whether the accounting policy and accounting evaluation varied or not in the latest three years; whether the company changed the accountant office or not; whether the changed accountant office presents objection or appeal; whether the accountant office which presides over the auditing of the annals supplies other kinds of services to the company or not; whether the supervisory board ever found and corrected counterfeit information in the financial report or not	Reflect the quality of the information disclosure
Timelines ($CCGI^{NK}_{52}$)	Whether the decisions of the shareholders conference are disclosed in time or not; whether the decisions by the board of directors are disclosed in time or not; whether the stated reports in the latest three years are disclosed in time or not; whether the financing entrusting is disclosed in time or not	Reflect whether the information disclosure is in time or not
Completeness ($CCGI^{NK}_{53}$)	Whether the decisions of the shareholders conference are disclosed completely or not; whether the decisions by the board of directors are disclosed completely or not; whether the decisions by the supervisory board are disclosed completely or not; whether the stated reports in the latest three years are disclosed completely or not; whether the financing entrusting is disclosed completely or not	Reflect whether the information disclosure is complete or not

Using the methods of experts rating and level analysis, the weights of the main factors and sub-factors in the information disclosure evaluation system can be identified. Synthesizing the suggestions by the experts group, we can determine the three main factors in the evaluation of information disclosure are authenticity ($CCGI^{NK}_{51}$), timeliness ($CCGI^{NK}_{52}$), and completeness ($CCGI^{NK}_{53}$), and their corresponding sub-factors. Again, based on the marks of all the indexes given by the experts, passing the judgment matrix and consistency test, the weight of each index (W denotes the weight) can be attained. The relational formulas, results and statistics are as follows:

$$CCGI^{NK}_{51} = CCGI^{NK}_{511}*W_{511} + CCGI^{NK}_{512}*W_{512} + CCGI^{NK}_{513}*W_{513} + CCGI^{NK}_{514}*W_{514} + CCGI^{NK}_{515}*W_{515} + CCGI^{NK}_{516}*W_{516}$$

$$CCGI^{NK}_{52} = CCGI^{NK}_{521}*W_{521} + CCGI^{NK}_{522}*W_{522} + CCGI^{NK}_{523}*W_{523} + CCGI^{NK}_{524}*W_{524}$$

$$CCGI^{NK}_{53} = CCGI^{NK}_{531}*W_{531} + CCGI^{NK}_{532}*W_{532} + CCGI^{NK}_{533}*W_{533} + CCGI^{NK}_{534}*W_{534} + CCGI^{NK}_{535}*W_{535}$$

$$CCGI^{NK}_{5} = CCGI^{NK}_{51}*W_{51} + CCGI^{NK}_{52}*W_{52} + CCGI^{NK}_{53}*W_{53}$$

Based on the data from the investigation about the authenticity, timeliness and completeness of the information disclosure of the Chinese listed companies, the descriptive statistics can be collated and appraised. Meanwhile, we can do some empirical research, expecting to pick up the existing problems and find out the relevant solutions.

Descriptive statistics of information disclosure of Chinese listed companies

Overall analysis

In general, the selected sample of listed companies do not behave well on the authenticity index, timeliness index, completeness index and the general index of information disclosure. Specifically, the indexes marked above 80 account for 13.96%, 15.68%, 16.01% and 9.13%, respectively. The percentages of the four indexes under 50 are 34.16%, 15.79%, 14.50% and 25.35%, respectively. We can say that the whole level of the information disclosure of Chinese listed companies is comparatively lower and the information transparency isn't high. Basically, the information disclosure index is consistent with normal distribution, but the values of the indexes are wholly on the low side, with the mean of 58.44. Moreover, there appear two peak values, which indicates the distribution of the information disclosure is reasonable as a whole, but still reveals imbalance. The quality of the information disclosure can be satisfied.

Frequency and proportion analysis

The authenticity index ($CCGI^{NK}_{51}$), timeliness index ($CCGI^{NK}_{52}$), completeness index ($CCGI^{NK}_{53}$) and information disclosure index ($CCGI^{NK}_{5}$) are stated in detail below.

Authenticity

The number of listed companies whose authenticity index reaches $CCGI^{NK}_{51}I$, $CCGI^{NK}_{51}II$, $CCGI^{NK}_{51}III$, $CCGI^{NK}_{51}IV$, $CCGI^{NK}_{51}V$ and $CCGI^{NK}_{51}VI$ is 11, 119, 46, 295, 142 and 318 respectively, accounting for 1.18%, 12.78%, 4.94%, 31.69%, 15.25% and 34.16% of the total sample companies respectively. The interval proportion with high evaluation marks (from $CCGI^{NK}_{51}I$ to $CCGI^{NK}_{51}III$) is 18.9% (1.18% + 12.78% + 4.94%); the value of the information disclosure between $CCGI^{NK}_{51}I$ and $CCGI^{NK}_{51}IV$ (above 60 marks) accounts for 50.59% (18.9% + 31.69%); the information disclosure value locating from $CCGI^{NK}_{51}V$ to $CCGI^{NK}_{51}VI$ takes the percentage of 49.41% (15.25% + 34.16%). The status discussed above illuminates that the information disclosure performed badly on authenticity.

Timeliness

The number of listed companies whose timeliness index reaches $CCGI^{NK}_{52}I$, $CCGI^{NK}_{52}II$, $CCGI^{NK}_{52}III$, $CCGI^{NK}_{52}IV$, $CCGI^{NK}_{52}V$ and $CCGI^{NK}_{52}VI$ is 138, 8, 531, 32, 48 and 174 respectively, accounting for 14.82%, 0.86%, 57.04%, 3.44%, 5.16% and 18.68% of the total sample companies respectively. The proportion of the indexes reaching the fine criteria (from $CCGI^{NK}_{52}I$ to $CCGI^{NK}_{52}III$) is 72.72%

(14.82% + 0.86% + 57.04%); the value of the timeliness evaluation between $CCGI^{NK}_{52}I$ and $CCGI^{NK}_{52}IV$ (above 60 marks) accounts for 76.16% (72.72% + 3.44%); the lower marks from the timeliness evaluation (from $CCGI^{NK}_{52}V$ to $CCGI^{NK}_{52}VI$, less than 60 marks) takes the percentage of 23.84% (5.16% + 18.68%). All of this data proved that the timeliness of information disclosure performed well, but the regulation still needs to be strengthened.

Completeness

The number of listed companies whose completeness index reaches $CCGI^{NK}_{53}I$, $CCGI^{NK}_{53}II$, $CCGI^{NK}_{53}III$, $CCGI^{NK}_{53}IV$, $CCGI^{NK}_{53}V$ and $CCGI^{NK}_{53}VI$ is 140, 9, 10, 2, 635 and 135 respectively, accounting for 15.04%, 0.97%, 1.07%, 0.21%, 68.21% and 14.5% of the total sample companies respectively. The proportion of the indexes reaching the fine criteria (from $CCGI^{NK}_{53}I$ to $CCGI^{NK}_{53}III$) is 17.08% (15.04% + 0.97% + 1.07%); the value of the completeness evaluation between $CCGI^{NK}_{53}I$ and $CCGI^{NK}_{53}IV$ (above 60 marks) accounts for 17.29% (17.08% + 0.21%); the evaluation value less than 60 marks, from $CCGI^{NK}_{53}V$ to $CCGI^{NK}_{53}VI$, takes the percentage of 82.71% (68.21% + 14.5%). Obviously, we can find that the completeness of information disclosure in China-listed companies is quite insufficient; what's more, this reveals polarization.

Information disclosure index

The number of listed companies whose information disclosure index reaches $CCGI^{NK}_{5}I$, $CCGI^{NK}_{5}II$, $CCGI^{NK}_{5}III$, $CCGI^{NK}_{5}IV$, $CCGI^{NK}_{5}V$ and $CCGI^{NK}_{5}VI$ is 17, 60, 127, 334, 158 and 235 respectively, accounting for 1.83%, 6.44%, 13.64%, 35.88%, 16.97% and 25.24% of the total sample companies respectively. The proportion achieving the higher values (from $CCGI^{NK}_{5}I$ to $CCGI^{NK}_{5}III$) is 21.91% (1.83% + 6.44% + 13.64%); the evaluation value of the information disclosure between $CCGI^{NK}_{5}I$ and $CCGI^{NK}_{5}IV$ (above 60 marks) takes the percentage of 17.29% (17.08% + 0.21%); the proportion of the information disclosure evaluation value less than 60 marks (from $CCGI^{NK}_{5}V$ to $CCGI^{NK}_{5}VI$) is 42.21% (16.97% + 25.24%). This kind of status shows that the whole quality of the information disclosure must be improved.

Extremes, mean and standard deviation analysis

Concerning the authenticity index of information disclosure evaluation of sample companies, the minimum is at around 0.4, the maximum is 100, and the mean is 54. Authenticity of information disclosure performed poorly. Furthermore, the standard deviation appears quite large (25%). It notes that there exists great differences on the authenticity of information disclosure within the sample companies.

The minimum of the timeliness index is at 0, the maximum is 100, and the mean is 66.38. Timeliness of the information disclosure performs better than both authenticity and completeness. The standard deviation of the timeliness index is 23.81%, less than that of authenticity of information disclosure.

Regarding the completeness index, the minimum, the maximum and the mean are 7.06, 100 and 59.05, respectively. That means the completeness of the information disclosure performed poorly. The standard deviation of the completeness index is 19.44%, less than that of the authenticity index and timeliness index.

As to the information disclosure general index, the minimum, the maximum and the mean are 4.72, 97.69 (the maximum is rather extreme), and 58.44, respectively. From an overall point of view, the information disclosure cannot be satisfactory. The means of the information disclosure index of the listed companies in services, industry, public utilities, agriculture, and integrated category are 60.83, 61.05, 63.15, 42.17 and 55.4, respectively, followed by the standard deviations of 14.76%, 15.26%, 13.97%, 26.93% and 18.89%. It is clear that the information disclosure of listed companies in the public utilities category seems better than other industries, and the internal differences are also the smallest. The information disclosure of listed companies in agricultural categories is the lowest index, with the greatest internal differences.

There appear two peak values in the evaluation index of information disclosure, which means the quality of information disclosure varies greatly. And there is a concentrated interval of normal curve positions in the 58th percentile, indicating that the overall level of information disclosure index is not high. Another peak value is 19, which means the companies on this interval are in a sizeable number, and the information disclosure index is significantly lower. This situation can be reflected through the specific projects of information disclosure.

Empirical research on the relationships between information disclosure, company performance and corporate governance

Through relevance analysis between the information disclosure index and corporate performance indicators, and between the information disclosure index and the corporate governance index, on the one hand we can judge the reasonableness of the design evaluation index of the information disclosure, and on the other hand we can still test the information disclosure hypothesis of the sample companies, and use disclosure of information of sample companies to explain the evaluation results.

Based on the earlier studies and analysis, we can make an assumption: there exists a correlation between the information disclosure index of Chinese listed companies and corporate performance (financial early warning value, equity expansion capabilities, and so on). The model can be established according to the assumption, testing the relationship between the information disclosure index and corporate performances, and the relationship between the information disclosure index and corporate governance levels. At the same time, in order to further test the relationship between the information disclosure index and shareholder governance, the board governance, the supervisory board governance, and the manager-governance, we create the following models:

$$CCGI^{NK}_5 = \beta_0 + \beta_1 \text{ FEVAR} + \beta_2 \Sigma \text{Indus} + \beta_3 \text{Ln(Asset)} + \beta_4 \text{Leverage} + \varepsilon \dots\dots (I)$$

$$CCGI^{NK}_{5i} = \beta_0 + \beta_1 \text{ FEVAR} + \beta_2 \Sigma \text{Indus} + \beta_3 \text{Ln(Asset)} + \beta_5 \text{Leverage} + \varepsilon \dots\dots (II)$$

$$CCGI^{NK}_5 = \beta_0 + \beta_1 \text{ SER} + \beta_2 \Sigma \text{Indus} + \beta_3 \text{Ln(Asset)} + \beta_4 \text{Leverage} + \varepsilon \dots\dots (III)$$

$$CCGI^{NK}{}_{5} = \beta_{0} + \beta_{1} CCGI^{NK}{}_{1} + \beta_{2} CCGI^{NK}{}_{2} + \beta_{3} CCGI^{NK}{}_{3} +$$
$$\beta_{4} CCGI^{NK}{}_{4} + \beta_{5}\Sigma I_{i} + \beta_{6}Ln(Asset) + \beta_{7}L + \varepsilon \ldots\ldots (IV)$$

Where *FEVAR* stands for financing early warning value; $CCGI^{NK}{}_{5}$ denotes information disclosure index; $CCGI^{NK}{}_{5i}$ represents authenticity index ($CCGI^{NK}{}_{51}$), timeliness index ($CCGI^{NK}{}_{52}$), and completeness index ($CCGI^{NK}{}_{53}$); *SER* stands for equity expansion capacity; $CCGI^{NK}{}_{1}$ is shareholders meeting governance index; $CCGI^{NK}{}_{2}$ is board governance index; $CCGI^{NK}{}_{3}$ is supervisory board governance index; $CCGI^{NK}{}_{4}$ is manager governance index; I_{i} represents industrial control variable (industry, agriculture, services, public utilities, integrated companies); *Ln(Asset)* is the logarithm of the total assets; *L* is liability/asset ratio.

The correlation analysis between the information disclosure and financing early warning value

Financial early warning value reflects the company's financial risk in the future. By analyzing the relationship between information disclosure index and the financial early warning, we can get the forecast value of the information disclosure index. Partha Sengupta (1998) suggested that the factor normally considered by the creditors and underwriters when they are forecasting the default risk for enterprises is the information disclosure policy. The possibility of hiding adverse information becomes one of the factors in evaluating the debt risk. The greater the uncertainty a company faces in the market, the more apparent the reverse relationship between the quality of the information disclosure and debt financing costs is. This study can help to understand the motivation of information disclosure and the information disclosure evaluation.

Information disclosure index and the financial early warning value existed correlation. By performing a co-linearity analysis of authenticity, timeliness and completeness, we find that the Pearson Relevance is all less than 0.7; that is to say, the co-linearity problem did not exist among authenticity, timeliness and completeness. In general, the three sub-factors of the information disclosure index are significant with the financial early warning value; R^2 reached 0.113. Thereunto, the regression value between authenticity index, completeness index and financial early warning value is 0.744 and 1.017, with significance level of 0.168 and 0.155 respectively. With the high level of information disclosure, the corporation's financial early warning value is correspondingly higher, which means lower financial risk. Similarly, if the corporation is endowed with lower financial early warning value (high financial risk level), its quality of information disclosure is lower (see Table 7.3).

Table 7.3: The correlation between the sub-factors and financial early warning value (Model II)

	Nonstandard correlation coefficient	Standard deviation	Standard correlation coefficient	t-value	Sig.
Authenticity	0.744	0.538	0.036	1.381	0.168
Timeliness	0.975	0.669	−0.046	−1.458	0.145
Completeness	1.017	0.715	0.039	1.422	0.155
Ln (total asset)	−0.517	0.122	−0.096	−4.226	0.000
Liability/Asset ratio	−6.366	0.196	−0.742	−32.423	0.000

Signaling theory assumes, in the context of information asymmetry, that a company of high quality possesses corporate governance information of high criterion (standard). The company with good governance would like to disclose relevant information about itself factually, duly and integrally. To alleviate the qualms of the stockholders and creditors, the managers signaled by disclosing the information actively that they didn't get lazy or make adverse decisions to lower the value of the company; accordingly the managers can be relieved of agent responsibility and can obtain market trust. The signal functions that it can supply the information user with the information of the status of the company. With the information disclosed directly, we can: understand the structure of corporate governance, the structure of capital, dividend policy, the choice of accounting policy, and so on; judge the value of the company; assess the possibility that the company goes bankrupt; judge the stability of accounting policy, and so on. If the information supplied by the operator to reflect the value of the company contains illusory ingredients, the showing function of the signal will give warning to the public. Once the information is disclosed, it will become a kind of public product. Analyzing in terms that the market is out of order and information is regarded as public product, evaluating the disclosed information is essential in order to improve the quality of the signals.

The power to disclose information for companies lies in obtaining the low-cost resources, real, timely and complete information to enhance the confidence of investors. In 1994, Chemmanur and Fulghieri proposed a theoretical model of how much force it takes the investment banks to assess the investment projects of listed corporations. Meanwhile, the model of Chemmanur and Fulghieri also discussed the transaction relationship between the listed companies and financial intermediation (investment banks) in the disclosure of information. In their model, the credibility of financial intermediaries, investment banks' positioning of the project evaluation criteria and the services compensation commercial stocks obtain from listed companies, as well as sales on stock markets, are endogenous. In fact this gives transactions theory analysis between the disclosure of information and compensation of listed companies.

The quality of information disclosure is determined by the following aspects: the detailed and explicit degree of quarterly reports and annual reports, whether the results discussed by management and a financial analyst are available, the frequency with which the company releases information via media, and so on. Empirical study discovers that the cost of raising funds of debt is lower when the company performs well in the above-mentioned aspects. One of the factors the creditors and distributors use to evaluate the risk of arrears is the possibility that the company concealed news that was not favorable to it. If the quality of the disclosed information in the past is

Table 7.4:   The matrix analysis on the relevance between the information disclosure index and the financing early warning value (Model II)

		Financing early warning value	Authenticity	Timeliness	Completeness
Pearson relevance	**Financing early warning value**	1.000	0.044	0.001	0.040
	Authenticity	0.044	1.000	0.489	0.114
	Timeliness	0.001	0.489	1.000	0.557
	Completeness	0.040	0.114	0.557	1.000
Sig. (1-tailed)	**Financing early warning value**	–	0.092	0.490	0.114
	Authenticity	0.092	–	0.000	0.000
	Timeliness	0.490	0.000	–	0.000
	Completeness	0.114	0.000	0.000	–

higher, the creditors and underwriters are of the opinion that the possibility the company concealed disadvantageous news is lower, so that the risk payment they demand is lower. When the uncertainty the company faces within is larger, the opposite relationship between the quality of the information disclosure and the cost of raising funds of debt is more obvious. In order to obtain resources, the company must meet the demand of the resource supplier on authenticity, timeliness, completeness and other aspects of information.

From Table 7.4, we can see the relationship analysis between the information disclosure evaluation and financing early warning.

The correlation between the information disclosure index and equity expansion capacity

By the relevance analysis of the information disclosure index and equity expansion capacity, when the control variable is liability / asset ratio, the logarithm of total property, the equity expansion capacity and the information disclosure index display some connection. When carrying on the analysis of regression by taking the logarithm of total asset, liability / asset ratio, and industry as the control variables, the correlation between the information disclosure index and the equity expansion capacity is quite obvious; adjusted R^2 achieves 0.104, and D-W value is 1.756. The stronger the equity expansion capacity is, the higher the quality of the information disclosure is; the relevance between the equity expansion capacity and the authenticity of the information disclosure is especially remarkable (see Table 7.5).

The stronger the ability of the company to survive and develop is, the better the authenticity of its information disclosure; otherwise, when the company falls into a difficult position, the authenticity of the information disclosure is decreasing. This can be tested from the financial scandals of Enron Corp. in America, the World Communications Company, Italy Pamalate company and Lan Tian joint-stock companies in China, and so on, a common feature of which is a serious shortage of capital stock expansion ability and obtaining social resources by false information. When the equity expansion capacity is strong, the control ability of the manager level is consolidated and maintained; when the equity expansion capacity is weak, the status of the manager level will be challenged. When the benefits of a destroyed agreement outweigh the benefits of a completed agreement, the violation of the information disclosure will possibly occur (see Table 7.5).

Contract theory considers firms as an aggregation of a series of contracts. There are different kinds of contracts in firms: credit contracts, compensation contracts, and so on. For example, the contracts between the firm and debtors, between owner and manager, between the firm and suppliers, between the firm and sale agents, between executives and subordinates, and between the firm and employees. If the market is efficient, the opportunism of one contractor will definitely damage the benefits of others. Therefore, the contracts should reduce the asymmetrical information and improve the transparence of the information. The manager will provide all information relative

Table 7.5: The correlation between information disclosure index and the corporate performance

		Authenticity	Timeliness	Completeness	Indexes of information disclosure	Profitability	Growth	Equity expansion capacity	Ln(Total Asset)	Liability/asset ratio
Authenticity	Pearson relevance	1.000	0.486	0.111	0.870	0.034	0.041	0.071	0.008	–0.037
	Sig. (2-tailed)	–	0.000	0.001	0.000	0.302	0.217	0.030	0.807	0.260
Timeliness	Pearson relevance	0.486	1.000	0.559	0.810	0.039	0.029	0.059	0.026	–0.008
	Sig. (2-tailed)	0.000	–	0.000	0.000	0.240	0.371	0.071	0.426	0.797
Completeness	Pearson relevance	0.111	0.559	1.000	0.529	0.034	–0.026	0.043	0.016	–0.024
	Sig. (2-tailed)	0.001	0.000	–	0.000	0.295	0.435	0.193	0.635	0.456
Indexes of information disclosure	Pearson relevance	0.870	0.810	0.529	1.000	0.045	0.030	0.079	0.018	0.034
	Sig. (2-tailed)	0.000	0.000	0.000	–	0.170	0.355	0.015	0.578	0.293
Profitability	Pearson relevance	0.034	0.039	0.034	0.045	1.000	0.204	0.410	0.240	0.366
	Sig. (2-tailed)	0.302	0.240	0.295	0.170	–	0.000	0.000	0.000	0.000

Table 7.5: The relevance between information disclosure index and the corporate performance *(cont'd)*

		Authenticity	Timeliness	Completeness	Indexes of information disclosure	Profitability	Growth	Equity expansion capacity	Ln(Total Asset)	Liability/ asset ratio
Growth	Pearson relevance	0.041	0.029	−0.026	0.030	0.204	1.000	0.036	0.032	−0.050
	Sig. (2-tailed)	0.217	0.371	0.435	0.355	0.000	–	0.276	0.334	0.125
Equity expansion capacity	Pearson Relevance	0.071	0.059	0.043	0.079	0.410	0.036	1.000	0.370	−0.466
	Sig. (2-tailed)	0.030	0.071	0.193	0.015	0.000	0.276	–	0.000	0.000
LN(Total asset)	Pearson relevance	0.008	0.026	0.016	0.018	0.240	0.032	0.370	1.000	−0.176
	Sig. (2-tailed)	0.807	0.426	0.635	0.578	0.000	0.334	0.000	–	0.000
Liability/Asset ratio	Pearson relevance	−0.037	−0.008	−0.034	−0.034	−0.366	−0.050	−0.466	−0.176	1.000

to the implementation of the contracts. As for the information spread and valuation, they are the results of internal negotiation. If too many people are involved, the contracts may fail, because the cost during this process is too high. Since the existence of principal–agent relationship between manager, owner and debtor, and the manager control of the information processing, minority shareholders pay much attention to the information quality. With respect to the various demands of information, managers and others have to come to an agreement about the information management. We can find another explanation from the point of Nash Equilibrium; that is, the presupposition of the commitment means that the gain of maintaining the contracts is bigger than of damaging them. With the change of the conditions, the original benefit equilibrium of every party in the game will make great change.

The relations analysis between information disclosure and shareholders behavior, board, supervisory board, and manager governance

The firm with better corporate governance is more likely to reveal performance completely and in a timely way. Because in order to reduce the worry of the stakeholders, the manager will passively send out the signal that he does not take the expense preference and goldbrick to reduce the valuation of the firm. Furthermore, it helps him to free from the agent responsibility or obtain the market resources. By using the information about the corporate governance structure, financial statement, managing strategy, the ability of risk management, and the accounting policy, the user of information will estimate the valuation, the possibility of bankruptcy, the steadiness of accounting policy, and so on. The relevance between the information disclosure and controlling shareholders, board, supervisory board, and manager governance is listed in Table 7.6.

Table 7.6: The correlation between the index of information disclosure and controlling shareholders, board, supervisory board, and manager governance

	Non-standard regression coefficient		Standard regression coefficient	t-value	Sig.
Controlling variable	B	Standard deviation	Beta		
Controlling shareholders' governance	0.07883	0.054	0.048	1.455	0.146
Board governance	−0.07059	0.037	−0.064	−1.888	0.475
Supervisory board governance	−0.01638	0.053	−0.010	−0.308	0.758
Manager governance	0.148	0.078	0.062	1.897	0.058

The regression value between the behavior of the controlling shareholders and the index of the information disclosure is 0.07883, and the P-value is 0.146; namely, the information disclosure is somewhat relevant with the efficiency of the behavior of controlling shareholders (15% reliability horizontal). To a certain extent, it can indicate the function of the shareholders meeting of China-listed companies works, especially for the "phenomenon of domination of a single shareholder." The behavior of controlling shareholders directly affects the quality of the information disclosure.

The regression value of the board governance and the index of the information disclosure of −0.07059, and the P-value of 0.475, indicates that it has not passed the significant examination; on the other hand, it explains that the influence the board governance of the China-listed companies has on the quality of the information disclosure is not obvious. The reason possibly lies in that the function of the board is attenuated or the quality of the information disclosure mainly comes from the influence of senior managers. For example, the registered accountants depend largely on the appointment of senior managers, rather than the board; senior managers control the accounting policies; and so on. The regression value of the governance and the information disclosure is −0.01638, the significance level is 0.758, not passing a significance test.

The regression value of the manager governance index and the index of information disclosure is 0.148, and the P-value is 0.058. It explains the managers governance of the sample companies has a positive impact on the quality of information disclosure (10% reliability level). The behavior of managers directly affects the quality of the information disclosure, which in other relevant research literature has also been proved. To win the trust of the owner, the manager layer will take the initiative and act to provide information and reduce information asymmetry. Rational managers would like to have a higher market value; the market value of the managers is enhanced in creating company value, but this conclusion is premised on the effective market. If the manager market is not perfect, the market will be devoid of effective constraints for the professional managers; the behavior of the managers will not be effectively evaluated, so that managers evade responsibility. Compared with the owners, creditors and government, managers have unique information superiority.

Information economics holds the point that only if the gain from producing and revealing the information is bigger than the cost will their be drive to produce and reveal. Otherwise, if the cost is bigger than the gain, there will be a lack of impetus to produce and reveal the information. We should compensate the information producer by an external mechanism. In this way, the impetus to produce and reveal the information will not be limited. Since the users of the information employ the public information freely, the producers will likely reveal the positive information, and hide the negative information about the firm. That is to say, the suppliers of information cannot meet the needs of different users. And the information supply brings the contradiction between the high quality of information demand and low quality of information supply. Considering many other factors, this contradiction should be solved by the non-market aspects.

In conclusion, the regression results from the index of information disclosure and financing early warning value, equity capacity expansion, behavior of controlling shareholders, board governance, supervisory board governance, and manager governance are shown in Table 7.7.

Table 7.7: The information disclosure index regressed on the financial early warning value, the equity capacity expansion, the behavior of controlling shareholders, the board governance, the supervisory board governance and the manager governance

Variables	Model (I)	Model (II)	Model (III)	Model (IV)
(Const)	16.526***	16.283***	0.473***	0.514***
$CCGI^{NK}_5$	0.424	–	–	–
$CCGI^{NK}_{51}$	–	0.744 (0.168)	9.545E–03** (0.051)	–
$CCGI^{NK}_{52}$	–	–0.975 (0.145)	–	–
$CCGI^{NK}_{53}$	–	1.017 (0.155)	–	–
Shareholder meeting governance	–	–	–	7.883E-02 (0.146)
Board governance	–	–	–	–4.092E-02 (0.475)
Supervisory committee governance	–	–	–	–1.638E-02 (0.758)
Management governance	–	–	–	0.148* (0.058)
LN Asset	–4.278***	–0.517***	1.361E–02***	–
Leverage	–32.523***	–6.366***	–3.02E–02	–
Adj_R^2	0.112	0.113	0.104	0.008
F(Sig.)	158.777**	123.921**	58.918**	1.717* (0.072)
D-W	1.995	2.004	1.756	1.269

Note: ***, **, * denote the significant levels of 1%, 5%, 10%, respectively.

Model (I): The relevance between the information disclosure index and financing early warning value.

Model (II): The relevance between the information disclosure sub-factors and financing early warning value.

Model (III): The relevance between the information disclosure and equity capacity expansion.

Model (IV): The relevance between the information disclosure index and the behavior of controlling shareholders, board, supervisory board, and manager governance.

Conclusions and suggestions

We conclude the above analyses concerning the information disclosure in China's capital market as follows, and some suggestions also are raised.

(1) The frequency of annual financial reports receiving non-standard audit with qualified opinions is high among the China listed companies during these three years. While most companies have changed their account policy, as well as account estimation, the companies are still asked by investors to document explicit interpretations, announcing to the investors the potential influences on decisions, thus protecting their interests. We also notice the adverse influence on the reliance of the information disclosure due to the change of accounting firms and additional services provided by accounting firms, which would lead to the damage of audit continuity and its reliability, respectively. Consequently the separation of assurance and consultation services needs to be considered further; at the same time it is significant to reinforce the supervision on the accounting market and encourage the accounting firms not to demur and to appeal to court.

(2) Basically the information disclosure issue is generally timeliness in China, but still more preparations should be done previous to and during audit work. On the other hand, the timeliness of irregular reports needs improvement. Big changes may happen unexpectedly, and the reports concerning these should also be published in a timely fashion. Both external and inner stimulus mechanisms would promote the voluntary disclosure, thus reducing the asymmetry of information between the management and external investors.

(3) The decisions made by both the shareholder meeting and the board have been disclosed by most of China's listed companies, however the bad performance still exists in the subject and big affairs information disclosure; the transparency of some sensitive problems such as financial trust deserves great notice.

(4) From the big sample we can find that in the index of information truthfulness, information disclosure timeliness and

integrity, including the general index of information disclosure, only a few companies perform well, indicating that the majority of companies are in the low level. What's more, we can also find the imbalance of information disclosure among different companies. The analysis of industries' documents shows that the companies in the Public Facilities industry perform better than those in other industries; there is also small inter-industry discrepancy. However, companies in the Agriculture industry get the poorest performance, indicated by their lowest information disclosure index and their great discrepancy among the companies. All these analyses require more certain information disclosure definition and its quality characteristics, and the construction of internal enterprise control systems, especially the internal accounting control system and the outer regulatory enforcement, with the help of market mechanisms to realize information disclosure evaluation, will play important roles in information disclosure improvement.

The empirical studies indicate that the general index of information disclosure of the overall sample is approximately 60.00 (it is 54.88); more than half the sample get the index higher than 60.00 (assumed to be qualified), similar to the results derived from other research institutions, suggesting the validity and reasonability of our evaluation system.

(5) From the correlation between the information disclosure index and corporate governance structure, the relationship between the behaviors of the board and the information disclosure index is not significant, which is the same with the behaviors of the supervisory committee. On one hand these correlations indicate the low efficiency of corporate governance structure; on the other hand, the information disclosure quality may rely more on external regulation, suggesting higher degree of external regulation enforcement. We admit that the existing supply–demand contradictory information, and the supply–demand is not only determined by the contracts between the suppliers and users, but also mediated by external mechanisms.

(6) The behaviors of the shareholders (controlling shareholder) and the management influence information disclosure, especially the influence from the behaviors of the

management, thus the governance or stimulus of the management is the key factor to improve information disclosure. For the sake of information transparency and to protect the interests of the stakeholders, it is essential to notice the behaviors of the management; for example, a change of the accounting policy and the accountant. And under the rational hypotheses, the subjects of the information disclosure are based on the given assumptions and the behaviors of the information users to determine their behaviors to reach their maximal benefits, indicated by the qualifications of financing, the company's value improvement and the building of the company's image.

CHAPTER

The Appraisal and Index Research of Stakeholder Governance: Evidence from China's Listed Companies

Stakeholder governance has been one of the key components in the corporate governance research framework. The stakeholder governance should be included in an integral corporate governance evaluation system, which aims to demonstrate an objective and comprehensive corporate governance status. Based on the above reasoning, stakeholder governance should not be neglected by any company seeking better and sound performance.

The index of stakeholder governance

Introduction

In the early 1980s, from the angle of company strategic management and business ethics, stakeholders have been firstly and comprehensively explored by some economists and management scholars, represented by Freeman (Freeman and Redd, 1983). Blair (1995) argues that an organization holds social responsibility and exists to create wealth for the whole society, so the key points for corporate governance are based on the fact that the management should be liberated from the pressure of the shareholders and transfer more rights to other stakeholders. However, the dominant position of the stakeholder is also highlighted by the Hampel Report (1998), the OECD Principles of Corporate Governance launched in June 1999, and the U.S. Business Roundtable. For simplicity, the China Corporate Governance Principles, drawn by the CSRC and the SETC in 2002, outlined in detail the definition of stakeholders, the stakeholder position in the company, and the rights and obligations of stakeholders; thus the protection for stakeholders participating in corporate governance has been set up fundamentally, especially from an institutional base.

The components of stakeholder governance appraisal

Though the significant position of stakeholders has been hotly supported, a corporate governance appraisal system all around the world, taking stakeholder governance into consideration, still cannot be found. The noted Standard & Poor's Corporate Governance Appraisal System (1998) only refers to "financial stakeholder," mainly concerning the shareholders, thus no other stakeholders are included. However the other stakeholders have been somewhat noticed in the Lyonnais Securities appraisal system, which focuses on the transparency, the restrictions of the management, the independence and accountability of the board, and the protection for the small and medium shareholders. But in Deminor and China Haitong Securities corporate appraisal systems, stakeholder governance appraisal hasn't been found.

We list the general components of stakeholder governance in Table 8.1, and for more details we conduct regression analyses for these indices.

Employee participation

It is common knowledge that the employees are the key stakeholders, in particular as part of knowledge and economic development which is guided by the human resources. On the one hand an effective channel for employees to participate in daily management and key decision-making would enhance the transparency of the company, and eventually rational decisions would be made; on the other hand, the employee could be stimulated and thus enhance the satisfaction degree and loyalty through efficient mechanisms. Consequently the following indicators are considered to investigate the employee participation degree:

- The employee–supervisor ratio, employed to investigate the employee participation in supervisor committee thus exploring their participation degree in corporate governance.
- The employee shareholding ratio, known as employee stock ownership plan, which is the capital and property rights on which the employees' participation in corporate governance is grounded, also taken as an important means to stimulate the employee in the form of property.

The indexes of realizing corporate social responsibility

Nature and the social environment have been demonstrating growing importance in corporate development, thus the corporate world should endeavor to take more care of the surroundings and social interests, thus a harmonious, coordinated and sustainable social-corporate relationship can be formed. Mainly we employ two indicators to investigate the corporate social responsible realization status.

Table 8.1:   The stakeholder governance appraisal system

Destinations	The indicators	The sub-factors	Instructions
The appraisal indicators of stakeholder governance	1. Employee participation ($CCCGI^{NK}_{61}$)	1. The ratio of employees in the supervisory committee	Investigate the employee participation in corporate governance
		2. The shareholding ratio of the employees	The employee shareholding ratio, known as employee stock ownership plan, which is the capital and property rights on which the employees' participation in corporate governance is grounded, also taken as an important means to stimulate the employee in the form of property
	2. Social responsibility realization ($CCCGI^{NK}_{62}$)	1. The commonwealth donation	Non-business expenditure of donation, which is used to investigate the contribution the companies make for the society or the community
		2. The environment protection measures	The measures of protecting the environment, which is used to investigate the environment protection status of the company
	3. The investor relationship management ($CCCGI^{NK}_{63}$)	1. The net station of the company and its renovation	The construction and updating of the company's network station, which is used to investigate the information disclosure and communication channels
		2. Whether investor relationship management measures have been set up	The investor relationship management system, used to investigate whether the company has set up a sound investor relationship management system. In our expectation, the special IRM system would undoubtedly pave the way for sustainable and continuous development
	4. The relation with the regulatory authorities ($CCCGI^{NK}_{64}$)	1. The output and income of the penalty	We take the penalty expenditure as the proxy for investigating the coordination degree to which different subjects act in the regulatory system
	5. The arbitrage and law suits of the companies ($CCCGI^{NK}_{65}$)	1. The existence of arbitrage and law suits of the companies	The law suits or the arbitrage the company is involved in will demonstrate the coordination and harmony degree between the shareholders, the suppliers, the clients, the consumers, the debtors, the employees, the communities, the governments and the company

(1) Non-business expenditure of donation, which is used to investigate the contribution the companies make for the society or the community.

(2) The measures of protecting the environment, which is used to investigate the environment protection status of the company.

The investor relationship management

There is a great amount of writing and scholarly publishing attaching much importance to the relationship between the company and its investors. In China, the *Administrative Guidelines on Management of Investor Relations of Companies Listed on Shenzhen Stock Exchange* has been published by Shenzhen Stock Exchange in October 2003, which details the relationship management. For simplicity we define that the investor relationship management (IRM), through effective information disclosure and sound communication, aims to establish a healthy investor relationship and advocate rational investment, thus enhancing the reputation among the investors to realize the value maximization of the company. However, in China creating IRM is still underway, and we take the following proxies to investigate the IRM status:

1. The construction and updating of the company's website, which is used to investigate the information disclosure and communication channels.
2. The investor relationship management system, used to investigate whether the company has set up a sound investor relationship management system. In our expectation, the special IRM system would undoubtedly pave the way for sustainable and continuous development.

The relationship between the regulatory authorities and the companies

There is sufficient evidence documenting the relationship between the regulatory authorities and the companies. We take the penalty expenditure as the proxy for investigating the coordination degree to which different subjects act in the regulatory system.

The arbitrage and law suits of the company

This indicator can be employed to represent the coordination and harmony degree between the company and all its stakeholders. The law suits and the arbitrage the company is involved in will demonstrate the coordination and harmony degree between the shareholders, the suppliers, the clients, the consumers, the debtors, the employees, the communities, the governments and the company.

Based on the predominant position and the outstanding functions of the stakeholder governance in the corporate governance system, and the characteristics of China's listed companies, all the above factors we set focus on the stakeholder rights protection and their participation in corporate governance. Actually, the higher degree of stakeholder participation would lead to higher protection of stakeholder rights, and higher probability that sound decisions will be made.

With the help of expert graders and an analytic hierarchy process the main factors and their sub-factors were weighted. For the suggestions raised by the fellow experts we fixed the main factors for the stakeholder governance appraisal, namely the employee participation ($CCGI^{NK}_{61}$), the corporate social responsibility ($CCGI^{NK}_{62}$), the investor relationship management ($CCGI^{NK}_{63}$), the relationship with the regulatory authorities ($CCGI^{NK}_{64}$) and the arbitrage and law suits of the company ($CCGI^{NK}_{65}$), and then we confirm the corresponding sub-factors which will be scored after that. Finally the consistency check and evaluation matrix will be introduced to generate the factor weight (represented by w_i). The corresponding calculations, as well as some necessary tests, are as follows:

$$CCGI^{NK}_{6} = W_1{}^*CCGI^{NK}_{61} + W_2{}^*CCGI^{NK}_{62} + W_3{}^*CCGI^{NK}_{63} + W_4{}^*CCGI^{NK}_{64} + W_5{}^*CCGI^{NK}_{65}$$

Data and statistical descriptions

All the data is collected from the database of the Corporate Governance Research Center of Nankai University; the sample consists of data from the listed companies of China's stock market in 2002.

The statistical description of the stakeholder governance in China

In general, the index of stakeholder governance in China is subject to normal distribution, however including some peak values, indicating the lopsided distribution of the index of stakeholder governance and different development levels of stakeholder governance mechanisms among the companies. Specifically, the mean of the stakeholder governance index is 57.05, with the maximum value 82.82 and minimum value 20.49, which provides evidence that weak stakeholder governance mechanisms exist in most of the companies whose index value is low, as well as a large discrepancy of the stakeholder governance mechanisms among them. From the statistical descriptions we can find the index value of 24.27% of companies from the overall sample are below 50.00, and only 9.56% of companies whose index value is above 80.00. Consequently we can conclude that there is still a lot of work to do in order to improve the stakeholder governance among most of China's listed companies, and the balance of development of different companies should also be noticed.

In particular, the mean value of the corporate social responsibility index ($CCGI^{NK}_{62}$) is 53.72, similar to the employee participation index ($CCGI^{NK}_{61}$), both of which are in the middle rank of the indexes. Obviously we can conclude that most of China's listed companies haven't attached too much importance to their social responsibility. Meanwhile the standard deviation of the corporate social responsibility index ($CCGI^{NK}_{62}$) is only slightly larger than that of employee participation, indicating a small deviation among the data.

The mean index of the relationship with the regulatory authorities ($CCGI^{NK}_{64}$) is 66.23, from which we can see no perfect coordination and harmony relationship status between the companies and the regulatory authorities, whose standard deviation reaches 34.03, also suggesting a great deviation among different companies.

The mean of the arbitrage and law suits of the company index ($CCGI^{NK}_{65}$) is 76.28, which serves as the top among the five main indexes; however there is still room left to improve the coordination and harmony degree between the shareholders, the suppliers, the clients, the consumers, the debtors, the employees, the community, the governments and the company. Moreover, the large deviation of the indexes among the companies can be verified by the standard deviation of 37.20, suggesting large different levels of $CCGI^{NK}_{65}$.

Finally, the last factor—that is, employee participation index, whose mean value is 53.92—plays a common role among the five factors, but its standard deviation is the smallest among them, indicating a similar level of this factor among the companies.

Based on the above analyzing, for the sub-index $CCGI^{NK}_{61}$, 30.08% of the sample gets a score below 40.00, and only 3.76% of the sample in this aspect gets a score more than 80.00, suggesting that most companies in China should endeavor to improve $CCGI^{NK}_{61}$. And 30.08% of the sample for another sub-index—$CCGI^{NK}_{64}$, which is used to investigate the relationship between the regulatory authorities and the companies—are also below 40.00; however, we also find that the sample whose $CCGI^{NK}_{64}$ is higher than 70.00 reaches 40.28%, showing that there may be a great discrepancy in this aspect for the companies in China.

Moreover, in the sub-index $CCGI^{NK}_{62}$ 50.08% of the sample is under 50.00, with 18.36% of the sample higher than 70.00. There are 142 listed companies whose $CCGI^{NK}_{62}$ is more than 80.00, above all indicating that the social responsibility hasn't been highlighted by the listed companies in China.

What is more important, the mean of $CCGI^{NK}_{63}$, which indicates the investor relationship management, only scores 41.48, performs the worst among the five sub-indices, and there is also 35.12% of the sample whose $CCGI^{NK}_{63}$ is below 40%. Only 0.43% of the sample is higher than 80.00. The above analyses indicate that the corporate investor relationship hasn't been attached importance to by China's listed companies, especially for the dominant small and medium investors and other stakeholders who are essential for the development of the companies. Accordingly the IRM system is essential for most of China's listed companies to set up, so the small and medium investors, as well as other stakeholders, can effectively participate in corporate governance to protect their own interests.

Lastly, 22.56% of the sample in the sub-index of $CCGI^{NK}_{65}$ gets a score less than 40.00, and 66.92% of the sample reaches the score of 80.00, which is similar to $CCGI^{NK}_{64}$, indicating the different levels of development of $CCGI^{NK}_{65}$ among the companies.

The stakeholder governance index analysis based on the nature of the first big shareholder

On average, the stakeholder governance index of the listed companies whose first big shareholders belong to non-bank financial institutions, SOEs, and the collective enterprises perform better than others; their averages rank as 59.45, 57.85 and 57.11, respectively. However, the companies whose first big shareholders are university or state-owned asset management corporations (AMC) and the companies controlled by the government perform worse in stakeholder governance mechanism, and their averages are 53.50, 54.91 and 54.50 respectively, significantly lower than the average of the whole sample. And at the same time, the standard deviations of the stakeholder governance index of the listed companies whose first big shareholders belong to non-bank financial institutions, SOEs, and the collective enterprises are significantly higher than that of the other companies. All the analyses suggest an imbalance in the development of the stakeholder governance among the listed companies in China.

The percentages of stakeholder governance index below 40.00 of the companies whose first big shareholders are universities, state-owned asset management corporations, private companies and foreign investment companies are 18.18%, 11.86%, 11.32% and 11.11% respectively. The high percentage indicates unhealthy development of the stakeholder governance for the companies listed above, thus more attention needs to be paid. On the contrary, there is no company whose first big shareholder is a non-bank financial institution that scores lower than 40.00. And only 2.50% of companies whose first big shareholders are collective enterprises score lower than 40.00. However, in another aspect, only three companies (that is, 0.57%) whose first big shareholders are state-owned companies and two companies (that is, 2.86%) whose first big shareholders are state-owned AMCs score more than 80.00. And in particular, all the companies whose first big shareholders are non-bank financial institutions and foreign companies scores less than 70.00, indicating their low level of stakeholder governance. There is a high ratio of the companies whose first big shareholders are state-owned enterprises or state-owned asset management corporations getting the index between 60.00 and 70.00; that is, 10.29% and 11.86%, respectively.

The empirical research of stakeholder governance index

Stakeholder governance and other governance mechanisms

Table 8.2 shows some conventional statistics of the stakeholder governance, and its score is 57.05. From the angle of the means, the stakeholder governance index is generally higher than the shareholder meeting and controlling shareholder behaviors index, the board governance index, as well as the management and supervisors' committee governance index, but slightly less than the information disclosure governance index. We propose that the stakeholder governance index is somewhat related to the indicators we choose and score standards we provide. And we should also take the limited information disclosed in the annual financial reports of the companies and the possible earnings management behaviors into consideration, because our appraisal is mainly based on the public information of the annual financial reports. It should be noted the mean of the investor management index—as an instrumental part of stakeholder governance—is significantly lower than that of stakeholder governance, which indicates that the investor management index should be paid special attention to by China's listed companies. Table 8.2 also demonstrates that the standard deviation of the stakeholder governance index, 10.60, is significantly higher than that of the corporate governance index, which explains the discrepancy and imbalance in development of the stakeholder governance.

Table 8.2: The comparison between the stakeholder governance and the other corporate governance mechanisms

Indices	N	Range	Minimum	Maximum	Mean	Standard deviation
Stakeholder governance index	931	62.33	20.49	82.82	57.047505	10.5978460
Shareholder meeting and controlling shareholder behavior governance index	931	72.93	10.40	83.33	53.7035	10.99475
The board governance index	931	72.95	1.56	74.51	43.4152	10.3755938
The management governance index	931	52.52	19.03	71.56	48.6420	7.59403
The supervisors' committee governance index	931	65.76	11.98	77.74	47.4450	11.2482825
The information disclosure index	931	92.97	4.72	97.69	58.437744	18.08333
The corporate governance index	931	35.97	30.79	66.76	49.649965	5.26162

Source: Database of Corporate Governance Research Center of Nankai University.

The empirical study of stakeholder governance

Hypothesis, model and variables

To explore the influence of stakeholder governance mechanisms on corporate performance and its value, we raise corresponding models to capture the stakeholder governance mechanism effect. Firstly, based on the corresponding literature reviews and the corporate governance practices we propose six hypotheses as follows:

- *Hypothesis 1:* Ceteris paribus, the employee participation appraisal degree ($CCGI^{NK}_{61}$) is positively related to the corporate performance and its value.
- *Hypothesis 2:* Ceteris paribus, the degree of corporate responsibility realization ($CCGI^{NK}_{62}$) is positively related to corporate performance and its value.

- **Hypothesis 3:** Ceteris paribus, the degree of corporate investor relationship management ($CCGI^{NK}_{63}$) is positively related to corporate performance and its value.
- **Hypothesis 4:** Ceteris paribus, the degree of relationship management with the regulatory authorities ($CCGI^{NK}_{64}$) is positively related to corporate performance and its value.
- **Hypothesis 5:** Ceteris paribus, the level of corporate arbitrage and law suits appraisal ($CCGI^{NK}_{65}$) is positively related to corporate performance and its value.
- **Hypothesis 6:** Ceteris paribus, the index of stakeholder governance ($CCGI^{NK}_{6}$) is positively related to corporate performance and its value.

Conventionally, we utilize the earnings per share (EPS), return on equity (ROE), NAPS, financial early warning Z value and Tobin's Q value as proxies for corporate performance and its value, and develop regression models taking the degree of employee participation appraisal ($CCGI^{NK}_{61}$), the corporate responsibility realization ($CCGI^{NK}_{62}$), the degree of corporate investor relationship management ($CCGI^{NK}_{63}$), the level of corporate arbitrage and law suit appraisal ($CCGI^{NK}_{65}$), the degree of relation management with the regulatory authorities ($CCGI^{NK}_{64}$) and the index of stakeholder governance ($CCGI^{NK}_{6}$) as independent variables[1], and we also control the influences from other corporate governance mechanisms and financial leverage, the time of going public and the companies' scale through taking the shareholder meeting and controlling shareholder behavior index ($CCGI^{NK}_{1}$), the board governance index ($CCGI^{NK}_{2}$), the supervisory committee governance index ($CCGI^{NK}_{3}$), the management governance index ($CCGI^{NK}_{4}$), information disclosure index ($CCGI^{NK}_{5}$), the financial leverage (DTA), the time of going public (YEAR), and company scale (LNTA) as control variables (Table 8.3). The models are listed as follows:

---

[1] Considering the influence on models from the multicollinearity problem, we bring the independent variables into the model respectively; after that, all the VIF of the variables are below 1.20 with the exception of industry dummy ones—the interpretability of the models rises.

$$\text{Dep} = B_0 + B_1 CCGI^{NK}_{61} + B_2 CCGI^{NK}_{62} + B_3 CCGI^{NK}_{63} + B_4 CCGI^{NK}_{64}$$
$$+ B_5 CCGI^{NK}_{65} + B_6 CCGI^{NK}_{1} + B_7 CCGI^{NK}_{2} + B_8 CCGI^{NK}_{3}$$
$$+ B_9 CCGI^{NK}_{4} + B_{10} CCGI^{NK}_{5} + B_{11} DTA + B_{12} YEAR + B_{14} LNTA$$

$$\text{Dep} = B_0 + B_6 CCGI^{NK}_{6} + B_7 CCGI^{NK}_{1} + B_8 CCGI^{NK}_{2} + B_9 CCGI^{NK}_{3} +$$
$$B_{10} CCGI^{NK}_{4} + B_{11} CCGI^{NK}_{5} + B_{12} DTA + B_{13} YEAR + B_{14} LNTA$$

Table 8.3: Variable schedule

Types		Name	Code	Definitions
Indispensable variables	Experiment variables	Employee participation	$CCGI^{NK}_{61}$	The appraisal of employee participation
		Corporate social responsibility realization	$CCGI^{NK}_{62}$	The appraisal of corporate social responsibility realization
		Investor relationship management	$CCGI^{NK}_{63}$	The appraisal of investor relationship management
		The relationship with the regulatory authorities	$CCGI^{NK}_{64}$	The appraisal of the relationship with the regulatory authorities
		The arbitrage and law suits of the company	$CCGI^{NK}_{65}$	The appraisal of the arbitrage and law suits of the company
		Stakeholder governance	$CCGI^{NK}_{6}$	The index of stakeholder governance
	Control variables	Shareholder meeting and controlling shareholder	$CCGI^{NK}_{1}$	The index of shareholder meeting and controlling shareholder
		Board	$CCGI^{NK}_{2}$	The index of board governance
		Supervisory committee	$CCGI^{NK}_{3}$	The index of supervisory committee governance
		Management	$CCGI^{NK}_{4}$	The index of management governance
		Information disclosure	$CCGI^{NK}_{5}$	The index of information disclosure
		Financial leverage	DTA	Financial leverage, 2002
		Time of going public	YEAR	The interval to 31 December 2002 accounted as the number of months
		Company scale	LNTA	The log total assets in 2002
Dependent variables		Earning per share	EPS	The earning per share in 2002
		Return on equity	ROE	The net return ratio on equity in 2002
		Assets per share	NAPS	The net asset per share in 2002
		The early warning Z value	Z	The earning warning financial value
		Tobin's Q value	QV	The Tobin's Q value in 2002

Source: Database of Corporate Governance Research Center of Nankai University.

Empirical analyses of regression models

Table 8.4 provides the results of the regression models; with the exception of Tobin's Q value, other models are all significant at the level of 5%. We also notice the low explanatory power of the models whose dependent variables are return on equity (ROE) and financial early warning Z value—their R square and adjusted R square are both below 0.05.

At the significance level of 10%, the robust tests of regression model whose dependent variable is earning per share (EPS) supports hypothesis 5 and hypothesis 6. Based on this, all others being equal, the higher the index of the arbitrage and law suit of the company the higher earnings per share will be. We cannot find significant effects on earnings per share from employee participation appraisal degree ($CCGI^{NK}_{61}$), the degree of corporate responsibility realization ($CCGI^{NK}_{62}$), the degree of corporate investor relationship management ($CCGI^{NK}_{63}$), and the degree of relationship management with the regulatory authorities ($CCGI^{NK}_{64}$). The regressions from the control variables demonstrate that a positive relationship exists between the management governance index and EPS, with worse EPS performance for the companies who have higher financial leverage and smaller company scale.

At the significance level of 10%, the models which take ROE as dependent variable are supportive of hypothesis 2, 5 and 6. So we can conclude that, all other things being equal, the realization of corporate social responsibility, the law suits and arbitrage of the company and stakeholder governance index are positively related to ROE. However the relationships between the employee participation, the investor relationship management, the relationship with the regulatory authorities and the ROE of the companies are not significant. And as shown in Table 8.4, the regressions on the control variables indicate a positive relationship between the company scale and ROE.

The regression which takes NAPS as dependent variable supports hypothesis 5 and 6 at the significance level of 10%, indicating that all other things being equal, the higher the appraisal of the law suits and arbitrage of the companies, as well as the higher the stakeholder governance index, the higher NAPS will be. However we cannot find statistical significance between the employee participation, the corporate social realization, the investor relationship management and the relationship with the regulatory authorities and the NAPS. And the regressions on control variables document that a positive relationship exists between the management governance index, the company scale and the NAPS, however a negative significant relationship exists between the NAPS and the shareholder meeting and controlling shareholder behaviors governance index, the supervisors' committee governance index, the financial leverage and the time of going public.

At the significance level of 10%, the model whose dependent variable is financial early warning value Z supports hypothesis 5, suggesting that, all other things being equal, the higher appraisal of the law suits and arbitrage of the company will lead to better financial performance—that is, higher financial early warning value—but the influences on the financial performance from the employee participation, the corporate social responsibility realization, the investor relationship management, the relationship with the supervisory authorities and the stakeholder governance index are still negligible. And the regression on corresponding control variables indicates the negative relationship between management governance index, financial leverage, the company scale and the financial early warning value, but positive relationship between the financial performance and the time of going public.

At the significance level of 10%, the regression taking Tobin's Q as dependent variable is not supportive of any hypotheses, thus we can infer that the stakeholder governance index, including its five main factors, has no influence on Tobin's Q, which is conventionally used to measure the market value of the companies. And these are almost similar to the control variables; only the information disclosure governance index is positively related to Tobin's Q.

The relationships between the stakeholder governance index and other governance mechanisms and the corporate governance index are shown in Table 8.5. Under the significance level of 5%, we cannot find any significant relationships with the stakeholder governance mechanism, including its five main factors, namely employee participation ($CCGI^{NK}_{61}$), the realization of corporate social responsibility ($CCGI^{NK}_{62}$), the investor relationship management ($CCGI^{NK}_{63}$), the relationship with the regulatory authorities ($CCGI^{NK}_{64}$), the law suit and arbitrage of the company ($CCGI^{NK}_{65}$), the shareholder meeting and controlling shareholder governance mechanism ($CCGI^{NK}_{1}$), the board governance mechanism ($CCGI^{NK}_{2}$), the information disclosure governance mechanism ($CCGI^{NK}_{5}$) and the corporate governance index. However, both the employee participation ($CCGI^{NK}_{61}$) and company investor relationship management ($CCGI^{NK}_{63}$) are positively related with the management governance index under the significance level of 1%, thus concluding the stakeholder governance index is also positively related with management governance index at the significance level of 5%, which suggests that the mutual promotion effect exists between them. Under the circumstance of higher employee participation and better investor relationship management, the internal employees and the investors would effectively promote and supervise the management to perform efficient governance mechanisms, thus improving governance levels to achieve better performance. Under the consummate management governance mechanisms and higher corporate governance level, the employees, as well as the investors, may better participate in corporate governance under a sound and efficient framework; consequently the investor management institutions and other corresponding measures would be more properly put to the test, improving the stakeholder governance level of the listed companies.

The employee participation degree ($CCGI^{NK}_{61}$) is negatively related to the supervisory committee governance index at the 1% significance level, which leads to a significantly negative relationship between the stakeholder governance index and supervisory committee governance index at the 1% significance level. The interpretation may be the inefficiency of the employee participation; on the one hand, for compliance with the company law at least one employee from the basic units of the companies is appointed as a member of the supervisory committee, who may face awkward situations among different stakeholders,

Table 8.4: Results of regression models

Models	EPS		ROE		NAPS		Z		QV	
	Model I	Model II	Model I	Model II	Model I	Model II	Model I	Model II	Model I	Model II
C	-2.438 (0.000)	-2.386 (0.000)	-192.706 (0.007)	-192.628 (0.006)	-7.673 (0.000)	-7.594 (0.000)	15.554 (0.000)	15.286 (0.000)	1.076 (0.548)	1.384 (0.421)
$CCGI^{NK}_{61}$	0.002 (0.127)		0.169 (0.380)		0.003 (0.215)		-0.001 (0.888)		7.70E-005 (0.987)	
$CCGI^{NK}_{62}$	-0.001 (0.504)		0.451 (0.015)		0.001 (0.701)		-1.06E-005 (0.999)		-0.001 (0.794)	
$CCGI^{NK}_{63}$	0.000 (0.761)		0.079 (0.620)		0.000 (0.829)		-0.001 (0.817)		-0.004 (0.270)	
$CCGI^{NK}_{64}$	2.61E-005 (0.955)		0.016 (0.858)		0.000 (0.801)		-0.002 (0.642)		0.000 (0.860)	
$CCGI^{NK}_{65}$	0.001 (0.017)		0.234 (0.004)		0.004 (0.002)		0.006 (0.053)		0.000 (0.811)	
$CCGI^{NK}_{6}$		0.003 (0.038)		0.820 (0.004)		0.011 (0.007)		0.010 (0.380)		-0.004 (0.599)
$CCGI^{NK}_{1}$	5.56E-005 (0.967)	0.000 (0.897)	0.076 (0.766)	0.035 (0.892)	-0.007 (0.069)	-0.007 (0.068)	-0.003 (0.774)	-0.004 (0.731)	0.001 (0.906)	0.001 (0.818)
$CCGI^{NK}_{2}$	0.002 (0.232)	0.002 (0.243)	-0.089 (0.743)	-0.096 (0.722)	0.005 (0.157)	0.005 (0.168)	0.006 (0.556)	0.006 (0.592)	0.008 (0.260)	0.008 (0.255)

Table 8.4: Results of regression models *(cont'd)*

Models	EPS		ROE		NAPS		Z		QV	
	Model I	Model II	Model I	Model II	Model I	Model II	Model I	Model II	Model I	Model II
$CCGI^{NK}_3$	0.002 (0.266)	0.002 (0.213)	0.332 (0.372)	0.364 (0.324)	0.015 (0.004)	0.016 (0.003)	-0.031 (0.042)	-0.030 (0.041)	0.000 (0.968)	0.000 (0.966)
$CCGI^{NK}_4$	7.90E-005 (0.953)	0.000 (0.889)	0.128 (0.616)	0.117 (0.639)	-0.008 (0.024)	-0.008 (0.016)	0.010 (0.345)	0.011 (0.297)	-0.001 (0.925)	-0.001 (0.925)
$CCGI^{NK}_5$	0.000 (0.614)	0.000 (0.651)	0.094 (0.546)	0.079 (0.614)	0.002 (0.356)	0.002 (0.389)	0.008 (0.232)	0.007 (0.254)	-0.007 (0.070)	-0.007 (0.080)
DTA	-0.443 (0.000)	-0.445 (0.000)	-4.401 (0.375)	-4.503 (0.362)	-0.994 (0.000)	-1.002 (0.000)	-6.417 (0.000)	-6.445 (0.000)	-0.030 (0.824)	-0.037 (0.781)
YEAR	-0.001 (0.325)	-0.001 (0.185)	-0.012 (0.903)	-0.041 (0.662)	-0.011 (0.000)	-0.011 (0.000)	0.007 (0.089)	0.006 (0.143)	0.003 (0.203)	0.003 (0.181)
LNTA	0.116 (0.000)	0.112 (0.000)	5.165 (0.091)	5.808 (0.052)	0.513 (0.000)	0.508 (0.000)	-0.480 (0.000)	-0.476 (0.000)	0.022 (0.768)	0.005 (0.950)
R^2	0.341	0.338	0.032	0.024	0.420	0.418	0.550	0.548	0.012	0.011
Adjusted R^2	0.331	0.331	0.018	0.012	0.412	0.412	0.550	0.543	-0.005	-0.001
F-stat	36.449 (0.000)	52.162 (0.000)	2.317 (0.005)	2.494 (0.008)	51.113 (0.000)	73.369 (0.000)	86.041 (0.000)	124.026 (0.000)	0.722 (0.742)	0.914 (0.513)
N	931	931	931	931	931	931	931	931	773	773

Source: Database of Corporate Governance Research Center of Nankai University.
Note: Probability in parentheses.

Table 8.5:   The correlation between stakeholder governance mechanism and other governance mechanisms and the corporate governance index

		$CCGI^{NK}_{61}$	$CCGI^{NK}_{62}$	$CCGI^{NK}_{63}$	$CCGI^{NK}_{64}$	$CCGI^{NK}_{65}$	$CCGI^{NK}_{6}$
Shareholder meeting and controlling shareholder	Pearson correlation	0.058	−0.051	−0.055	0.056	−0.001	0.011
	Sig. (2-tailed)	0.077	0.119	0.095	0.087	0.968	0.732
	N	931	931	931	931	931	931
Board	Pearson correlation	0.007	0.004	−0.028	0.013	−0.059	−0.036
	Sig. (2-tailed)	0.821	0.903	0.401	0.701	0.072	0.268
	N	931	931	931	931	931	931
Management	Pearson correlation	0.095**	0.020	0.103**	−0.062	0.054	0.078*
	Sig. (2-tailed)	0.004	0.541	0.002	0.059	0.102	0.018
	N	931	931	931	931	931	931
Supervisory committee	Pearson correlation	−0.225**	−0.021	−0.047	0.021	−0.015	−0.098**
	Sig. (2-tailed)	0.000	0.526	0.153	0.522	0.655	0.003
	N	931	931	931	931	931	931
Information disclosure	Pearson correlation	0.006	−0.016	−0.047	0.034	−0.009	−0.008
	Sig. (2-tailed)	0.860	0.628	0.150	0.300	0.795	0.800
	N	931	931	931	931	931	931
Corporate governance index	Pearson correlation	−0.035	−0.034	−0.060	0.045	−0.030	−0.040
	Sig. (2-tailed)	0.280	0.302	0.069	0.174	0.368	0.224
	N	931	931	931	931	931	931

Source: Database of Corporate Governance Research Center of Nankai University.
(*, ** denote significance level of 0.05, 0.01, respectively (2-tailed T tests))

as well as weak self-governance ability, and the usual result is that the higher the percentage of employee supervisors in the supervisory committee, the more possibility the supervisory committee mechanism will not work. On the other aspect, though the internal employees may be good for the corporate governance, their functions may be mitigated by their relatively small shareholding. Both of these findings may well explain the negative relationship between the employee participation index ($CCGI^{NK}_{61}$) and the supervisory committee governance management index.

Conclusions and implications

Stakeholder governance has been an indispensable part of modern corporate governance. The appraisal of stakeholder governance will pave the way for us to explore the stakeholder governance status, as well as the protections of stakeholders. According to the predominant position of stakeholder governance in the corporate governance framework, we set the indicator system to measure the coordination and harmonization of stakeholder governance.

(1) The low stakeholder governance index, as well as its high discrepancy among the companies, indicates the weak stakeholder governance status in China. Only a few companies have sound stakeholder governance systems, and in particular the corporate investor relationship management should be enhanced.

(2) We found that the employee participation indexes are not significantly related to the company's performance and value. And similarly, the prime operating revenue ratio, the prime operating profit ratio, the profit ratio after taxes and Tobin's Q value are not significantly related to the stakeholder governance index, including its five main factors.

(3) A significantly positive relationship does exist between the stakeholder governance index and EPS, the ROE, as well as the NAPS. These findings indicate that better stakeholder governance mechanisms and higher stakeholder governance indexes would improve profitability, as well as indicators of

development such as NAPS. Consequently, as the scholarly literature has pointed out, the stakeholders should be stimulated to join in corporate governance effectively and appropriately, and their rights should be considered in the mechanism of corporate governance.

(4) The inefficacy of employee participation in corporate governance may be used to explain why it has a weak impact on the performance and value of the company. The nominal and inessential position of employees is not enough to demonstrate the effects of employee participation. However, the above analysis is not evidence of unimportance of employee participation, but leaves us room to enhance and consummate its effectiveness.

(5) The pronounced positive relationship between the corporate social responsibility realization and the performance of the company, shown in Table 8.4, gives us an instrumental clue to the realization of corporate responsibility; thus, in possession of good relationships and reputation, the harmonization and coordination with the environment would be propitious to the profits for the companies. Naturally the sustainable development atmosphere can be improved.

(6) Investor relationship management for the companies is critical, though a significant relationship cannot be found in the results of regression models. Through effective information disclosure and communication, and the promotion of investor relationship management, rational investment can be enhanced and thus the credit reputation can be set among the investors. In light of the early stage of development of investor relationship management in China's capital market, sound institutions and mechanisms should be established for further development of IRM.

(7) Obviously, the fewer arbitrages and law suits the companies are involved in, the higher the EPS, ROE, NAPS and financial early warning value will be. It is common knowledge that unfavorable arbitrages and law suits impair financial performance, thus hampering the potential development of a company.

(8) We conclude that for most of China's listed companies, all the corporate governance mechanisms, including the stakeholder governance mechanism, are in the stage of foundation,

consummation or gradual establishment; accordingly their influences are not powerful enough to significantly affect the performance of the companies and their value. It is a long journey to the establishment of corporate governance mechanisms, so the enhancement of corporate performance is also a long way away. However, it is common sense that we should improve the corporate governance mechanisms, including the stakeholder governance mechanism, to improve the general performance of China's listed companies.

CHAPTER

Research on Evaluation and Index of Private-oriented Listed Enterprise Governance

Private enterprises are the outcome of the Chinese economy development, reformation and opening up, and play an important role in the increase in the Chinese economy. With flexible operation mechanisms, private enterprises exert more impact on the Chinese economic development and economy structure and regulations. Based on the evaluation of listed company governance in the previous chapter, this chapter emphasizes particularly the evaluation of private listed enterprise governance status, analyzing the relationship between governance status and corporate performance and comparing the governance characteristics of private-oriented listed enterprises.

Literature review on governance of private enterprises

In view of there being scarce literature about evaluation of private listed enterprise governance, we mainly analyze general research literature about private enterprises. We research on private listed enterprise governance from trust mechanism, organization manner and other angles, mainly surrounding the family system characteristic of private enterprises. Seen from the angle of corporate governance, some scholars do research on private listed enterprise governance by the comparison of different ownership structures. With the relationship between human capital and currency capital, some scholars point out it should not be overemphasized that the single aspect of owners of human capital and currency capital, and beneficial guarantee of both sides be brought into corporate governance. There are some scholars who do the research on the problems of private technology enterprises and small–middling enterprises' governance. For instance, Bai Yu (1999) and others emphasize private enterprise governance mode which emphasizes particularly external governance, and put forward that it should carry out multiple aspects of supervision; Guo Yong (2000) emphasizes innovation of governance subject and suggests that private enterprise should adopt some employees and creditors into directorate and supervisors' committee; Li Weian (2001) summarized governance mode from the angle of corporate governance system and research on family governance mode.

Origin of private enterprise governance issues

At present, the theory is in agreement on the essential cause of private enterprise governance issues' origin. The extension on this issue is just the analysis formed by the theory about the origin of private enterprise governance issues.

Firstly, the ownership and operation right of private enterprise cannot realize the separation. After private enterprises reach a certain scale, the owner and the operator's knowledge and experience cannot meet the need of further corporate development as a result of increases of production variety and technology content, and so on, so the necessity of rights separation dramatically appears. However, those rights have to meet two postulates: one is corporate property clarity, the other is mobile professional management. At present, in our country these two postulates are not carried out completely. Firstly, the mechanism of private enterprises is not advanced and the property is unclear. The whole property of private enterprises is clear—that is, the ultimate ownership of enterprises is clear—however, the relationship of different components is unclear. It is mainly because Chinese private enterprises are at the primary development phase. According to relative source, even in Wenzhou, the most developed area, only 48% of private enterprises carry out sharing systems while a majority of private enterprises give priority to the individual system and partnership.

Lastly, the phenomena of private enterprises' family system and focus are quite serious. Chinese private enterprises are family-system firms at large, and the biggest deficiency of family system firms is with the focus on human governance instead of law governance. The most difficult problem the family system enterprises face is scientific decision-making. At the beginning of private enterprises' foundation, on the one hand, capital is limited; on the other hand, technology, management, information and other resources are seriously scarce. However, the family resource can make up the deficiency, and with the connection of consanguinity and kindred people, private enterprises have stronger unity. Meanwhile, traditional culture exerts profound impact on private enterprises' formation. A family system is not necessarily a bad criterion—it remains to be seen whether it blocks corporate long-term development. Speaking of some large private enterprises, to break out of the family system is imperative.

The governance mode of private enterprises

For governance mode of private enterprises, different scholars have different points of view. Some of them think the private enterprises of China should manage a standard enterprise system, therefore the corporate governance mode should also choose relevant shareholder-dominated governance mode consistent with this kind of corporate organization system. Some other scholars consider that the existence of China's private enterprise family system is reasonable, thus our private enterprises ought to act in the corporate governance mode of this family system.

The governance mode of enterprises includes the organization and system's arrangement in the relationship of stockholders' responsibilities, rights and benefits regulated by enterprises. It is the reasonable distribution of enterprises' rights of demand and control, which is also mechanized. The family governance mode is "a governance mode that the enterprises' main control rights is distributed in family members, while the ownership and operation rights of the enterprise are not separated and the enterprise and the family are synergetic."[1]

The main research contents of the family governance mode include the following aspects:

- *The equity structure and capital structure of enterprises:* The equity structure of enterprises consists of two levels of meanings: one is who shareholders of enterprises are; the other is how much the share quotient of each of the shareholders is. Capital structure is the structure of long-term capital sources and its proportional relationship. The equity structure and capital structure are principle contents of family governance mode. The equity structure affects the practice of enterprises' incentive mechanism, merger and acquisition (M&A) mechanism and supervision mechanism; while capital structure influences the question of spare demand and control rights between shareholders and creditors. It is worth mentioning that nowadays the tendency of family enterprises' development worldwide is to achieve the separation of ownership and operation rights; that is to say, the rights relationship of family members is embodied through enterprises' equity relationship.
- *The selection of management and the incentive and restriction mechanism of enterprises:* To implement the effective stimulation to management and making management's actions stay consistent with the targets of the enterprise is one of the objectives of every governance model, certainly including family governance. Although family enterprises do not engage superior managers, they engage secondary management. Therefore, incentive and restriction questions exist too. Effective incentive mechanisms include two aspects at least.

---

[1] Gan Dean, *Chinese family enterprises research*, China Society Science Press, 2002.

One is a psychological incentive mechanism, which is to increase managers' individual achievement and satisfaction by various incentive measures; for instance, more challenging working arrangement, promotion opportunities, and career development. The other is a substance incentive mechanism in order to improve employees' quality of life. One important method of that is a payment incentive mechanism, such as an increasing salary plan, additional benefits, and equity incentive plans.

- *The organization structure construction and function mechanism of enterprises:* The organization structure construction mentioned here mainly refers to questions about shareholders' meeting, enterprises' directorate, supervisors' committee, the setting of management structure, and so on. Function mechanism means the distribution of rights between shareholders' meeting, directorate and supervisors' committee, the decision procedure of enterprises, the rights restriction relationship between each department, and so on. In theory, the shareholders' meeting is the most superior rights structure in enterprises, whose responsibility is electing directors of enterprises' directorate and voting in representatives to build the supervisors' committee in order to supervise the directorate's work. However, in reality, since family members hold most of an enterprises' stocks in family enterprises, the directorates of family enterprises are mouthpieces of the family's interests. Because this kind of mechanism can easily damage the interests of small and medium shareholders, this is an important question of family governance to be settled in the future.
- *Cultivate and select entrepreneurs:* Entrepreneurs play a critical part in the free market economy society. They take charge of searching for potential profit in the market and taking action to transfer this chance to realistic profit; they take on the enterprises' managing risks. In many cases, the entrepreneurs' decisions are so determinative

that they lead eclipsed enterprises to prosperity again. For family enterprises, passing rights between different generations is a vulnerable operation. In order to ensure the successful procession of this rights passing, the principle task is to select and cultivate excellent future entrepreneurs to become the enterprises' key people.

In all, the exchange cost of internal enterprises is relatively low because of the combination of ownership and operation rights in family enterprises. Since there is no agency problem, the supervision cost is low too. In addition, enterprises' management serving as shareholders have the responsibility of two positions, so conflict problems which lie in normal enterprises do not exist, and managers will not depart from shareholders' beneficial target, which highly reduces risk and moral cost. Therefore, the family governance mode fits well with the lack of capital and technology situation at the beginning phase of Chinese private enterprises. It is a low-cost and highly beneficial model. Certainly, the family governance model also has many disadvantages, and it needs perfecting. Family governance has both supporters and detractors.

Research on governance evaluation and index of private enterprises

Corporate governance is the consolidation of mechanism adaptability and efficiency. Private enterprises possess natural synchronization with a market economy, and research on private listed corporate governance is quite valuable for Chinese corporate governance reformation. And the start of all work consists of the development of an evaluation of private-oriented listed enterprises and the summing-up of private-oriented listed enterprises' specific governance mechanisms.

Research sample

We make an analysis of private-oriented listed enterprises' governance status with the application of an evaluation and index of corporate governance offered by the task group, the

Corporate Governance Research Center of Nankai University. According to investigation of corporate governance status offered by the Corporate Governance Research Center of Nankai University, we select private-oriented listed enterprises to conduct special analysis. The investigated sample contained 1,307 Chinese listed companies; however, there were only 931 effective samples, selected according to information entirety and including no unwanted data, and 146 of which have private enterprises as largest shareholders.

In the private-oriented listed enterprises, industry distribution is asymmetric. The highest level is Manufacturing Industry, accounting for 70.7%, and the second highest is Service Industry, accounting for 12.3%, then Miscellaneous, 11.3%. The proportion of Agriculture and Public Utility is less. Industry proportion shows great differences when comparing with the industry distribution chart of the whole sample, which may be related to the manner of coming into the market of listed enterprises. Most of private enterprises (over 90%) adopt the way of buying a shell, however as most of the shells available in the market are poor performance manufacturing enterprises, characterized by the low direct buying cost and high hidden and indirect cost, some private enterprises plunge into trouble, as when KLH bought AC Steel Company.

Another significant difference consists in synthetically (multi-industry) listed companies. Private enterprises account for a higher proportion (in the entire sample, synthetic firms number 44, only accounting for 4.7%, while private enterprises amount to 12). We think the main reason is that it is very significant for private enterprises' diversified development. In addition, some private enterprises carry out a diversified strategy in order to disperse the risk of the industry. Regarding the state-owned companies, diversity takes place in the level of group.

Evaluation system and method of private-oriented listed enterprises governance

The Corporate Governance Research Center of Nankai University published the research of application and evaluation of China company governance—Chinese corporate governance evaluation indicators system. The main evaluation method of the book comes from this research. The setting of evaluation system of corporate governance of Chinese listed companies is based on the governance environment Chinese listed companies face, including dominant shareholders' behavior, directorates, supervisors' committee, top management, information disclosure, and stakeholders—emphasizing particularly corporate inside governance mechanism, information disclosure, shareholders' behavior, independence and supervisors' participation in corporate governance.

Analysis on governance evaluation of Chinese private-oriented listed enterprises

General analysis of evaluation of private enterprise governance

Based on the evaluation of the text above, we make an analysis of the whole governance of private-oriented listed enterprises. Mean value of the general index of private-oriented listed enterprises is 50.63, a little higher than that of the 931 samples. If we only make comparison between private-oriented listed enterprises and non-private-oriented listed enterprises, the difference itself is more significant. The whole level is located above CCGI^{NK}V, a grade higher than CCGI^{NK}VI of all of listed companies. The general index of samples presents a normal distribution tendency. The variation of different private-oriented listed enterprises' indexes is quite large, the maximum and minimum of which are 73.38 and 38.53 respectively. There are 64 companies beyond the level of CCGI^{NK}V accounting for 60.38%; there are 42 private enterprises at the level of CCGI^{NK}VI accounting for 39.62%. Comparing with the 931 effective samples (the maximum and minimum are 78.71 and 30.79 respectively, distributing among CCGI^{NK}III, CCGI^{NK}IV, CCGI^{NK}V, and CCGI^{NK}VI), the difference of private-oriented listed enterprises' governance status is a little smaller. It is worth taking note that in all of the effective samples, 46.51% of listed companies are at the level of CCGI^{NK}VI while the proportion of the private-oriented listed enterprises is 39.62%, the difference being quite significant.

As the majority of listed companies are state-owned listed companies, we make comparison between private-oriented listed enterprises and state-owned listed companies. The majority of private-oriented listed enterprises come from Household Electric Appliances, IT, Medicine and other highly competitive industries, which all belong to corporation control (at the aspect of equity concentration, the proportion of the top five shareholders' equity is less than that of state-owned listed companies; in other words, they do very well in the diversity of property rights) with the core function of operation experience, managing the enterprises' development and pullulating. The appearance of private-oriented listed enterprises solves the problem of property body personification and there are not problems of double agency as with state-owned listed companies (at first the state regulates the enterprise group and then top management; in other words, there is one agency above the shareholders). Many private enterprises have not separated the ownership and operation rights, with higher management stock position and more sufficient incentive on directorates and top management than state-owned listed companies, so their governance status is relatively better. Accordingly, as the proportion of state-owned listed companies which are deficient at the aspect of property rights structure and have not taken measures on equity incentive and possess characteristics of "insiders' control" and owners' absence is relatively higher, state-owned listed companies are disadvantaged comparing with private-oriented listed enterprises, which we think will not change in a short period.

In addition, it cannot be ignored that private-oriented listed enterprises have relative fewer burdens while state-owned listed companies want to take responsibility of enterprises' reformation, and most of them are peeled off when coming into market, so it will be inevitable that the result is prevalent related transactions (dominant shareholders can control the decision-making of directorates easily). Comparatively, private-oriented listed enterprises do better than state-owned listed companies in related transactions. In order to analyze the corporate governance status of different industries, we select the first 35 companies with a higher index.

Industry analysis of evaluation of private enterprises' governance

A number of the best enterprises are from Miscellaneous, Services, and Public Utility—these three kinds of private-oriented listed enterprises are higher than the whole level. As there are only two listed Public Utility companies, the worse governance status of them may be contingent and hence cannot mean much. However, the better governance status of Miscellaneous is a good trend and worthy of paying more attention to. Seen as a group, telecom and computers have the best performance, ranked at the first two. We think it is not a coincidence that private-oriented listed enterprises with diversity have good corporate governance, and the reasons are:

- Firstly, generally only when owning quite strong or superfluous capital, technology and market exploitation capability do private-oriented listed enterprises carry out diverse operations in order to make use of spare resources. Private-oriented listed enterprises with diverse operations have high-quality management from a range of backgrounds and can make full use of this, which means management experience from one industry is applied to a new industry.
- Secondly, diversity of operation can promote the governance level of top management, because it is beneficial to stimulate the passion of all of management. There will be conditions for managers' promotions as the number of subsidiary companies increases.
- Thirdly, under present circumstances, as industry upgrades more quickly and production lives are shortened, diverse operations face more uncertainty and it is more difficult to obtain market dominance, which demands industry experts consult widely (private-oriented listed enterprises engage independent directors with industry experience; for example, as UFIDA engage Yang Yuanqing of Lenovo as an independent director). Meanwhile, enterprises have to intensify decision-making, strengthen capability in the market and control market risk.

- Fourthly, parts of diversified companies pay more attention to strategy investments in new market opportunities, with private-oriented listed enterprises changing markets fast. According to the analysis of the relationship of capital operation and company governance, capital operation must be based on company governance. So, private-oriented listed enterprises keep dwelling on making company governance better in the course of capital operations. Besides, capital operation is good for diversity and socialization of property rights and company governance development for private-oriented listed enterprises.

Take a Chinese dot-com company for example; due to various limitations on the national stock by China's authorities, there are seldom dot-com companies going public directly in the domestic stock market, and those dot-com companies are also examined and approved strictly when going public overseas. In addition to the infant venture capital market, many private-oriented listed enterprises increase their revenue through merger and acquisition of small dot-com companies. Haihong share, which is ranked the fourth of corporate governance evaluation, is doing quite well through this. At the peak point of its business, Haihong holds Zhonggong Net and Lianzhong and is a participant in Meilinzhengguang.

There is an attractive point that the four private-oriented listed enterprises that have the best corporate governance are all in Real Estate, but both the commerce sub-industry and tourism sub-industry did not appear in the best governance group. This indicates that the private-oriented listed real estate enterprises take corporate governance more seriously, because the real estate industry is a capital-concentrated enterprise with higher capital risk.

For example, at the end of 2002, in order to reduce the misconduct of commercial banks on mortgage loans provided to the real estate enterprises, The People's Bank of China (PBC), the central bank of China, required commercial banks to deflate loans to real estate enterprises, and terminate loans to the real estate enterprises that do not have the necessary qualifications or have not enough self-possessed funds and capital. And the consequence was that many real estate enterprises faced the capital inferior problem. In 2003, the PBC added fuel to the flames by drawing a new regulation on mortgage loans, which gave real estate enterprises higher pressure on operation capital. Generally, 30% of a typical real estate enterprises' capital comes from the self-possessed fund, 30% comes from the trade credit, and 40% comes from bank loans. This kind of capital structure is very easily affected by the fluctuation of capital markets. In the case of state-owned real estate enterprises, they usually have more financial strength, and have more channels to get loan support, in addition to more opportunities to get higher quality land through participating in municipal construction.

Regarding private enterprises in real estate, the financing channel is not so smooth. The main ideal of guarding against capital risk is to develop a variety of financing channels, in which using capital markets by coming into the market is an important part. Most of the real estate private enterprises come into the market with a financing plan. In order to successfully achieve refinancing or actualize financing with low cost, optimizing corporate governance becomes a crucial problem that they have to think about carefully. At the same time, the furious competition in the real estate industry forces each private enterprise to enhance the incentive mechanism. The clearness of property rights of private enterprises can benefit in improving the governance level of management.

The multi-dimensions analyses of the private-oriented listed enterprises' corporate governance

From the aspects of controlling shareholder's behaviors, board governance, the supervisors' committee governance, management governance and information disclosure, we explore and conclude the corporate governance of the private-oriented listed enterprises as discussed below.

The appraisal of the controlling shareholder's behavior

The mean of the controlling shareholder's behavior index is 52.66, which is close to 53.70, the mean of the total sample. But a great discrepancy exists among the companies, with the lowest value 12.80 and the highest 73.61. For more details, the independence index, the small and medium shareholder protection index and the general meeting of shareholder index are 63.60, 13.83 and 66.52 respectively. With the exception of the independence of the companies, all other indexes we get for the private companies are higher than those of the state-owned companies. We also notice that the performance of the controlling shareholder's behaviors of the private-oriented listed enterprises is better than that of the state-owned companies, especially in the aspects of related trade and the general meetings of the shareholders.

Additionally, for the benefit of definitive industry structure, the independence of the private-oriented listed enterprises is at a high level (from the sample, there are plenty of companies which do not set up the group companies structure), and in state-owned companies, the "one dominant shareholder" phenomenon is prevalent. However, the controlling shareholder's behaviors index for the private companies is lower than that of foreign capital listed companies (that is, the first big shareholder is a foreign investment company, such as Hainan Aviation), indicating that controlling shareholder's behaviors of the private companies still needs to be improved, especially the standard of operation. In general, we believe that the controlling shareholder's behaviors are determined by the nature as well as the destination of the control shareholders; meanwhile the heterogeneity of the industry competition also leads to their different behaviors.

The appraisal of the board governance

The maximum value of the board governance index is 66.00, with a minimum value of 20.85 and a mean of 45.12, which gets closer to that of the total sample. As far as the private companies are concerned, there is still a long way to go for the improvement of board governance. The corporate governance structure of private companies basically comprises two meetings and four rights in appearance (that is, the board, supervisors' committee and management occupy the ultimate control rights, supervisory rights and business operation rights respectively.)

However, the board is actually controlled by the big shareholders. Because of concentrated ownership structures, the board cannot be independent, so the operation mechanism and the appraisal mechanism of management are in urgent need of attention, just as Wangbin (2000) argues that the governance road of the private companies will be from the family governance to board governance; that is, realizing the reasonable investment policies and decision policies, and promoting and supervising both the institution and organization construction, thus making all these processes programmed, transparent, and reasonable.

The appraisal of the supervisory committee governance

The maximum value of the supervisory committee governance index is 74.45, with a minimum value of 15.64 and a mean of 49.42, which is slightly higher than that of the total sample (48.64). In general, the performance of the supervisory committee governance for private-oriented listed enterprises is better than that of state-owned companies, as the executives and organizational structures almost remain the same after the privatization reforming for the latter. For state-oriented listed companies, the modern governance structure of the general shareholder meeting, the board and supervisory committee is operating in parallel with the old structures—the CPC Committee, the Worker's Congress and the Labor Union—and hence limits the supervisory committee's daily operating.

The appraisal of management governance

The maximum value of the management governance index is 68.29, with a minimum value of 22.84 and a mean of 50.04, which is higher than that of the total sample (47.44). We list the reasons that the management governance of the private-oriented listed enterprises is better than that of the total sample as follows: as mentioned above, compared with the state-owned companies, the stimulus for the management, as well as the restraint imposed on the management in the private companies, are much stronger. Furthermore, the big shareholders in the private companies attach much importance to the firm's development, and a majority of private companies actually implement executive stock ownership. However, for the sake of the capital's safety, the big shareholders of the private-oriented listed enterprises stress the constructions of internal control and risk early-warning systems.

The appraisal of information disclosure

The maximum value of the information disclosure index is 91.01, with a minimum value of 14.55 and a mean of 58.54, which is higher than that of the total sample (47.44). Generally speaking, we cannot be satisfied with the present status of information disclosure of the private companies. Some probable reasons may lie in: the family management and family governance may lead to the low level of socialization and transparency in private companies, and there is no obvious changes in these fields after they went public. As we all know, the non-family employees may find it hard to join in the operation control, and external supervision for private companies is still absent.

In particular, we find that in China, some company groups didn't go public but some of their subsidiary companies have gone public, thus the "integrated operation" may exist, and much critical information cannot be disclosed in a timely way. The "tunnelling" effect may be significant due to special relations between the parent and subsidiary companies, and consequently the interests of the external investors may be exploited.

References

1. Li Wei-an. *Corporate Governance*. Tianjin, Nankai University Press. 2001

2. Li Wei-an. *Researches on Contemporary Corporate Governance: Capital Structure, Corporate Governance and the Reform of State-Owned Enterprises*. Beijing, China Renmin University Press. 2003

3. Li Wei-an, Zhou Xiao-su and Wu Li-dong. *Frontiers of Corporate Governance Theory and Practice*. Beijing, China Financial & Economic Publishing House. 2003

4. Li Wei-an and Zhang Jun-xi. *Frontiers of Corporate Governance*. Beijing, China Financial & Economic Publishing House. 2003

5. Li Ya. *Corporate Governance of Private Enterprises*. Beijing, China Integrity Press. 2003

6. Ye Ying-hua, Li Cun-xiu and Ke Cheng-en. *Corporate Governance and Appraisal System*. Taipei, BusinessNews Publishing. 2002

7. FASB. *Conceptual Framework of Financial Accounting*. Beijing, China Financial & Economic Publishing House. 1992

8. Carlock, Randel S. and John L.Ward. *Strategic Planning: For the Family Business Parallel Planning to Unify the Family and Business*. China Citic Press. 2002

9. Salmon, Walter J., *Corporate Governance. Beijing*, China Renmin University Press. 2001

10. Chen Jia-gui and Huang Qun-hui. The Comparison and Improvement of Corporate Governance Structure for Different Ownership Enterprises. *China Industrial Economy*. Iss. 7, 2001

11. Chen Ling. Information Characteristic, Transaction Cost and Economic Plan *Economic Research Journal*. Iss. 7, 1998

12. Cheng Xin-sheng. Analysis on Several Modes of Monitoring and Controlling on the Corporate Accounting. *Accounting, Iss. 6, Research* 2002

13. Ge Jia-shu and Chen Shou-de. Study on Assessment of the Quality of Financial Reporting. *Accounting Research.* Iss. 11, 2001

14. Hu Xin-wen and Yan Guang-hua. A Review of Contemporary Corporate Theory and Private Enterprises Governance. *Finance and Trade Research.* Iss. 5, 2003

15. Li Wei-an and Li Jian-biao. Stock Ownership, Management by Board of Directors, and the Integrity of China's Listed Companies. *Management World.* Iss. 9, 2003

16. Li You-gen. Study on the Board Composition and Corporate Performance of Listed Companies. *China Industrial Economy.* Iss. 5, 2001

17. Liao Hong and Zhang Juan. Analysis on MBO Performance of Chinese Listed Companies. *Audit Research.* Iss.4, 2004

18. Ma Lian-fu. Study on Indices System of the Board Governance Assessment in the Corporate Governance. *Nankai Business Review.* Iss. 3, 2003

19. The Project Team of the Research Center of Corporate Governance of Nankai University. Corporate Governance Evaluation, Governance Index (CCGINK) and Performance: Evidence from Chinese Listed Companies. *Management World.* Iss. 2, 2004

20. The Project Team of the Research Center of Corporate Governance of Nankai University. A Study of Appraisal System of Corporate Governance for Chinese Listed Companies. *Nankai Business Review.* Iss. 3, 2003

21. Xie Yong-zhen. Study on Indexes System of the Independent Director Governance Assessment in the Corporate Governance. *Nankai Business Review.* Iss. 3, 2003

22. Pei Wu-wei. A Study of Appraisal System of Corporate Governance. *Securities Market Herald.* Iss. 9, 2001

23. Sun Yong-xiang. Scale of Board, Corporate Governance and Performance. *Business Economics.* Iss. 10, 2000

24. Shi Xi-min. Improving Corporate Governance and Innovating on Management Accounting. *Accounting Research*. Iss. 4, 2001

25. Su Qi-lin, Wan Jun-yi and Ou Xiao-ming. International Comparison of Familial Controlling and Family Business Governance. *Foreign Economies & Management*. Iss. 5, 2003

26. Tang Yue-jun. Insider Control and Moral Hazard in Transitional Economy. *Economic Review*. Iss. 6 2002

27. Tian Kun-ru and Tang Yue-jun. Study on Indices System of IPO Funds Management and Information Disclosure Assessment in the Corporate Governance. *Nankai Business Review*. Iss. 3, 2003

28. Wang Fu. The Development of Private Enterprises on the point of Corporate Governance Structure. *China Non-governmental Science Technology and Economy*. Iss. 1, 2001

29. Wang Hui. Stakeholders in the Corporate Governance Principle. *Nankai Business Review*. Iss. 1, 2001

30. Yu Li, Ma Li-bo and Sun Ya-feng. Three-circle Mode in the Family Business Governance Structure. *Economic Management*. Iss. 1 2003

31. Zhang Guo-ping and Xu Bi-lin. Study on Indexes System of Board of Directors Governance Assessment in the Corporate Governance. *Nankai Business Review*. Iss. 3, 2003

32. Zhang Wei-ying. The Adjustment of Global Microeconomic Mechanism and Chinese Choice. *International Economic Review*. Iss. 1, 1998

33. Welch, David. The Rest and the Worst Board. *BusinessWeek*. Iss. 11, 2002

34. Coffee, John C. Market Failure and the Economic Case for Mandatory Disclosure System. *Comparative Economic and Social Systems*. Iss. 1, 2002

36. AICPA. *Improving Business Reporting: A Customer Focus*. New York: AICPA, 1994

37. AICPA. *Quality of Accounting Principles-Guidance for Discussions with Audit Committees, Practice Alert.* New York: AICPA, 2000

38. Beatty, R. and J. Ritter. Investment Banking, Reputation and the Underpricing of Initial Public Offerings. *Journal of Financial Economics*, 1986, 15: 213–232

39. Blair, Margaret. *Ownership and Control: Rethinking Corporate Governance for the 21st Century.* Washington: The Brookings Institution, 1995. 36–192

40. Blue Ribbon Committee (BRC). *Report and Recommendations of the Blue Ribbon Committee on Improving the Effectiveness of Corporate Audit Committees.* New York: BRC, 1999

41. Boioth, J. and R. Smith. Capital Raising, Underwriting and the Certification Hypothesis. *Journal of Financial Economics*, 1986, 15: 261–281

42. Chemmanur, T. J. and P. Fulghieri. Investment Band Reputation, Information Production, and Financial Intermediation. *Journal of Finance*, 1994, 49: 57–79

43. Durnev, Art and E. Ham Kim. To Steal or Not to Steal: Firm Attributes, Legal Environment, and Valuation. Working Paper, University of Michigan Business School, 2002

44. Freeman, Redd. Stockholders and Stakehoders: A New Perspective on Corporate Governance. *California Management Review*, 1983, 25: 83–106.

45. Gale, I. and J. Stiglitz. The Informational Content of Initial Public Offerings. *Journal of Finance*, 1989, 44: 469–477

46. Gampers, P. J. L., Ishi and A. Metrick. Corporate Governance and Equity Prices. *NBER Working Paper*, 2001

47. Hampel Committee on Corporate Governance. The Hampel report on corporate governance. the European Corporate Governance Institute's (ECGI) website, published on 29 January, 1998

48. Hermalin, Benjamin, Michael Weisbach. The Determinants of Board Composition. *Rand Journal of Economics*, 1998, 19: 589–606

49. Jensen, Michael C. The Modern Industrial Revolution, Exit, and the Failure of Internal Control Systems. *Journal of Finance*, 1993, 48: 831–880

50. Klapper L. F. and I. Love. Corporate Governance, Investor Protection and Performance In Emerging Markets. *World Bank Working Paper*, 2002

51. Lipton, Martin and Jay W. Lorsch. A Modest Proposal for Improved Corporate Governance. *Business Lawyer*, 1992, 48: 59–77

52. OECD *(Organization for Economic Cooperation and Development).* OECD Principles of Corporate Governance. Paris: www.oecd.org, 1999, 2004

53. Partha, Sengupta. Debt Cost and the Quality of Information Disclosure. *The Accounting Review*, 1998, October: 98–117

54. PriceWaterhouse & Coopers. *The Opacity Index*. http://www.opacityindex.com, 2001

55. Rothschild M. and J. Stiglitz. Equilibrium in Cooperative Insurance Market. *Quarterly Journal of Economics*, 1976, 90: 629–649

56. Spence, A. M. *Market Signaling*. Cambridge, MA: Harvard University Press, 1974

57. Standard & Poors'. *Standard & Poors' Company Transparency & Disclosure Survey 2001*. S&P/IFC Emerging Asia, 2001

58. Standard & Poors'. *Standard & Poors' Corporate Governance Scores: Criteria, Methodology and Definitions*, 2002, 2004

59. UNCTAD (Prepared by M. Zubaidur Rahman). *The Role of Accounting Disclosure in the East Asian Financial Crisis: Lessons learned?* 1998

Index